G000115750

Springer Series on Social Work

Albert R. Roberts, D.S.W., Series Editor
Graduate School of Social Work, Rutgers, The State University of New Jersey

Advisory Board: Gloria Bonilla-Santiago, Ph.D., Sheldon R. Gelman, Ph.D., Gilbert J. Greene, Ph.D., Jesse Harris, D.S.W., Michael J. Smith, D.S.W., Barbara Berkman, Ph.D., and Elaine P. Congress, D.S.W.

Margaret Gibelman, DSW, is Professor and Director of the Doctoral Program at the Wurzweiler School of Social Work, Yeshiva University, in New York. She teaches in the areas of social welfare policy, management, and child welfare. She has also taught at Rutgers University and The Catholic University of America.

Dr. Gibelman has worked in the human services as a clinician, supervisor, educator, and manager. In the latter category, she has served as Executive Director of the National Association of School Psychologists and the Lupus Foundation of America. She was also Associate Executive Director of the Council on Social Work Education, the accrediting body for social work education programs in the United States. She is a frequently contributor to scholarly journals on nonprofit management, privatization, professional education, women's issues, and service delivery systems.

Harold W. Demone Jr., PhD, is currently a Visiting Scholar at Florence Heller School for Advanced Studies in Social Welfare, Brandies University and an Emeritus Professor II in Social Work and Sociology and former dean of the School of Social Work at Rutgers University. His publications on the human services exceed 120 in number.

With a professional career spanning more than 40 years, about equally divided between the practice and academic arenas, Dr. Demone has had frequent opportunities to both practice and observe many of the facets of privatization, even long before it was known as such. Dr. Gibelman and Dr. Demone have teamed on several articles on the subject of privatization and co-edited *Services for Sale: Purchasing Health and Human Services* (Rutgers University Press, 1989).

The Privatization of Human Services

Policy and Practice Issues

Volume 1

Margaret Gibelman, DSW
Harold W. Demone, Jr., PhD
Editors

 Springer Publishing Company

Copyright © 1998 by Springer Publishing Company, Inc.

All rights Reserved

No part of this publication may be reproduced, stored in a retrieval system, or transmitted in any form or by any means, electronic, mechanical,
photocopying, recording, or otherwise, without the prior permission of
Springer Publishing Company, Inc.

Springer Publishing Company, Inc.
536 Broadway
New York, NY 10012–3955

Cover design by Margaret Dunin
Acquisitions Editor: Bill Tucker
Production Editor: Pamela Lankas

98 99 00 01 02 / 5 4 3 2 1

Library of Congress Cataloging-in-Publication Data

The privatization of human services : policy and practice issues /
 Margaret Gibelman, Harold W. Demone, Jr., editors.
    p.   cm.—(Springer series on social work : 28)
  Includes index.
  ISBN 0-8261-9870-8
  1. Human services—Contracting out—United States.
 2. Social work administration—United States.
 3. Privatization—United States. I. Gibelman, Margaret.
 II. Demone, Harold W. III. Series.
 HV95.P737 1997
 361.973—dc21   97-28506
                                                    CIP

Printed in the United States of America

Contents

Foreword

No reader of professional journals, agency reports, or the daily press needs to be told that Professors Gibelman and Demone have assembled a volume of contributions to a very lively debate. The two words highlighted, "privatization" and "contracting," sum up the prescriptions of many for social service reform and the anxieties of others who question the new strategies.

The pace and scale of developments over the past 2 decades sometimes allows us to forget that the subject has a long history. Privatization may be thought of as involving public turnover to the private sector of responsibility for services it has been delivering. Or it may be the public sector arranging for the private sector to take on new services that the public wishes to encourage or for which it accepts responsibility. The transaction usually involves public funds.

The historical story, however, is not one of public temporal primacy. One can go back to the ancient world for early examples of simultaneous public and private contributions to what would today be thought of as welfare services. The private component was either individual charity or was usually based in religious institutions. Or, one can begin with the break up of feudalism and the transition to mercantilism. The evolving state needed to develop new provisions (through poor law) where church institutions, mutual aid, and charitable individuals had once sufficed. As it matured, poor law eventually involved intertwined local government and the local private sector, with some public subsidy of the latter. The process was more strongly delineated by the 19th century, when the "requirements" of the developing wage system created a new, more limited and punitive poor law; an expanded middle-class humanitarianism provided a much-needed safety valve (sometimes with and often without government financial support). Now there were programs for the "deserving" and for the others. Private agencies were to become "more" eligible, less stigmatizing.

Modern social services and modern social work developed from the Progressive Era, but the scale and nature of the social welfare enterprise changed with the entry of the federal government, a result of the New Deal. The process gathered momentum in the public and private social services and mental health after World War II—but especially during the Great Society. It was the expansion of scale and scope from the mid-1960s to the 1980s that encouraged and supported the large, publicly assisted, voluntary service expansion, some of it associated with successive thrusts of public welfare "reform" and much of it categorically organized around social problems or troublesome symptoms. All of it remains with us today and the process continues.

The backdrop for social service developments of the last 2 decades is the "liberal" turn in economic thinking in capitalist welfare states, exemplified and led by the Thatcher era in Britain and the Bush–Reagan terms in the United States. (Reference here is to liberal economic policy in the European meaning, with the resultant emphasis on deregulation, government downsizing, privatization, and the insistence on the use of market devices, whenever possible, as vehicles for efficiency.) As of this writing, most of the leading industrialized societies (as represented by the European Union [EU], the Organization for Economic Cooperation and Development [OECD], the World Bank, and the International Monetary Fund) are preaching, enforcing, and exporting a process of governmental downsizing, free trade, and privatization, which, despite some resistance and recent challenges, continues to dominate.

But it is one thing to privatize armament manufacture, telecommunications, transport, or even garbage collection, fire fighting, and road maintenance. The products or services are or can be standardized, units can be counted, costs and cost-benefits can be computed. The terms of the debate and the nature of the policy choices can be arrived at (and there is by now an extensive body of empirical literature as a result). What of the social services, whether narrowly or broadly defined? What is a standard expected unit of child protection, family support, child guidance intervention, and how does one describe standard expected impact? The social services, nonetheless, are part of the general culture so that, inevitably, public leaders, legislators, and the media expect them to behave as do all institutions, and the ideologies that motivate public policy in other domains are applied to them as well. This is indeed a time of change.

But how does it work? And does it work? What are the processes and mechanisms that will create effective systems? How has privatization and contracting evolved in a political culture which has cut funding for social services significantly since the Reagan years and has recently decentralized some major functions to the states"? Surprisingly, little is known. The answers must be sought "on the ground."

Contracting, or purchase of service, has been the most prevalent privatization mechanism in the social services in recent decades. The general arguments offered—economy, efficiency—are similar to the general arguments for all privatization, but the empirical case is weak if one demands standard research. If one cannot standardize inputs and outputs, how does one measure? Is progress being made in these regards? Further, there are also hints of other arguments and rationales beyond economy and efficiency that deserve attention and testing: quality, diversity, innovation.

For now, we must return to the immediate questions: What do we know? What is the experience? What is the case for privatization/contracting? What are the choices? What are the mechanisms? Gibelman and Demone have assessed the state of affairs very well. They know that we need case materials, records of experience, fresh and sharp thinking, and a vehicle for debates. This timely book, and its companion volume, will be welcome and used.

ALFRED J. KAHN
Professor Emeritus
Columbia University
School of Social Work
New York, NY

Preface

Hardly a day goes by without newspaper headlines announcing the privatization of some process or product, in the United States or in any other part of the world. The word "privatization" is now part of our nomenclature. Although technical and common use definitions may vary, privatization is widely understood in concept. This broadly encompassing term refers to the divesting of government responsibility for the funding and provision of products or services, mostly services in the United States, as government has not played a major role in the direct manufacture of products.

Within the human services area, the subject of this book, privatization, is more rhetoric than reality; private market forces are not able to address issues of the distribution of resources within our society that are required to meet the psychosocial, economic, and employment needs of citizens. An intermediary step in privatization widely used in the human services is that of purchase of service (POS). Here, the government retains a primary role in service funding, but delegates, through contracting, service delivery responsibility to the private sector (Demone & Gibelman, 1989; Gibelman, 1995).

Privatization is certainly not a new concept or practice, but its boundaries have been continuously expanding over the past decade across functional areas, international boundaries, and levels of government. It is an encompassing term, with many variations spanning the gamut from total abdication of a government role to heavy government financial subsidization of the private sector.

Traditionally, state and local governments have elected to meet a part of their responsibilities through financing the provision of care and services by nongovernmental organizations. The general satisfaction with these arrangements is evident in their continued and expanded use. Although the practice of contracting is far from new, its expanding scope and boundaries calls forth an array of practical, ethical, legal, and interorganizational issues that demand exploration.

Much public attention, through the media, has been focused on this transfer of functions. In some cases, the goal is to move government out of its funding role, as well as that of manager or provider. In other cases, where the public commitment is more firmly entrenched, the intent is to change delivery auspices. In the latter instance, government maintains its fiscal responsibility for the service, but transfers service provision to the private sector.

For a tradition as well-established as purchase of service, the scholarly base is remarkably thin. The literature on the subject tends to be ad hoc and sporadic in nature, and few scholars have written more than once on the subject. Kramer (1966, 1979, 1994), Savas (1977, 1982), Rathbeg Smith (1994), DeHoog (1984), Kettner and Martin (1987, 1993), Kamerman and Kahn (1989) and Smith and Lipsky (1993) are among those who have contributed to the scholarly base, and several chapters of this volume and its companion volume *The Privatization of Human Services, Volume II. Case Studies in the Purchase of Services,* published by Springer represent the work of some of these authors.

Without exception, the researchers and commentators have been consistent in expressing concern about the dearth of empirical information. Given the state of the art, it is not surprising that there are many opinion pieces: pro, con, and in between. Remarkably, the themes are similar, and as data trickle in, the speculation has not always been found to be wrong. In the absence of data to contradict prevailing beliefs, the purchase of services is hailed as a means to save money, increase efficiency, reduce conflict of interest, and diminish the direct public provider role, thus decreasing the size of the bureaucracy. Questions of quality are less often raised and less easily answered.

The two editors of this volume joined the exchange with their own perspectives on purchase of service. Earlier in his career, Harold W. Demone, Jr. served as a public administrator overseeing the direct operation of a statewide direct service alcoholism program. Several years later, he assumed responsibility for a program in another state that contracted for all direct services. These experiences in two state health departments stimulated a long-standing interest in the merits and pitfalls of direct versus indirect service delivery approaches and the related variables.

Margaret Gibelman directed several government-funded contracts, including a state-sponsored training program under university auspices and a national demonstration project on staff development and training.

Having some clear opinions about contracting, she decided to test the premises empirically, conducting one of the earliest studies on the relative impact of purchase of service versus direct public service delivery on client services, with specific regard to the field of child protection. Demone and Gibelman found that they agreed on the importance of purchase of service as a major trend affecting the process and outcome of public and private organizational roles and responsibilities and the interaction between them. They contend that the growth of purchasing represents one of the most significant trends in human services delivery and suggests a fundamental and pervasive alteration in the government's role and the nature of public-private sector relations.

In 1989, the two editors collaborated on *Services For Sale: Purchasing Health and Human Services.* Since then, the march toward privatization has continued and strengthened, and the mechanism of contracting has become both more sophisticated and deeply entrenched. Experience offers an important framework for the quest to develop a theoretical and practical base to contracting.

There is no single explanation for the multidimensional phenomena of contracting, but rather several possible theoretical bases. Which, if any, framework is correct is not yet apparent. More likely, some new combination of existing theoretical principles is necessary. What is clear is that for such a widely used service delivery mechanism, some greater understanding of its principles, assumptions, practices, rationale, and basis in history and tradition is required.

Theory is best tested in practice. With relatively clear motivations for privatization, including its more specific form of purchase of services, what has been the actual experience? Moving from the theme of the relative merits of purchase of service as a mechanism for delivering goods and services, this volume focuses on the implementation of contractual arrangements, including performance, role delegation and delineation, interorganizational relationships, accountability, and service outcomes.

Given the enormous industry that has evolved to implement POS (rate-setting systems, contract administration, negotiating and compliance monitoring procedures, etc.), how POS works to achieve its intended public purposes is a subject of utmost importance. The high expectations surrounding purchase of service, despite a growing list of documented problems, also suggest the need for a comprehensive exploration of the implementation and outcome of these arrangements. An emphasis on outcomes also helps to focus on the people ultimately intended to benefit by improved methods of service delivery: the consumers of services.

This volume thus focuses on POS in implementation and examines, through case studies, a number of human service areas in which services are now being purchased. These services share in common their goal of preventing, ameliorating, or resolving health, mental health, social or environmental problems which afflict individuals, families, groups, and communities.

This volume is the first of two volumes exploring the implementation of purchase of service and its policy implications. The chapters in this first volume provide an overview of the contracting experience in regard to selected service areas—mental health, mental retardation, and alcohol and drug treatment, as well as an overview of some of the overarching issues that have emerged in recent years, with special attention to account-ability demands and the impact of contracting on a subset of human ser-vice agencies, those that are sectarian-based. One chapter looks at purchase of service from a cross-national perspective and shows that many of the issues identified in the United States have their counterparts elsewhere.

The second volume, *The Privatization of Human Services: Volume II. Case Studies in the Purchase of Services* focuses more extensively on case studies to provide an in-depth look at purchase of service experiences. Both of the volumes are published by Springer Publishing Company of New York. These examples of POS contracting for human services are selected to show the range and breadth of such arrangements and their impact on consumers of services, agencies, government, and the interrelationship between the public and private sectors. The nine case studies of purchased services, which appear in the second volume, are explored in relation to the rationale, implementation experience, trends, lessons, and future prospects associated with this method of service delivery. The majority of chapters focus on purchase of service at the state or local level, the tra-ditional locus of most direct human service delivery programs within the province of government.

The case studies in both volumes are authored by individuals who have expertise in the particular area of purchase of service and have engaged in substantial research of a qualitative or quantitative nature. Several have written dissertations on the subject (Gibelman; Etta; Regan); others have conducted independent or organizationally sponsored research (H. Davidson, Hickey, Camberg, M. Davidson, Kern, & Kelly; Canter; Fishbein & McCarty; Kettner & Martin; Rathbeg Smith; Wieman & Dorwart). Still others have personal experience in contracting from the perspective of government and/or private providers (e.g., Dukakis, Johnston, Gibelman, Demone, Kraft). Substantive areas of purchase practice include sectarian family and children's services, mental health services, substance abuse, and mental retardation services. The companion volume adds to the service list and includes case studies related to child welfare, school-based psychological services, veteran's services, and homemaker/home health aide services. These examples of purchased services are explored in relation to the rationale, implementation, experience, and trends and future prospects associated with this method of service delivery.

Several of the cases focus on contracting experiences in the Commonwealth of Massachusetts. Although not intentional, it is also not accidental that Massachusetts is overrepresented, given this state's long history with contracting and the extent of its use.

As we become increasingly sophisticated about organizational behavior, blatant structural–functional constraints inherent in government have come to be of increasing concern to many public administrators, politicians, and citizens. In the search for options, purchase of service has been seen as one option to ease conflict of interest. Others, looking for increased efficiency, cost reduction, improved quality, and diminished bureaucracy have similarly looked to purchase of service. Thus, interest in purchase of service by the public sector has accelerated to an unprecedented level.

Although extensive literature on the purchase of human services is lacking, the range of participants and interests is substantial. Public administrators seek to improve public sector performance. Public employees' unions are concerned with the potential loss of members that may accompany the purchase of services. Accountants and economists, legislators and administrators are concerned with economy and cost benefits, for example, efficiency and expenditure control. Political scientists inquire about structure and function. Client advocates are concerned about accountability. There are concerns about the potential effect of purchase of services on consumers of services, for example, has the use of contractual arrangements made possible the more effective provision of quality services and more positive client outcomes? Others are concerned with the elusive public interest.

IMPLEMENTING PURCHASE OF SERVICE: A CASE STUDY APPROACH

American culture has long supported the concept and practice of individual or group purchase of needed goods and services; this is a fundamental tenet of the free enterprise system (Mills, 1985). The application of this value to the human services has had a less certain history, in part because of the paternalism that has characterized support of public health, welfare, and social services. Nevertheless, the growing body of experience with POS in the human services is suggestive of the range, advantages, and pitfalls of these kinds of arrangements.

Regan applies organizational theory to help explain what he terms "an alarmingly high rate of organizational failure" within the Massachusetts purchase of service system, with particular attention to services for the mentally retarded. These provider agencies are typically nonprofit organizations operating at the community level for the delivery of services. Blame for this high rate of organizational morbidity has been leveled against both the Commonwealth and the community-based providers, with little explanation as to the underlying forces which may be influencing the system in this way.

Regan explores the notion that there are environmental forces which are endemic to the POS system itself and which have an overall negative effect on the organizational health and longevity of provider agencies. The rise of these environmental forces are seen as a function of the history and development of the POS system in Massachusetts, and their continuing adverse influence on provider agencies is dependent on the present structure of the POS delivery model. Regan concludes by discussing how his findings can be applied to ongoing proposals to reshape the Massachusetts purchase of service system.

Rathbeg Smith examines contracting for substance abuse services in North Carolina from a public management perspective, noting their vulnerability to budget cuts due to the nature of the service and the dependence of many of those served by public programs such as Medicaid. Data are drawn from research conducted during 1994–1995 on contracting for substance abuse services in North Carolina. Recent and pending changes in public policy are a particular threat to the many substance abuse services provided through private agencies. The North Carolina example of the effect of budget cuts on contracted services is illustrative of the policy trade offs of the decentralized program structure currently favored by many policymakers. Further, this case study underscores the potential fallout of a sharply reduced federal role in social and health policy.

Levine details a number of questions that arise for sectarian agencies from purchase of service arrangements in relation to agency practices, values, and core purposes. His chapter provides a brief history of sectarian agencies and purchase of service contracting and analyzes key practice issues, such as the extent of government funding to this sector, dependence on government funds, interagency competition, and issues pertaining to personnel and boards of directors. Salient philosophical and value conflicts are reviewed. The chapter then draws examples from the literature and the field of social welfare and presents a case study of the experience of one organization to further explore how sectarian agencies respond to the challenges of government funding. A concluding section summarizes prospects for and ongoing implications of continued funding of sectarian agencies in the future.

The United States has its own special blend of issues relating to and flowing from contracting for services. Some issues have parallels in other nations. POS contracting is relatively new in the United Kingdom's (UK) social services system, and has aroused considerable hostility, especially among sections of the nonprofit sector. Richardson and Gutch examine the reasons behind the introduction of POS and compare the reality of implementation with the hopes and fears that greeted the policy. They argue that the "contract nightmare" conjured up by opponents of the policy shift has failed to materialize, in part because implementation has been only partial, but also because many of the fears about contracting arose from a vision of the shape of the market for care that has not been borne out. Although ideology was the primary force behind the policy, practical considerations have driven implementation. Contracting has been a difficult change for many nonprofits, but in many cases it served merely to rectify chronic undermanagement that would have had to be tackled even without POS. Finally, the authors argue that the real threat of contracting may lie in for-profit competition. Without the levels of charitable subsidy seen in the US, or the institutional biases of continental Europe, UK nonprofits are uniquely vulnerable to for-profit competition. Contracting may serve ultimately to shift UK social services from overwhelmingly statutory provision to overwhelmingly for-profit provision, with nonprofits occupying only niche markets. The competition between the for-profits and nonprofits in the United Kingdom for scarce contract dollars is also surfacing as a major issue in the United States.

The majority of authors perceive contracting to be a "mixed bag." They agree, further, that the continuation of these arrangements is a given, and that fiscal dependency has largely replaced earlier motivations for the public–private relationship. Contract funds have come to represent the greatest source of revenues for many private agencies. The programs that they support have developed constituencies of their own, and there is internal agency, board, community, and client pressure to preserve them. A number of service delivery problems plague both public and private agencies as they attempt to respond to the range of responsibilities they are expected to fulfill, including comprehensive planning, service provision, and service monitoring and evaluation. The difficulties inherent in the breadth of functions delegated to providers of human services are evident across sectors and are compounded, in some cases, by contractual arrangements. For example, state public health agencies may serve as allocators, contractors, service providers, comprehensive health planners, regulators, and overseers of services delivered by external sources. Similarly, the United Way has attempted to play comparable roles, exclusive of direct service delivery. In both examples, comprehensive planning has suffered. Negative results are not surprising as role conflict becomes more evident. Studies by several management consulting firms underscore the point.

The growth in contracting has been accompanied by increased formalization and accountability demands. Accountability has evolved to include more than fiscal reporting and process adherence. The demand is more and more for documenting the outcome of services and there is movement toward reimbursement systems based on outcome measures. This portends of things to come.

With the more widespread use of POS and in the wake of some negative experiences, demands for accountability have grown. Drawing on their two national studies of state purchasing practices, Kettner and Martin trace the evolution of accountability demands and practices. In the early days of contracting, arrangements were "loose," and available providers in the community were approached for their existing expertise. Contract requirements were general in nature, typically specifying only the time period, dollar amount, general population to be served, and the type of service. Reporting requirements were also minimal. This situation was to change with relative speed. According to these authors, during the 1980s, planning and controlling the human services system became a dominant theme, including attention to measuring performance and outcomes. This emphasis on performance has become more pronounced in the 1990s.

Kettner and Martin conclude that contracting in the future will include increased attention to lower costs, which tends to support increased competition and accountability, both fiscal and programmatic components. The emphasis on performance measurement is part of an overall federal strategy, including mandates in the Government Performance and Results Act, which specifies that by 1998 all federal agencies must develop 5-year strategic plans linked to measurable outcomes.

The ability to measure outcomes has matured. Similarly, progress has been made in establishing contract expectations, monitoring contracts and accurately calculating the cost and price of services. Few states have developed the data processing and information management capacity needed to move purchase-of-service accountability to the next level, however. Clearly, the measurement of outcomes will receive even more emphasis in the future.

Demone's concluding chapter in this volume highlights the role of political thought and politics in human services contracting. Privatization can no longer be considered a passing fad. The quest for smaller government is a worldwide phenomenon.

EMERGING ISSUES AND FUTURE PROSPECTS

There are many advantages and disadvantages attributed to contracting. What is an advantage to some organizations or individuals may be seen as a disadvantage by others. As the case studies in this volume suggest, these perceived advantages and disadvantages are crystallized in contract implementation.

Contracting for service has become big business with big stakes. Often, voluntary and for-profit providers are pitted against each other in competition for contract funds. Sophistication in marketing one's agency has become essential for success in this competitive environment.

The "big business" side for government is the amount of dollars (and discretion) they have to offer. For potential and actual contracted service providers, the stakes are high. As Levine observes, the cumulative impact of contracting can be an alteration of the client population served and services offered. Even when boards of directors and management are aware of the "costs" of contracting to their mission and purpose, the enticement of dollars may neutralize these concerns. Practicality often rules.

Perhaps in an ironic twist, even the accountability function may be subject to contracting out. Fishbein and McCarty, in a chapter in the companion volume on quality improvement for contracted substance abuse services, suggest that monitoring and accountability processes can be contracted out in much the same way that services are purchased. The breadth of accountability requirements are now taxing public agency capability. The Massachusetts State Department of Health, Bureau of Substance Abuse Services, in collaboration with alcohol and drug abuse treatment and prevention services, has replaced much of its quality-assurance process with a contract that supports the development of continuous improvement systems in programs that contract to provide addiction treatment and prevention services.

As more and more experience is gained with POS, issues of planning, performance, role delegation and delineation, interorganizational relationships, service monitoring and evaluation and accountability, among others, have surfaced. As the case studies illustrate, contracting for services is not without its problems. As is true with any mechanism for the delivery of services, experience may deviate from intent.

By the mid-1980s and well into the 1990s, purchase of service had come under considerable attack and scrutiny, to which human services contracting has not been immune. Criticisms range from inadequate accounting procedures to ineffective services. The *New York Times* and *Washington Post*, two of the major national newspapers, contain consistent and numerous articles about allegations, investigations, and outright scandals concerning contracted services. Although a majority of these reports have concerned the defense industry, by virtue of the sheer volume of defense contracting, contracting problems related to the human services have also surfaced in the media. In Volume II of the series, Demone provides an example of the role of the print media in the contracting for human services.

Experience suggests that purchase of service arrangements are likely to be an increasingly used tool to provide human services, particularly in light of political and social pressures to diminish the size and role of government. Even if government maintains fiscal responsibility, the appearance of divestiture is made possible through the contract method. And despite a checkered history, the weight of evidence is in favor of continued and widespread use of purchase of services.

AUDIENCES

Potential users of this volume include public policymakers, public and private human service managers, and social service practitioners. Procurement agents, contract and grant managers, and financial officers at the federal, state, and local levels will also find both volumes to be relevant and useful. Educators who seek to prepare students for the realities of current practice will find the case studies adaptable for classroom use.

The volume can also stand alone or in combination with its companion volume as a text in masters and doctoral level public policy and social administration courses in the fields of social work, public health, political science, and public administration. Finally, interested citizens concerned with how their tax dollars are being spent or how the human services works to promote or inhibit high quality service delivery may find this volume instructive.

REFERENCES

deHoog, R. H. (1984). *Contracting out for human services.* Albany, NY. State University Press.

Demone, H. W., Jr. & Gibelman, M. (1989). *Services for sale: Purchasing health and human services.* New Brunswick, NJ: Rutgers University Press.

Gibelman, M. (1995). Purchasing social services. In R. I. Edwards (Ed.), *Encyclopedia of social work* (19th ed., pp.1998–2007). Washington, DC: NASW Press.

Kramer, R. M. (1966). Voluntary agencies and the use of public fund: some policy issues. *Social Service Review. 40,* 15–26.

Kramer, R. M. (1979). Public fiscal policy and voluntary agencies in welfare states. *Social Services Review, 53,* 1–14.

Kramer, R. M. (1994). Voluntary services and the contract culture. "Dream or nightmare". *Social Services Review, 68,* 7–35.

Kamerman, S. B., & Kahn, A. J. (1989). *Privatization and the welfare state.* Princeton, NJ: Princeton University Press.

Kettner, P., & Martin, L. (1987). *Purchasing of service contracting: Two models.* Beverly Hill, CA: Sage.

Kettner, P., & Martin, L. (1994). Purchasing of service at 20: Are we using it well? *Public Welfare, 52,* 14–20.

Mills, J. E. (1985). Moving toward a tripartite marketplace in the human services. In *The social welfare forum* (pp. 108–116). Washington, DC: National Conference on Social Welfare.

Savas, E. S. (Ed.). (1982). *Privatizing the public sector: How to shrink government.* Chatham, NJ: Chatham House.

Savas, E. S. (Ed.). (1997). *Alternative for delivering public services.* Boulder, CO: Westview Press.

Smith, S. R., & Lipsky, M. (1993). *Nonprofits for hire: The welfare state in the age of contracting.* Cambridge, MA.: Harvard University Press.

Contributors

Andrea Canter, PhD
School Psychologist
Minneapolis Public Schools
Minneapolis, MN 55409

Robert A. Dorwart, MD, MPH
Professor of Psychiatry
Harvard Medical School and
    Harvard School of Public
    Health
Harvard University
Cambridge, MA 02138

Richard Gutch
Chief Executive
Arthritis Care
London, NW1 2HD
England

Peter Kettner, DSW
Professor
Arizona State University
School of Social Work
Tempe, AZ 85287-1802

Eric M. Levine, DSW
Associate Executive Director of
    the Annual Campaign
United Jewish Appeal-Federation
    of Jewish Philanthropies of
    New York
New York, NY 10022

Lawrence Martin, PhD
Associate Professor
Director, Social Work
    Administration Program
Columbia University
School of Social Work
New York, NY 10025

Steven Rathgeb Smith, PhD
Associate Professor
University of Washington
School of Public Affairs
Seattle, WA 98105

Paul S. Regan, EdD
President
Steward Ministries
Barrington, IL 60010

James Richardson
Contracts Information Officer
  and Acting Head of Research
National Council for Voluntary
  Organizations
London, WC2 H9AT
England

Dow A. Wieman, PhD
Research Fellow
Mental Health Policy Working
  Group
John F. Kennedy School of
  Government
Harvard University
Gloucester, MA 01930

1

Theory, Practice, and Experience in the Purchase of Services

Margaret Gibelman

PURCHASE-OF-SERVICE FRAMEWORK

- Government is too big.
- There is waste and duplication in the delivery of services.
- Competition drives down prices.
- The private sector can do it better.
- Innovation is promoted through privatization.

These prevailing beliefs and attitudes, as applied to the human services, form the parameters in which to articulate, redefine, and implement alternative strategies for financing and delivering human services. The system, itself, has become the identified problem.

The use of the private sector is a strategy that has widespread political and citizen support. The ultimate goal is to have the private sector assume responsibility for both service delivery and service funding, and to encourage the use of market criteria to control costs and ensure quality. The compromise is the use of the private market through the continued growth of purchase of service, with government maintaining its role as chief financier, but requiring increased cost-sharing on the part of the private sector. This incremental approach is politically and fiscally expedient, builds upon established and successful alternative service delivery models, and potentially addresses many of the weaknesses long identified in the delivery of services.

As a political symbol, privatization constitutes the polar extreme of the welfare state (Leat, 1986). The reality, at least in the human services field, is a modified form of privatization in which government delegates service provision responsibility but maintains some or all policy and fiscal responsibility. Purchase of service falls within this latter category and encompasses the concept of public-private partnerships. Government, at the federal, state, and local levels, purchases services from for-profit organizations, from proprietary groups, from other governmental units, and from not-for-profit organizations.

Purchase of service thus concerns both the act of transmitting public funds to private service providers and decisions about how services are to be delivered. It is an organized procedure by which an entity of government enters into a formal agreement with another entity for goods or services. In the case of POS for human services, the focus is on those services provided to individuals, groups, or communities to prevent, ameliorate, or resolve environmental, physical, or psychosocial problems (Demone & Gibelman, 1989).

The original intent of POS was to provide an alternative means of delivering services that would better achieve public purposes in the public interest (Gibelman & Demone, 1989). As the concept and practice has evolved, however, POS has become a means to further the goal of reducing the size and scope of government. As defined in the Reagan and Bush administrations, privatization has meant divesting government of as many functions as possible. President Clinton, too, has sought to trim government; "reinventing government" through streamlining has been a major theme of his administration (Clinton, 1993). These include not only operations, but also planning, administering, monitoring, and sometimes even licensing and regulating of services. Public services ranging from air traffic control to management of prisons have been considered fair game for contracting out.

Government contracting of human services has traditionally been smaller in scale than contracting for other government services, such as defense, and has, until more recent years, been primarily confined to relationships with the not-for-profit sector. Privatization of the human services marks an about-face of social policy development since the Great Depression, which substantially increased the roles and responsibilities of the public system (Gibelman & Demone, 1989).

The absolute and relative extent of POS depends not only upon the perceived wisdom of contracting out, but also on the dollars available within the federal or state budgets in a particular service or functional area. Purchased services may be provided to targeted groups of people, for example, AIDS education oriented to teenagers in public schools; or to special populations, such as runaway youth or children who have been abused. In some cases, the type of service or number of people to whom services may be rendered within a group may be limited by statute, regulations, or agreement, or it may be open-ended. As budgets tighten, open-ended arrangements are less frequently found, a fact highlighted in several of the case studies in this volume.

The dollar amount of contracting within the human services arena began as relatively small and grew exponentially. For example, Johnston, in the companion volume, (Gibelman & Demone, Vol. II, 1998) notes that in Massachusetts, during the period 1984–1991, contracting increased from about $400 million per year to $1 billion per year. Demone, also in the companion volume, cites 1996 figures which estimate the total Massachusetts contracting at between $4 and $5 billion or, using this higher estimate, approximately 30% of the state's operating budget. Purchasing services from not-for-profits, alone, has grown into a $15 billion a year industry annually (Smith & Lipsky, 1993). If the Massachusetts experience were to be generalized, the national figure would approximate $150 billion, not $15 billion. Although it is clear that estimates vary considerably, the scope of contracting remains significant.

THE EVOLUTION OF PURCHASE OF SERVICE

Traditionally, state and local governments have elected to meet a part of their responsibilities through financing the provision of care and services by nongovernmental organizations. The general satisfaction with these arrangements is evident in their continued and expanded use. POS is as much a practical, freestanding technology as it is an ideological preference.

Purchase of service is not a new or unique invention. George Washington established several precedents. Included was the purchase of goods and services and, conversely, the expression of complaints about several contractors who supplied military hardware (Sharkansky, 1980). Wedel (1976) points out that purchase of service has been practiced since colonial days and that purchased services can be traced throughout the history of the American social welfare system. Specific financial modalities have included grants, per capita payments, tax concessions, and lump sum subsidies. He notes that contracting has often been the preferred mode.

The use of purchase of service thus has historical roots. A review of historical trends in the delivery of health, welfare, and rehabilitation services in the United States shows this type of arrangement to be pervasive. In fact, as one views the 300-year development of social welfare in the United States, the interaction between the private and public service delivery systems provides an important vantage point (Cruthirds, 1972; Kramer, 1964).

The extent to which purchase of service dominates a particular health and human services field is subject to a wide range of influences, including political and philosophical forces and social values and preferences. Purchase of service is reflective of, and integrally related to, changing conceptions of the roles and functions of the public and private sectors of this society. Increases or decreases in the use of purchase of service must thus be understood within the context of prevailing priorities, values, and preferences affecting social welfare policies and programs. Far from a static phenomenon, "contracting out" for the delivery of services may, at different times, be seen within a continuum of a preferred solution or new type of accountability and administrative problem (Demone & Gibelman, 1989).

Purchase of service has its origins in the very first systems established in the United States to provide for the public welfare. During the colonial era, a rudimentary form of public relief, based on the English Poor Laws, provided a type of last-resort assistance when family and individual resources were exhausted. The rudimentary system of outdoor relief administered by some local public authorities at this time was augmented by a system of "contracting out" and a related practice of "auctioning off" the aged, orphaned, and poor to private individuals for care (Cruthirds, 1972; Wedel, 1976). Expectations concerning the extent of governmental intervention on behalf of the needy were limited, as were the resources to meet social and individual needs. The public sector was slow to accept responsibility for maintaining adequate social welfare supports and services, particularly in comparison with other Western industrialized nations (Wilensky & Lebeaux, 1965). That government would assume a monopoly on service provision to those with problems associated with economic, physical, or social dependency was simply antithetical to prevailing views. Accordingly, voluntary forms of assistance developed through the church, mutual benefit societies, and private philanthropy, concurrent with a very modest assumption of government responsibility in this early period (Kramer, 1964).

The complexities and variations in the interrelations between these two systems has been a dominant theme throughout this country's history.

Despite emphasis on the relative merits of one system over the other at various times, there is repeated evidence of governmental bodies electing to discharge their responsibilities through nongovernment service provision.

In reaction to the many abuses that became evident in the early system of private contracting, reformers in the first part of the 19th century urged changes. This successful reform effort resulted in a movement toward a policy of public indoor, or institutional, relief and the initiation of a subsidy system for private institutions. These earlier contractual agreements took the form of direct subsidies to voluntary welfare organizations. Many of the arguments concerning the subsidy system for social welfare services, as advanced at the turn of the century, linger to this day, and continue to influence the range and scope of purchase of service arrangements between the public and private sectors (Gibelman & Demone, 1989).

The financial support of the private sector through subsidies was seen as less costly than building new public facilities; subsidized institutions could be free of political interference and capable of maintaining high standards without government control (Burian, 1970). Kramer (1964) further notes that the readiness to use tax funds to subsidize existing private institutions may also relate to pressures exerted by voluntary agency leadership, which had a vested interest in utilizing its own facilities to the fullest.

Subsidy arrangements, however, were not without their critics. Kramer (1964), for example, points to the long controversy over the practice of public subsidies as exemplifying prevailing sentiments about the respective character and roles of government and voluntary agencies. According to Kramer, those arguing against the public–voluntary agency partnership, through the mechanism of the subsidy system, identified the following flaws, among others:

- It was not real economy because so many duplicate institutions were necessary, one for each sectarian group, and since intake policies were not controlled, funds were used to support the care of the "inmates" at private institutions;
- Special pressures were put on legislatures to influence appropriations;
- Subsidies tended to dry up other sources of private funds; and
- This system destroyed the freedom of the voluntary agency.

One of the first comprehensive studies of public subsidies to private charities was carried out by Amos Warner in the 1890s. Based on survey

data, Warner and his associates summarized the arguments for and against
the use of public subsidies. Among the arguments in favor of their use
were financial savings when care for dependents was provided by a private voluntary organization, better quality of care, more professional business operations, and less stigma attached tor the poor and aged. The
arguments cited against subsidies included loss of public control and waste
and duplication.

The debates were not limited exclusively to matters of public–private
relations. They also concerned the quality of care, eventually leading to
more experimentation. One purported advancement was the establishment of local public almshouses for paupers. The almshouses, operated
by public officials, were, for a while, considered to be a cheaper and better deterrent of malingering and to be more efficient than other forms
of care (Mencher, 1967). Despite such "innovative" practices, varying
degrees of contracting continued to be practiced. Most popular was the
public purchase of special care, particularly in regard to the care of dependent children. Ironically, it was the deplorable conditions for and concerns about children in institutions and almshouses that served to stimulate
further the growth of subsidy arrangements in child welfare. A solution
had again become the problem—a recurrent theme in regard to service
delivery mechanisms. Many states began to seek alternative forms of child
care, either by establishing separate state institutions for children or by
subsidizing the already existing private institutions (Randolph, 1976).

Despite expressed concerns and arguments, the subsidization of private institutions evolved into a strongly entrenched system for financing
social services, reaching its zenith during the early 1930s and then losing
ground to the emerging pattern of financing entitled purchase of service
(Cruthirds, 1972). These financial arrangements were to have long-last-
ing implications for the nature of the relationship between government
and private agencies. The effects of the subsidy system included the early
and widespread growth of private child agencies through the assurance
of continued public support. Rather than supplementing, subsidies often
supplanted the government-operated agency system. Further, recurring
conceptions of agency character, roles, and relationships were articulated.
In a debate over subsidies, the public agency was frequently associated
with almshouses, political corruption, and lack of empathy. Voluntary
agencies, on the other hand, were seen as undertaking innovative and
quality programs (Gibelman & Demone, 1989).

Lourie (1979) comments that the increase in subsidized or purchased
services in this country in the 1890s and early 1900s was fraught with the

same ambivalence and dilemmas as is the case today. The question was asked then, as it is now: Is accountability possible when employees are not your own? Lourie also argues that the civil rights revolution and War on Poverty programs were significant influences on the present popularity of the purchase of social services. Decentralization and community control were advocated, and, by implication, so was private delivery, to avoid the perils of a large, distant government. Even local government was distrusted.

THE EMERGENCE OF THE MODERN SOCIAL WELFARE STATE

Most pronounced among the changes occurring during the 1930s was the enormous growth in social welfare expenditures; for the first time, the amount expended by government exceeded that of voluntary agencies (Wedel, 1976). The reasons, of course, are well documented in history. The level of social need created by the Great Depression demanded public intervention; this came in the form of Franklin Roosevelt's New Deal. The voluntary sector was simply unable to respond effectively to the demands of the day. Government was the only possible source of sanction, dollars, and programs. It is noteworthy that the New Deal also marks the ascendancy of the federal government into the business of selected social welfare institutions (Karger & Stoesz, 1994; Trattner, 1994). Again, the magnitude of need demanded a unified and far-reaching response.

During this period, the relative importance of public subsidies to voluntary agencies also diminished, due to the rapid expansion of functions directly assumed by government agencies. Some, fearing that voluntarism would be eradicated, urged a sharing of responsibility between the two sectors in the delivery of services, echoing past preferences for role delegation. With the advent of a strengthened public system, the key question concerned the nature of public-private interrelationships: Should there be such a relationship and, if so, how and to what degree?

Between 1935 and 1962, several amendments were added to the Social Security Act, separately and in combination, having the effect of enlarging government's role in the funding and provision of services to a client population increasing in size. One significant trend was the adoption of a "service" philosophy to assist recipients of public welfare, rather than simply the provision of cash or in-kind benefits. In part, this service approach was based on the assumption that the problems associated with poverty went beyond a lack of money, and that "rehabilitation" was necessary if the poor were to attain social and financial independence. Significantly, this approach was also seen as integral to diminishing, permanently, the ever-increasing size of the welfare rolls.

Although the purchase of social services has been practiced in some form since the earliest days of American social welfare, it was not until the early 1960s that POS became a major alternative for service delivery. The 1962 amendments (P.L. 87-543, 76 Stat, 173) to the Social Security Act (P.L. 90-248, 81 Stat, 82) authorized states, for the first time, to enter into agreements with other public agencies for services that could be more economically provided by these agencies (Slack, 1979). The 1967 amendments to the Social Security Act extended the authority of states to purchase services from nonprofit or proprietary providers, in addition to other state or local public agencies.

In the 1962 amendments to the Social Security Act, Congress initiated a series of programs to strengthen the rehabilitation approach, granting implementation authority to the public sector. Through an open-ended federal appropriation, P.L. 87–543, 75% matching funds were provided to states that would establish and implement defined social services under any of the public assistance titles they elected. Another important feature of the 1962 amendments was the official recognition of already prevailing beliefs: that services could be used to prevent some vulnerable persons from becoming or remaining dependent on public assistance. Two other features of these amendments are particularly relevant in terms of both present and future, unanticipated consequences. The federal financial match was increased to 75% from its prior 50% level as an incentive for states to undertake or expand services to a more broadly defined population eligible for services. Second, states were, for the first time, authorized to enter into agreements with other public agencies (such as health and vocational rehabilitation) for services that could be more economically provided by these agencies (Slack, 1979). Thus, purchase of service was introduced into the social services programs. In fact, the inclusion of this provision merely extended purchase of service practices to the social services; heretofore, such related fields as vocational rehabilitation and health had long made significant use of this service delivery mechanism.

There were those in Washington who were convinced that the "loopholes' in the 1962 amendments were responsible for the spiraling growth in the Aid to Families with Dependent Children (AFDC) program. Thus, in response to the growing size of AFDC rolls, the 1967 amendments to the Social Security Act were enacted. Although reaffirming the federal commitment to social services, this legislation sought to introduce certain measures that would tie social services more closely to the labor market. Rather than services, preparing people to enter or return to paid employment became the rallying cry. Thirty years later, now called welfare reform, the call was renewed. (The change was in degree, not kind.)

In keeping with the "get people back to work" philosophy, the 1967 amendments expanded available day care services. Purchase of service provisions were also modified. Under the new law, states were granted authority to purchase services from nonprofit or proprietary agencies, or from individuals or other state or local public agencies.

A growing disenchantment with the value of public services, as well as increased skepticism about the efficacy of public service provision, resulted in a new emphasis on private sector linkages. By 1969, nearly all restrictive language about the use of POS had been dropped from regulations, with new rules promulgated to require states to increase their use of contracting (Gibelman & Demone, 1989). State plans were to "assure progressive development of arrangements with a number and variety of agencies . . . with the aim of providing opportunities for individuals to exercise a choice with regard to the source of purchased service" (Derthick, 1975, p. 20). Subject to the limitations prescribed by the secretary of the then Department of Health, Education, and Welfare (DHEW), contractual arrangements were to be used for services that, in the judgment of the state agency, could not be as economically or effectively provided by the staff of such state or local agencies and were not otherwise reasonably available to individuals in need of them. At the same time, Medicaid and Medicare were implemented through private vendors, institutionalizing the large-scale use of the private market for the delivery of publicly funded services.

Broadened statutory authority for POS resulted in the escalated use of these arrangements. Such authority is found in each successive amendment to the Social Security Act and related human service legislation, such as the Comprehensive Employment and Training Act (93-203, 87 Stat. 839), which encouraged the use of community-based organizations to develop training and educational programs; the 1973 amendments to the Older Americans Act (Older Americans Act of 1965. P.L. 89-73, 79 Stat. 218), which required states to create local area agencies on aging using appropriate community providers to actually deliver services; and the Family Planning Services and Population Research Act of 1970(P.L. 94-69, Stat. 1504), authorizing grants and contracts to provide voluntary family planning services (Gibelman, 1995; Terrell, 1987). Other stimulating factors included federal financial incentives to develop such arrangements;

states' interest in maximizing federal funds; and the perceived advantages of private sector delivery, including increased flexibility, higher standards, cost-effectiveness, and control of staff size (Gibelman & Demone, forthcoming).

The original intent of POS was to provide an alternative means of delivering services that would better achieve public purposes. It was, in essence, a tool to achieve specific ends that was developed incrementally. As the concept and practice has evolved, however, POS has become, for some, a means to further the goal of "the least government is the best government." The Reagan and Bush Administrations made clear that the private sector was the provider of choice, and any remaining constraints to POS were removed. President Clinton has remained firm in the conviction that government should get out of the business of "doing." In this respect, POS and privatization have been viewed as ideologically compatible, with POS representing one means to accomplish public divestiture. It represents a midpoint between predominantly government provision and total privatization (Gibelman, 1995; Gibelman & Demone, forthcoming).

The use of contracting to purchase work-related services had been a dominant trend in several War on Poverty programs, such as the Job Corps; this established pattern presumably influenced the decision to expand purchase provisions for the renewed focus on work programs rather than a psychosocial rehabilitation approach. Accordingly, earlier attitudes of caution about the use of purchase of service were disregarded in favor of using the stronger capabilities and proven expertise of the private sector in this arena (Gibelman & Demone, 1989). There had been other recent and successful experiences in the public purchase of voluntary services, fueling the decision to proceed with this type of delivery mechanism. For example, the Vocational Rehabilitation Administration relied heavily and with positive results on purchasing, concluding from its studies that this method increased flexibility, improved standards, was cost-effective. controlled staff size, and created a network of organizational allies within the purchase of service network.

SPIRALING SOCIAL SERVICE COSTS

A combination of features, including broadened statutory authority for purchase of service, federal encouragement to develop such arrangements, states' interest in maximizing federal funds, and the support of the private sector resulted in rapid increases in the use of public social service dollars by the states. It should be recalled that, under the public assistance titles, there remained no fixed dollar limitation on spending. States sought to maximize the federal contribution through the use of purchase of service. The first goal of the states was very clear. Contrary to legislative intent, they sought to substitute federal expenditures for state expenditures. The quantity of services would likely remain essentially unaltered, certainly an unanticipated outcome. Some states permitted service expansion using voluntary matching dollars as state funds became a smaller component of the total.

As is customary in such matters, expenditures inflated and Congress and the administration reacted. They simultaneously put a ceiling on appropriations, focused the expenditures, and paradoxically granted the states more flexibility within the new set of parameters.

In October 1972 P.L. 92-512, the General Revenue Sharing Act (86 Stat. 20), was enacted, fixing a $2.5 billion ceiling on total federal expenditures for social services under the several Social Security Act public assistance titles. It also restricted 90% of the federal funds to expenditures for family planning, child day care, foster care for children, mental retardation, and alcoholism and drug abuse services. This $2.5 billion ceiling, which was carried over into the Title XX amendments of 1975 (P.L. 97-35; 95 Stat. 828) and was later retained with an inflationary index (though cut by 25% with the enactment of the Omnibus Budget Reconciliation Act of 1981 [P.L. 97-35; 95 Stat. 357]), applied to states according to a simple, population-based formula, unrelated to the proportion of welfare recipients (Slack, 1979).

With the passage of P.L. 93–637, the Social Service Amendments of 1974, which constituted Title XX of the Social Security Act, the nature of public social services was fundamentally changed. Henceforth, states would be given responsibility for not only defining services, but for deciding where, how much, and to whom these services should be provided. States now had significantly increased latitude to determine how federal funds would be used. Likewise, the role of the federal administrative agency (then the Department of Health, Education and Welfare [DHEW]) in the provision of public social services would be limited largely to technical assistance, with the granting of explicit responsibility for assisting states with their program content and with the newly established administrative requirements.

Title XX was to remain the predominant source of authority and funds for public social services until 1981 when, with the passage of the Omnibus Budget Reconciliation Act of 1981, states and localities were given substantially more authority and flexibility to design their human services programs than had existed under the earlier legislation, but with less money. This act authorized a social services block grant program, among other block grants, consisting of the earlier Title XX social services program, the Title XX training program, and day care. To the pleasure of many governors and mayors, a majority of the federal regulations governing the public social service programs were eliminated, but on the negative side, the level of federal funding was reduced by 25%. States would no longer have to meet a 25% match of the federal contribution, a feature of earlier Social Security Act amendments, but were encouraged by the Reagan Administration to make up for this difference in federal funding and finance "real" service costs by promoting private donations and state voluntary contributions.

Among the choices states faced with the enactment of the Omnibus Reconciliation Act of 1981 was the determination of when and how to use the private sector in the financing and delivery of services. The Reagan message was clear: the private sector should have a more expansive role in the planning, financing, and delivery of human services. Partnership building between the public and private sectors was, in the administration's view, an opportunity to overcome many of the perceived weaknesses in the public service system. However, the administration misread both the strength of its persuasiveness and the economic realities. As Salamon (1984, p. 271) notes: "Instead of forging a new coalition in support of a positive program of cooperation between government and the voluntary sector, the administration relied primarily on exhortation and on the expected success of its economic program to suffuse the country with voluntaristic spirit."

Cuts in the federal financing of social services had an immediate and profound impact on voluntary agencies. In FY 1981, it is estimated that federal financial support of nonprofit institutions had reached over $46 billion, 38% of the total revenues of nonprofit, charitable service organizations (Salamon & Abramson, 1982). In addition to direct funding, there are two other primary ways in which voluntary agencies benefit from federal policy. First is tax policy, particularly in regard to charitable-giving provisions. The second means is through purchase of service contracts grants, or third-party payment methods that flow from government to the nonprofit sector. One way in which states could reduce, quickly, their level of social service expenditures was to terminate purchase of service contracts. By so doing, states could redirect the dollars saved to maintain public agency operations. Conversely, states might opt to continue the level of contracting with voluntary agencies, but pass along to them a form of matching funds; for example, contracted providers could be asked to assume a portion of the costs in a modified version of cost-sharing. These two state options, in the face of diminished federal resources, would severely affect the financial status and service-rendering capability of the nonprofit sector. Holding the line on the dollar allotment for contracts was the least likely strategy for states which faced a 25% reduction in federal funding.

The impact of decreased federal revenues is starkly illuminated by comparing the amount of fiscal support nonprofit organizations receive from government with their other sources of revenue. Contributions to these organizations from individuals, foundations, and corporations was approximately $22 billion in 1980, 55% less than the revenues received from government. For social services, federal support totaled 58% of all revenues (Salamon, 1984).

For the nonprofit sector to make up the difference caused by decreased federal funding, and holding constant the high probability of cutbacks in the level of contracting, charitable contributions would have to be increased. The issue here, however, is that simultaneous changes were proposed (and finally enacted in 1986) in tax policy, again with a potentially adverse affect on voluntary agencies. The specific issue of concern was a decrease in tax rates. People in the higher tax brackets gain the most from charitable contributions. As the individual's tax bracket lowers, the "real cost" of giving rises, thus discouraging giving. Reagan's tax plan, however, benefitted most those who, heretofore, had contributed the most, with the net effect of reducing incentives to, and likelihood of, such charitable contributions.

Under the best of circumstances, the expected level of charitable giving was of growing concern to the nonprofit sector. One discernible trend in relation to charitable contributions is that the rate of giving has been falling behind increases in overall personal income. Concurrently, more and more taxpayers have been opting to take the standard tax deductions, decreasing the likelihood of their making charitable contributions, because this would no longer count as a tax break (Salamon, 1984). The net result of changes in tax law was to decrease even further the likelihood of charitable giving.

There are at least two other themes of recent administrations that concern the use of purchase of service arrangements. One is the consistently echoed desire to promote stronger linkages between the public and private sectors and, to the extent possible, to shift heretofore public functions and responsibilities to the private sector. This theme, new only in its extreme, comes under the rubric of "privatization." The emphasis on partnership-building will be discussed at greater length later in this chapter.

Closely associated with the desire to enhance collaboration between the sectors is the emphasis on federalism. Clearly, the current thrust is to reverse the historic and pervasive reliance on centralized decision making, that is, the federal establishment, favoring, instead, the discharge of public responsibility through state and local governments. It is believed that this decentralization of planning and delivery functions will result in greater responsiveness to the needs of citizens, and more accountability and efficiency. The relevance of Reagan federalism to purchase of service lay in its underlying premise that public responsibilities—no matter what the level of government—should be met by delegating functions to the private sector. Ideally, this delegation would include a direct role for the private sector in financing service provision, as well as delivering services.

In summary, a number of features of the Reagan and Bush domestic agendas, and largely in line with the thinking of President Clinton, tended to favor the use of purchase of service as a logical, practical, and proven method of furthering political goals and priorities. The Reagan, Bush and Clinton Administrations shared a basic commitment to reducing the size and power of government, a philosophy based on the assumption that the private sector can conduct business more efficiently and effectively than government (Rowen, 1986). POS has thus proven to be remarkably consistent with the basic philosophical bent that the less government is the best government, government should get out of the business of direct service delivery, and heretofore government functions should be relegated to the private sector.

POS AS AN ALTERNATIVE TO
PUBLIC SERVICE PROVISION

Purchase of service helps to achieve practical political purposes. Dating back to the presidency of Jimmy Carter, there have been consistent efforts to trim the size of the bureaucracy. In 1993, President Clinton introduced a plan to "reinvent government," a response designed to address the negative sentiments about government. The President's plan aimed to cut 252,000 federal government positions over a 5-year period, reducing the Civil Service by 12%. If achieved, this reduction in force would result in a bureaucracy smaller in size than it has been since 1966 (Barr, 1993a).

This initiative is part of a systematic effort to cut costs while improving services and program effectiveness. Reducing the size and cost of government has broad-based political and popular appeal.

President Clinton's expanded domestic agenda is compatible with a decreased bureaucracy. POS offers the administration a logical alternative to accomplish both goals, building on established and popular precedent. Over the past 30 years, we have witnessed a steady erosion in government's service delivery role, with the gradual transfer of functions to the private sector through purchase of service. Although it is difficult to determine exactly how much money is saved by contracting out, the *appearance* of substantial cost savings serves an important symbolic agenda (Gibelman, 1995).

Although there is a tendency in some quarters to view purchase of service as unplanned and an accident of history, this overview of the growth in the use of contractual arrangements indicates their philosophical and ideological consistency with shifts in political priorities and legislative agendas. Particularly in recent years, the evolution from a predominantly federal system of planning, funding, and delivering social services to a system characterized largely by state and local (and increasingly, private-sector) responsibility has made purchase of service a significant mechanism by which to accomplish explicit objectives.

DEFINITIONS

Definitions of purchase of service tend to reflect the narrow range and special interests so dominant in this field. The government purchases services from for-profit organizations, from self-employed individuals, from groups of practitioners, from other governmental units, and, in the case of much of human services contracting, from the nonprofit sector.

Purchased services may be provided to targeted groups of people—a corporation, a neighborhood group, or special populations, such as child abusers or runaway youth. Public responsibility for certain services, such as child and adult protective services, and concerns about equity will influence some of these choices. In some cases, the type or number of people to whom services may be rendered within a group may be limited by statute, regulations or agreement, or may be open-ended. As we move increasingly toward oversight of dollars spent, more limited contracts are a likely scenario.

Purchase of service is, in fact, one part of two larger categories. One is concerned with the transmission of public funds to private bodies, individually or collectively. The other concerns the delivery of services. Throughout this volume, focus is on organized procedures by which an entity of the government enters into a formal agreement with another entity—public, private for-profit, private not-for-profit, or individual purveyor of services. The purchase may be for goods or services, but the focus here is on services and, almost exclusively, those services provided to individuals, groups, and communities to prevent, ameliorate, or resolve environmental, physical, or psychosocial problems (Demone & Gibelman, 1989; Gibelman, 1995)).

Purchase of service constitutes only one of several options to plan and deliver services. Government has the choice of providing a service directly, such as investigating cases of child abuse and neglect by state or local agencies, or turning to another organization, which may be another government unit, a nonprofit agency, a proprietary organization, or an individual contractor, to provide the product or service. Government may also choose a hybrid model, in which it directly provides a service, such as child protective services, but concurrently purchases the same service from community agencies (Gibelman, 1995).

Purchase of service thus concerns the act of transmitting public dollars to private service providers. Inherent in this transfer are decisions about how services are best delivered.

Clearly, purchase of service represents one arrangement by which the government may relate to the nongovernmental sector. There are several other commonly used mechanisms, however, for linking public and private interests. Government may induce change by using tax concessions. The use of tax inducements has a long tradition in the United States and has been of significant importance to organized religion, voluntary associations, foundations, and others. During the last two decades, various tax reforms have been proposed and some enacted by Congress. In each instance, there has been some tightening of the freedom of individual not-for-profit organizations to receive tax benefits. In the mid-1990s, various proposals for limiting the lobbying and advocacy activities of not-for-profits receiving public dollars have been set forth by Congress. To date, no action has been taken by Congress, but the issue is one that is likely to linger on the political agenda.

Tax benefits for the profit sector have a more pendulum-like history than is the case for not-for-profits. Clear trends are generally lacking. Use of tax inducements to produce desired goods and services may be considered an indirect intervention into the private marketplace. Purchase of service, in contrast, involves a direct buyer-seller relationship.

It should be emphasized that purchase of service constitutes only one of several ways to plan and deliver services. Options include:

- direct government provision, as in the case of veterans' services;
- grants, which tend to be more open-ended than contracts;
- vouchers;
- free-market;
- voluntary services; and
- self-help or self-services outside of mainstream organizations.

These mechanisms, in implementation, may and do overlap. One government unit may even elect to purchase a service (seldom a good) from another government unit and, in fact, the public purchase of other public services has been quite pervasive within the human services. Agencies (public and private) may be recipients of grants and contracts. Their clients may also be eligible for vouchers. Some of these same agencies may also compete in the open market to attract consumers.

RATIONALE FOR PURCHASING SERVICES

The justifications for purchase of service and the possible problems relating to its use are remarkably consistent, whether identified at the turn of the century, in the late 1950s, or now. It should be noted that the number of arguments posed pro or con are less significant than the cogency of each argument. The numbers are not as relevant as the weighting attributed to each factor.

Purchase of service is an attractive service delivery option from the perspective of both government and the private sector. In recent years, there has been a growing body of knowledge about the process and outcome of contracting for services and the issues arising from its use. Claims and counterclaims have been set forth concerning the weaknesses and strengths of this form of service delivery based on the respective experiences of government and contracted agencies. Various rationales have been offered both in favor of and against POS. The advantages cited include: cost savings, administrative efficiency, quick program startup and termination, program flexibility, lack of bureaucratic "red tape," enhanced quality of services, higher level of professionalism, flexible use of personnel, partnership-building with the private sector, promoting innovation and competition, political climate and citizen preferences, and reducing the size and role of government (Demone & Gibelman, 1989; Ferris, 1993; Gibelman & Demone, in press; Ruchelman, 1989).

The same arguments have sometimes been used by both opponents and proponents of POS. For example, proponents argue that the use of these arrangements lead to cost savings, while opponents set forth the view that cost savings are largely illusive and unsubstantiated. When both sides lay claim to the same benefits, empirical support is typically lacking.

The identified disadvantages of POS include the loss of public control and accountability, the lack of mechanisms to ensure standards, the increased cost of service, poorer quality services, the tendency of voluntary agencies to "cream" the better clients and not service the most needy, the unreliability of contractors, and the difficulty of monitoring purchased programs and services. Arguments against POS have also been made from the perspective of contracted agencies. These include the potential loss of autonomy for private agencies and the problems associated with subjecting private agencies to public policy shifts (Gibelman & Demone, in press; Smith & Lipsky, 1993).

BOUNDARIES

The boundaries of purchase of service arrangements are continually expanding, within the broader context of the desire to privatize as many government functions as possible. Relative to the human services, several areas that were exclusively within the province of government are now being re-examined to identify alternative delivery methods, including social security (Kenworthy & Dewar, 1990). To date, POS has been applied to group homes, day care, child protective services, substance abuse services, foster care, mental health services, and residential care, among others. Very few areas remain untouched by contracting. A notable exception is in the area of protective services (adult or child), where the service includes a legal determination process and cannot easily be delegated by government to another provider.

The increased use of POS must thus be understood within the context of prevailing priorities, values, and preferences affecting social welfare policies and programs. The use of not-for-profit and for-profit human service providers as an alternative to public service delivery is politically expedient and a realistic and effective way to circumvent negative public sentiment about government's size and role. Its use is likely to continue unabated, despite some real or alleged problems that have surfaced in contracting experience.

Government contracting for social services has traditionally been smaller in scale, both absolutely and proportionately, than contracting for other government services, such as defense. Nevertheless, POS is now the dominant means for delivering social services. By the early 1990s, contracting for social services with nonprofits had become a $15 billion-a-year business (Smith & Lipsky, 1993). Government spends about $200 billion a year to purchase goods and services, of which approximately $105 billion goes to service contracts (Barr, 1994a). Such service contracts range from janitorial and food services to human services.

The use of voluntary and proprietary agencies to provide government-financed services does not alter the public nature of the service. Government pays for these services through taxes or user fees (Ruchelman, 1989). The decision to finance a human service and the decision about how to produce or provide that service may be made on the basis of very different criteria.

Virtually any human service can be purchased, and the potential variations in contracting across the states and localities fits with federalization and decentralization values and currents. The possibilities are as broad as the entire human services industry. The goal and intended outcome is to fulfill society's social welfare responsibilities in the most cost-effective, efficient, and qualitative manner, utilizing the expertise of the private sector. In the process, heightened competition among and between not-for-profits and for-profits to provide services is seen as enhancing private sector capability.

To best understand this increasingly complex mosaic, sets of constraints have been identified as if to represent pure either-or polarities: public versus private, not-for-profit versus profit. Marxists, Keynesians, liberals, traditionalists, pragmatists, neoconservatives, and conservatives, each convinced of their own perspective, are engaged in ongoing debate about the various merits of direct public service delivery versus partial or full purchase of service. For example, Stoesz (1981) described the prevalence of contracting for service as the "end of the welfare state" (p. 398). The issue of what form of service delivery works best for what problem and population at risk seems at times less relevant than ideological positions.

For many adherents of increased use of purchase of services, the issue is not whether "the least government is the best government," but how government can best achieve its objectives in the public interest. Society and its political representatives still maintain some commitment to meeting essential human needs, but are increasingly disenchanted with the means. The conservatives reject both ends and means; they want the government out of the human services "business." A nominal "safety net" is permissible. Then there are the pragmatists, those persuaded of the legitimate need for human services and structures to deliver these services. They merely want to know how best to achieve ends within realistic economic and social limitations (Demone & Gibelman, 1989).

It is not possible to identify all human services that are purchased because of the variations in contracting across the states and localities and, within each jurisdiction, the changes that occur over time in decision making about what should be purchased. Services purchased include mental health, emergency shelters for the homeless, group homes, day care, child protective services, foster care, mental health services, residential care, mental retardation services, services to pregnant and parenting teenagers, substance abuse counseling, pupil personnel services, and psychiatric hospital care. In some instances, the decision to purchase services may be motivated by the more rapid start-up capability of the private sector and its perceived responsiveness to the need for innovative programming. In other instances, precedent may play an important role in decision making.

The boundaries of purchase of service arrangements are continually expanding. Service areas that were exclusively within the province of government are now being reexamined to identify alternative delivery forms. The maintenance and ownership of jails is one example. Community fire and police services are two other areas in which heretofore public functions are now being delegated to the private sector by use of the contract method. Deficit-plagued state and local governments are increasingly turning to contracting as a means to save money and are examining what services may be turned over to private hands: garbage collection, transportation, automobile and building inspections, road maintenance, and cleaning public parks and buildings (Mathews, 1991; "Privatizing city services," 1994). Elected officials have embraced privatization. Mayor Guiliani of New York, as an example, has made sweeping proposals toward this end, including hiring private firms to operate some of the city's hospitals ("Privatizing city services," 1994). California's governor, Pete Wilson, has supported contracting out and privatization as partial solutions to the state budget deficit (Mathews, 1991). In an editorial, the *New York Times* ("Privatizing city services," 1994) offered its opinion: "Privatization, judiciously administered to foster healthy competition between city workers and the private sector, holds real promise for improving services and for saving money."

Almost the only exception to the utilization of contracting is in the area of national security or individual protection. In the former instance, it is only government that can protect the national security and provide for defense systems. Even here the government purchases all of its goods and an increasing proportion of its services. Despite some serious problems in the procurement practices of the Department of Defense, the fact remains that it continues to rely heavily on the use of purchase arrangements for products and services. With individual protection, some states may legislate that adult and child protective services are exclusively a public function. However, in the latter instance, there are already several precedents for the use of a private sector delivery model.

The extent to which purchase of service dominates a particular human services field is subject to a wide range of influences, including traditional practices, political and philosophical forces, and prevailing social and political values and preferences affecting social welfare policies and programs. Changing conceptions about the roles and functions of government and the private sector within this society affect the degree to which preference is given to alternative service delivery methods.

THE CHANGING NATURE OF
PUBLIC–PRIVATE RELATIONS

Purchase of service has been heralded as a means of forging stronger linkages between the public and private sectors, thereby promoting a partnership approach to the design, financing, and delivery of services. This emphasis on the positive benefits to accrue from a mixed service delivery system was expressed by Presidents Nixon, Ford, and Carter. The Reagan and Bush plans were merely an extreme version of a recurrent theme, to which purchase of service, as a means to an end, is philosophically and ideologically consistent.

The explosion in the use of POS arrangements has permanently altered the relationship between government and the voluntary and proprietary sectors. Many of the impacts have been positive. Voluntary agencies have had to develop new management competencies, ranging from contract negotiating skills to sophisticated financial accountability. POS has also resulted in the introduction of programs and services not previously available, as well as the start-up of new voluntary agencies and/or an increase in the scope of the services provided by existing voluntary agencies (Gibelman, 1995).

One example of service expansion through purchasing is in the area of services for victims of crime, a category of provision that had been largely nonexistent prior to the early 1980s, with the exception of child abuse. New authorizing legislation at the federal and state level resulted in the initiation or expansion of voluntary agency services to victims of crime. From government's point of view, a key advantage in initiating services to victims of crime through contracts with voluntary agencies was the quick start-up capability of nonprofits and the ease of terminating the contractual agreement when funding lagged (Smith, 1989). From the viewpoint of the voluntary agencies, federal funds, even when accompanied by regulations and program requirements that altered the way in which business was conducted, provided a means to expand services. The downside, of course, was the impact on these same agencies when there were cutbacks of contract funds.

The greater interaction between the public and private sectors that has been the natural consequence of purchase of service has intensified the dialogue about the appropriate relationship between the two sectors. A component of the debate concerns the perceived dichotomy between government's search for accountability and nonprofits' desire to preserve autonomy (Gibelman, 1995). As Ferris (1993) notes, voluntary agencies have always been accountable, but their primary constituency group was typically their board of directors, donors, and volunteers in charitable markets. Now, government has instilled its own set of accountability requirements, which may be instead of, in addition to, and/or in conflict with the nonprofits' traditional accountability channels.

In the earlier days of POS, voluntary agencies were in a positive position. In the absence of precedents, the public and voluntary agencies worked together as partners to define and implement contractual arrangements. Voluntary agencies could propose and initiate the contracting process; they had the expertise that government needed. In general, government funds through contracts represented only one of several diverse funding sources for voluntary agencies; while contracts were an attractive source of revenue to expand services or fund new services, procurement of such funds typically was an issue of augmentation, rather than survival.

Goldstein (1993) bemoans the transformation of private charities into "agents of the state." Voluntary agencies have come to depend on contract funds. The resulting financial dependence has dramatically altered the power relationship between the sectors. Bureaucratic rules and regulations governing contract negotiations, rate-setting, and monitoring and evaluation multiplied as a consequence of a new POS specialization within the public sector and implementation experience, also complicating public-private relationships.

The rise of a contract industry within the public sector encumbered the contracting process, adding to the complexity of negotiations and inevitable time delays. Rules were instituted that focus not only on the outcome of POS services, but also the process in which programs and services are carried out. For example, contracting specifications may prescribe the number of worker-client contacts or detail client eligibility criteria that allows little room for discretion.

POS regulations now authorize government to purchase from proprietary agencies. Thus, voluntary agencies now not only compete with other voluntary agencies for contracts, but vie with for-profits as well. The for-profits generally have developed a high level of technical competence in contract writing and negotiating compared to nonprofits, in large part because they have devoted personnel and resources to capacity-building in this area.

The cumulative effect of these several factors, according to McMurtry, Netting, and Kettner (1990, p. 68), "was that a recently enlarged voluntary service sector suddenly faced the combination of fluctuating demand, declining availability of resources, and increased inter- and intra-sectoral competition for both clients and dollars."

Nonprofits' competitive advantage thus gave way to a more defensive and reactive posture. Year-to-year funding creates a degree of financial uncertainty that taxes the ability of agencies to engage in long-range program and fiscal planning and leaves staff uncertain about their future employment (Gibelman, 1995). As the proportion of total agency revenues from purchase of service increases, voluntary agencies also find themselves "resource-dependent" on government. The greater the dependence of an organization on resources which are controlled by an outside source, the greater the influence of that external funding source (Hasenfeld, 1992). Resource dependence also tends to rechannel organizational time and energy to maintain inter-organizational relationships that promote or enhance the agency's competitive position.

Goal Displacement

With the proliferation of Request for Proposals (RFPs) for new and expanding services, many voluntary agencies responded by enlarging their domain. This domain expansion has been described as vertical integration, in which the range of target groups served or types of services offered is broadened (McMurtry et al., 1990). Two primary issues resulted from this expansion. First, the areas of expansion followed the money trail, and were not necessarily related to program development priority areas determined by the agency's board of directors. Second, once the new program or service is initiated, typically with the agency assuming planning and start-up expenses, it develops a constituency of staff and clients. Thus, in the eventuality that purchase of service funds dry up in the particular area, pressure would likely be brought to bear on the agency to continue the program or service as part of the agency's core offerings. The contracted program is justified on the basis of its quality, the added resources it brings to the organization, and the needed void it fills within the community.

Many nonprofits now face a dilemma: to what extent should organizational maintenance and growth needs take precedence over organizational mission? The association of Jewish sectarian agencies with government agencies, as highlighted in this volume by Levine (Chapter 5), suggests the magnitude of the issue. Because the shifting of program resources, size, and priority may occur over time, program directions are decided by default, rather than by established agency decision-making processes. When and if the contract funds are cut back or terminated, the agency faces critical issues about how organizational resources are to be used.

The tendency for purchase of service arrangements to encourage, if not directly lead to, goal displacement is one of the important unintended consequences with long-term implications for voluntary social welfare agencies. Further, when organizations seek to take advantage of available funding, the start-up costs involved in program development must be considered, as well as the potential impact on the cohesiveness and morale of staff (Edwards & Yankey, 1991). The potential of goal displacement is diminished in for-profit agencies, since they operate on the basis of profitability: a program or service must, at a minimum, be self-supporting.

The environment in which nonprofits function has become more turbulent as a result of POS, primarily due to the decrease in the level of control nonprofits can exert over decision-making processes that affect them. The advent of a contracting industry within the public sector, discussed above, has subjected nonprofits to the schedules and bureaucratic processes of government (Gibelman, 1995). Delays in contract negotiations, particularly in regard to program renewals, can have devastating effects on the cash flow of the voluntary agency and can even necessitate staff layoffs or the search for other external funds to continue the program or service (McMurtry et al., 1990). The repercussions for the voluntary agencies can be long-term—overload and burnout of staff, loss of valuable staff, and disruptions of operations. For example, at the national level, the Clinton Administration's initial delay in appointing senior officials involved in contract decisions hampered the flow of government contracts worth hundreds of millions of dollars, thus threatening the operations and even survival of companies dependent on these funds (Southerland, 1993).

POS has also impacted upon the internal operations of voluntary agencies. Fiscal management, with multiple reporting sources and perhaps different financial monitoring procedure requirements, has made fiscal operations much more complex. Similarly, different funding sources may have different accountability requirements, tending to increase the time and effort devoted by professional staff to paperwork. The only real power the voluntary agency can exercise over these requirements and the more general uncertainties inherent in the contract relationship is to say "no" to the contract process or product. It can request, negotiate, manipulate, or bargain for timely contract renewals, reasonable rate-setting, less paperwork, or more discretion. But, ultimately, the only absolute power the not-for-profit has is to withdraw from the relationship.

Standards for Contracting

An example of the legitimacy and common use of contracting for services is found in the incorporation of content related to their use in standards of national organizations which accredit social service agencies, such as the Child Welfare League of America and the Council on Accreditation of Services to Families and Children (COA). New COA standards (COA, 1997), for example, include among requirements for all agencies a section on "Contractual Relationships and Provider Alliances":

> The organization which engages in contractual agreements as a purchaser or vendor of services or as a cooperating provider in an alliance or network complies with the following standards:
>
> - Contracts and formal alliances or networks entered into by the organization are related to the organization's purpose and congruent with the policies of the governing body.
> - Policies and procedures, trends, and relationships with regard to purchase or vendorship of services are reviewed by the governing body.
> - The organization, whether the purchaser or vendor in a particular con-

tractual relationship, uses written purchase of service agreements or written contracts which contain all terms and conditions.

- The terms and conditions of contracts define the persons to whom service is to be provided, the services, the expected outcomes of the service, the methods for resolution of disputes, and the plan and procedures for payment.
- The organization which provides services as a vendor establishes safeguards against over- and under-billing which could jeopardize future funding or weaken the organization's financial condition and such safeguards include:
  - an accurate account of units of service provided;
  - timely submission; and
  - compliance with applicable regulations.
- The organization which provides services as a vendor reviews all contractual agreements to ensure that policies and operational procedures regarding confidentiality of persons served and professional conduct and practices are not violated by complying with the terms of the contract. (pp. 45–46)

Similarly, in regard to public agencies which contract out, COA standards specify that:

The public organization which is an applicant for accreditation and which also contracts with providers for a component or an array of services carries out the contracting process in accord with established procedures and with due regard for standards of best practice.

- The public organization which purchases services on behalf of eligible persons establishes a system of standardized procedures for contract management as a guide to its own personnel and for potential contractors.
- The availability of contract funds is made known through a formal bid or request for proposal issued by a public organization, in which explicit criteria are set forth.
- The public organization develops formal procedures for rating proposals and selecting providers.
- The public organization which is a purchaser of services from other providers develops procedures for administrative and programmatic accountability, for reporting on the quantity of service delivered under the contract, and for performance evaluation.
- The public organization which purchases or contracts for services establishes expectations that:
  - the majority of the contractors have a plan to meet national accreditation standards within a reasonable period of time; and
  - the contractors meet applicable licensing standards. (p. 46)

Other standards related to the purchase of services permeate the full gamut of standards. For example, in regard to quality assurance, standards require that the organization which purchases some of its services have a system in place to monitor, evaluate, and improve those contracted services (COA, 1997, Standard G2.6.05).

These standards are suggestive of the range of issues facing the non-profit world toward the beginning of the 21st century. Their content verifies some of the concerns discussed above in regard to goal displacement, boundary blurring between sectors, and service quality. For example, agencies accredited by COA are expected to enter contracts only in line with their purpose. Contracting policies and procedures are to be formalized through board review and oversight. Contracts are not to compromise organizational policies and procedures about client confidentiality. Standards of best practice are to be a baseline for the public agency in selecting a provider. The process is to be competitive. The fact that POS figures prominently in the revised COA standards points to the breadth of contracting relationships in which many, if not most, not-for-profits engage.

POS AS A VEHICLE OF SOCIAL CHANGE

Purchase of service has played an important but rarely articulated role in fostering larger social change purposes. A case in point is the use of the "power of the purse" through contracts to force compliance of the private sector with public sector goals. Affirmative action is a notable example.

In 1961, President Kennedy issued Executive Order 10925 which created the President's Committee on Equal Employment Opportunity. This Committee was charged with recommending "affirmative steps" that executive branch department and agencies could take to more fully integrate the federal work force. The Order went further in prohibiting discrimination on the basis of race, creed, color, or national origin by federal contractors. In fulfilling their contracts, these contractors were ordered to take affirmative steps to hire African Americans and other racial minorities (Wells & Idelson, 1995).

In 1965, President Johnson, through Executive Order 11246, expanded President Kennedy's earlier order by requiring contractors to take affirmative steps in all business operations, not just in fulfilling federal contracts (Pecora, 1995). (Gender protection was added as an amendment to the Executive Order in 1967.) This Executive Order was prompted by the perceived inadequacies of the 1964 Civil Rights Act; the law was not sufficiently effective in increasing economic and educational opportunities for targeted populations. Companies were required to submit their "numerical goals and timetables" used in carrying out their affirmative action plans (Wells & Idelson, 1995). In 1969, President Nixon further endorsed goals and timetables through Executive Order No. 11478. And, again, doing business with government through contracts was the means to force compliance (Gibelman, 1997). The U.S. Department of Labor, Office of Federal Contract Compliance Programs (OFCCP) requires contractors and subcontractors that employ 50 or more people and receive $50,000 or more in federal contracts to develop and maintain affirmative action programs for people of color, women, and persons with disabilities (U.S. Commission on Civil Rights, 1995).

In 1991 the Act was amended, through Title VI (P.L. 102-166, Nov. 21, 1991, 105 Stat. 1071), to prohibit discrimination based on race, color, or national origin in any program or activity that receives federal government financial assistance (Wells & Idelson, 1995). Included in this category would be programs that receive loans, tax breaks, or grants and contracts from the government.

The sheer scope of contracting ensured some degree of achievement of affirmative action goals. Affirmative action has a direct bearing on the internal policies and practices of agencies with which government does business, particularly in regard to employment practices. It suggests that positive steps must be taken to achieve equality in admissions to institutions of higher education, in hiring and promotion in employment settings, and in other arenas. Inequities must be reduced and eliminated through active intervention (DiNitto, 1991; Pecora, 1995). The implementation of affirmative action was left to employers and educational institutions, most of whom have developed affirmative action divisions or departments to create and monitor institutional policy. It is up to the businesses coming under this policy to demonstrate that they are in compliance with equal opportunity laws. If they want contracts, they need to comply. Social change has been fostered in this way.

The Small Business Administration (SBA) Minority Enterprise Program has also broadly impacted on achieving larger social change goals. This program applies to companies that are 51% owned, controlled, and operated by individuals considered to be socially and economically disadvantaged. *Economic disadvantage* is defined as a net worth of less than $250,000, excluding home equity or business investment. *Social disadvantage* refers to members of racial and ethnic groups, as well as white men and women who can demonstrate economic disadvantage based on prejudice (NASW, 1996).

The continued justification for the SBA program is based on several

Supreme Court decisions. The Supreme Court, in 1980, in *Fullilove v. Klutznick* (448 U.S. 448) found compelling evidence that minority-owned businesses had been denied effective participation in public contracting opportunities. The Court upheld the Public Employment Works Act of 1977 (P.L. 95-28, Stat. 116 [1988]), which required that "10 percent of all federal funds granted for local public works projects be used to procure services or supplies from minority owned or controlled businesses" (U.S. Commission on Civil Rights, 1995, p. 22). In 1989, in the case of *City of Richmond v. J.A. Croson Co.*, (488 U. S. 469) the Supreme Court upheld the "strict standard of review to remedial race-conscious measures" adopted by Virginia and the City of Richmond (National Association of Social Workers [NASW], 1996, p. 3).

As we approach the 21st century, the concept, policy, and practices of affirmative action have come under substantial criticism and review. In *Adarand Constructors, Inc. v. Federeco Pena* (No. 93-1841, 132 L. Ed. 2d 158), the Supreme Court ruled in 1995 that strict standards must be met to justify any contracting or hiring practices based on race, which might include correcting documented cases of discrimination and correcting specific instances of discrimination (NASW, 1996). Despite the application of stricter standards of review for programs to provide business opportunities in government contracting for racial minorities, the Court has not, as of this writing, ruled out the continuation of affirmative action and the Minority Enterprise Program. The majority of states have sought to document that their minority contracting programs are justified by current and past racial discrimination through studies to determine if there is a gap between the number of willing and qualified local minority firms and their share of contracting dollars (Henderson, 1992).

Indeed, there is evidence that these programs have worked. For example, a study of 77,000 companies with a collective total of more than 20 million employees found that minority employment increased by 20% and female employment by 15% after affirmative action programs in contracting had been implemented (National Council of LaRaza, 1995).

THE TECHNOLOGY OF CONTRACTING

Types of Contracting

Purchase of service is not a unitary concept. The arrangements by which government may purchase services from other public units or the private sector can take several forms. These range from the straightforward purchase on a unit basis of service on the open market to formalized contracts between the public agency and provider that define the type, conditions, and intensity of services to be purchased. The primary issue is the degree of control government will exercise over the services to be delivered, including the selection of clients/patients, the means and frequency of delivery, and the systems instituted for implementation, monitoring, and evaluation.

Purchase of service can take several forms, with variations in type of contractual arrangements often depending on the desired buyer-seller relationship and the nature of the service(s) to be purchased. One method is to purchase the service(s) for particular individuals or classes/categories of individuals. The premise here is that there are certain individuals, with identified problems or needs, who are deemed eligible by virtue of their problem or need to receive services. The service provider, be it an organization or individual, determines whether or not to sell the service. The Vocational Rehabilitation Administration, through its state agencies, is a classic user of this kind of arrangement. These agencies often pay market prices to educational institutions and medical rehabilitative facilities to provide services to particular clients who have specific, identified needs. Such contractual arrangements may be long or short term. The seller may offer services based on selective screening or serve all who are referred by the public agency who fall within a particular category or type of problem (Demone & Gibelman, 1989). These types of purchasing arrangements are typical within the human services.

The provider may offer services based on selective screening or service all who are referred by the contracting agency who fall within the established criteria; this will depend on the specifications of the contract. The amount of discretion that may be given to the voluntary or proprietary service provider has, historically, raised concerns that they may "cream" the "better" clients, those who are likely to achieve positive results from the service and are thus easier to "treat " (Gibelman, 1981).

The contract period may be for 6 months to several years. Contracts may, however, be terminated if the provider fails to live up to the agreement or if public funds are reduced or eliminated.

Time-limited, task-oriented contracts constitute another form of purchase of service. Such arrangements are generally initiated to prepare a product or deliver a service of a one-time nature; that is, once the service is delivered or the product completed, the contract will be terminated. Health research and defense contracts best illustrate this model. In the case of defense contracts, the U.S. Department of Defense may contract with a corporation, such as General Electric or Lockheed, to produce a new engine for an airplane. Once the engine is completed in the specified quantities, the contract is concluded. Most often, time frames for the completion of the work are built into the contract itself. In research, a medical school, research firm, or health association might be contracted to conduct an assessment of patient characteristics in public and private hospital emergency rooms.

The time-limited contracts, characterized by a high degree of specificity in terms of the product and production deadlines, may have a number of substantial effects on the seller. One disadvantage from the perspective of the service provider is that a substantial start-up period is often necessary to initiate the contracted tasks, with the possibility that the contracted organization will have to disband if the contract is not renewed, when the task has been completed, or if public interests and priorities have shifted (Demone & Gibelman, 1989). When Congress, for example, decided to cut the defense budget, the need for military aircraft decreased and contracts with Boeing were curtailed. There was a dramatic and severe impact not only on the company, but on the entire Seattle area, which is home to Boeing.

The costs to the seller of implementing and disbanding may be substantial and not necessarily covered by the contract budget. For example, the costs of hiring a staff of experts or expanding the physical plant may not be fully compensated or may be of dubious value in terms of time and effort. However, from the point of view of the public agency, these task-oriented contracts are extremely cost-effective and imply a responsible use of public funds in that no long-term commitments are implied. These contracts also allow for assessment and evaluation of the value of the service and contractor on the basis of specific and isolated pieces of work and places the major burden of start-up, personnel dislocation, and project termination on the service provider.

Another common purchase arrangement is for government to write a contract on a more extended time basis. These longer term commitments assume that the service or product will be needed indefinitely. As Richardson and Gutch point out in this volume (Chapter 6), there is an assumption that the vendor will sustain high service delivery capability over time. Components of these longer-term contracts may be quite specific, for example, the populations to be served, the types of services to be offered, and eligibility criteria. Similarly, the focus of the service may be narrow or broad in scope, such as diagnosing health problems or providing treatment and cure.

The Office of Economic Opportunity, the U.S. Department of Education, and the Job Corps Program, among others, have experimented with performance contracting. As Kettner and Martin (Chapter 7) note in this volume, recent federal legislation mandates that all federal agencies initiate outcome-oriented evaluations of their programs and services. Performance contracting is one way of distinguishing the successful from the unsuccessful.

As concerns about accountability have increased, purchase-of-service contracting has tended to become more formalized. Contracts often require the delineation of the kinds of service to be delivered and the standards for conducting these services. Specification of the target population, types and levels of service, intake eligibility procedures, budget and record keeping, personnel assignments and staff qualifications, and various reporting mechanisms may also be mandated. Such requirements may be seen as overwhelming and counterproductive by the provider and may impact on the length and complexity of the negotiating process. The provider agency may be required to submit a formal proposal to the public agency providing the program rationale and detailing its elements. This proposal is then negotiated until a final form, acceptable to both parties, is achieved. Time frames for completion of service activities and evaluation of the services provide a more legitimate basis by which the public agency can monitor performance and assure quality.

A major objective of policymakers and administrators is to ensure that services are provided in the most cost-effective manner. Several important matters of policy can be identified in relation to the financing of services, including reimbursement procedures and rate-setting for particular services or programs. Equity and incentives, rationality, level and types of payments, responsible record keeping, and assignment of public and private sector roles are all considerations in determining purchase-of-service cost structures (Gibelman & Demone, 1989).

The private sector is not expected to subsidize a new weapons system for the U.S. Department of Defense, but private human services providers are often expected to contribute, in cash or kind, to the cost of purchased social services. The difference has to do with attitudes about public and private responsibility. Rarely is it argued that the national defense is within the purview of private sector responsibility; even our Constitution allocates powers of defense and war to government. The assignment of responsibility for human services is less clear. Consistent with earlier Republican administrations, President Clinton, a Democrat, has also rallied behind the concept of privatization. The return or delegation of many service delivery functions to the private sector and the fostering of public–private partnerships is one important means to share responsibility, even if government still maintain partial or full funding responsibility. Requiring private agencies to match a portion of public funds may, in the view of recent presidents, prod the private sector's conscience to do what it is expected to do.

Deficit financing, as an alternative to purchasing units of service, is also a feasible model. In this case, a contracted individual or agency has an agreement to provide a service to a specific population or to all of those applying for service with a particular kind of problem. The service provider is seen as the primary financier of such services, the dollars of which may come from a variety of sources. Assuming that the service is consistent with public priorities and that the provider has met the conditions of imposed or applicable quality assurances, the government makes up the deficit between what the provider is able to secure from other sources and the actual cost of operating the program/service. For example, a half-way house may be able to secure 80% of its annual operating budget from United Way contributions, payment of fees by the residents of the house, and fund-raising activities.

Another pattern, more formalized, is the vendor agreement. Under vendorship arrangements, funds are allocated by the public agency to purchase specific services for clients. A simple contract may specify the rate of reimbursement for the services rendered. The number of clients to be served may be open-ended or estimated. As characterized in the field of rehabilitation services, purchase orders may also be issued by case managers to obtain products or services on the open market (Gurin & Freidman, 1989). An extension of the purchase-order contract is to give the consumer the power and responsibility to secure services for himself or herself. The client is then reimbursed directly at a predetermined rate. A variation of this theme is the use of vouchers. Because of the widespread attention to the potential use of vouchers, this mechanism deserves special mention.

Are Vouchers a Viable Alternative for Service Delivery?

Vouchers represent the extreme form of purchase of service, in which the decision about service provider is left to the individual consumer who then purchases the service directly. This model for social services, however, has been more widely discussed than implemented, and its immediate application has been sought mostly in housing and education. In the health industry, Medicare and Medicaid, following the traditional third-party health insurance model, have been largely based on the voucher system.

Vouchers involve the transfer of income to an individual to enable that person to purchase a specified type of good or service (Struyk & Bendick, 1982). Vouchers differ from cash equivalents in that they are restricted to specific uses. Thus, although vouchers pay homage to consumer choice, that choice is, in fact, limited to the goods or services within the eligible category. Recipients in this model are given cash equivalents by the public agency to purchase the necessary services in the market. The market may be open or constrained. For example, allowable competitors may be limited to not-for-profit organizations previously solicited by the public agency or with whom it has contracts. Psychotherapy may be limited to medically trained psychiatrists.

Several studies of experimental voucher programs have indicated positive results. In housing, substantially lower costs for private housing were found in comparison to units provided through government-operated public housing. Low-income families generally proved to be capable shoppers and obtained good value for their money without the need for assistance in searching for or procuring housing units (Struyk & Bendick, 1982). However, the positive results in regard to obtaining a house, per se, were not necessarily generalizable to other program objectives. Housing vouchers were provided instead of cash because of the desire to provide purchasing power only for housing. Struyk and Bendick (1982) found that recipients used their housing vouchers to substitute for money they were already spending on rent. The result was that only a small proportion of the value of the vouchers went for housing expenses; the rest was used for basic necessities. The objective to control recipient behavior was not achieved.

More recently, another problem associated with housing vouchers has emerged. The Section 8 housing subsidy program, which provides rent vouchers that entitled persons can use wherever they choose, has had the unintended consequence of increasing the density of already poor neighborhoods (Robberson, 1996). Although in theory the subsidy can be used to rent a unit anywhere on the open market, in fact the amount of the subsidy is insufficient. The federal government sets maximums on the voucher on the basis of family size. Thus, recipients of Section 8 vouchers frequently end up in poverty-stricken neighborhoods. The intent of the program—to assist low-income people to integrate into mainstream neighborhoods—is thwarted (Robberson, 1996).

To date, most of the experience with vouchers has been in the field of education, although third-party reimbursement in the health industry has many voucher characteristics. Their extended use could involve the certification of providers to provide quality control, in which public and private agencies could compete. Proposals have recently been debated about the merits of giving Medicare recipients vouchers so that they could buy coverage from private insurers or health maintenance organizations. The perceived benefit is in the potential cost savings, since private sector costs have, in recent years, risen less rapidly that Medicare costs (Rich, 1995).

Voucher systems could probably not be easily applied to service areas in which a regulatory/supervisory public justice function is involved, such as child protective services, corrections, and police protection. In these areas, the services delivered claim public uniqueness and cannot be left to consumer choice (Demone & Gibelman, 1989).

Although the efficiency of the private market, through the use of vouchers, may lead to lower costs, better quality, or both, the ability of taxpayers to impose their own preferences on the behavior of recipients is weakened. As we approach the 21st century, issues of behavior control are on the political agenda. Examples include provisions of the Welfare Reform Act of 1996. Drawbacks to voucher schemes also include the perception of limitations of consumers' ability to make informed judgements; the reliance on marketplace mechanisms in an environment of incomplete information; and the abdication of reliance on professionalism and expert knowledge.

These devises are all instrumentalities to make government assistance centered on the individual rather than on the institution, thus bypassing the major human service agencies as "brokers." As noted, they are intended to restore a measure of marketplace forces to induce and stimulate a degree of competition among providers, ideally allowing the consumer to determine the best source of services (Kahn, 1973).

Despite its simplicity and face validity, the widespread use of vouchers has many obstacles. Both conservatives and liberals doubt the wisdom of giving the poor and minorities authority to make their own decisions. That they might purchase frivolities (such as toothpaste or beer with their food stamps) worries the conservatives. The liberals fear that without controls and expanded resources, the poor might be exploited. "Otherwise, vouchers might become a way for government to abrogate its responsibility for making and implementing social policy" (Brilliant, 1973, p. 393).

REIMBURSEMENT AND COST STRUCTURES

The financial components of purchase-of-service contracts usually reflect more than the dollar value placed on a service or product. Matching requirements are a notable example of the political overtones of such fiscal arrangements; here, prevailing attitudes about role assignments and auspices may be one such factor. Market considerations, more broadly based than one particular contract, also impact on reimbursement rates and cost structures. Lack of competition among private sector providers, a common situation in weapons or aircraft production, places the seller in a much more opportune position to negotiate favorable financial arrangements. Providers of day care, a service for which there is substantial competition, must promise a lot and bid low in order to win a contract and, in fiscal negotiations, are in a far less advantageous position than providers of services for which there are few or no competitors.

As noted, claims that purchasing services are a means to reduce costs are often at the forefront of rationales supporting this form of service delivery. However, such claims are most often made on the basis of assumptions rather than on hard data. A few studies do support the proposition that purchasing services is less expensive than directly providing them. However, these seldom measure qualitative differences or account for administrative costs to the public agency to negotiate, monitor, and evaluate contracted programs. (It should be noted however, that this deficit in measurement applies equally to public agencies. When measuring public agency costs for the delivery of direct services, indirect costs, especially those not in the operating agency, are seldom measured.) Most frequently, cost comparisons focus on the dollar amounts expended by contracted agencies versus the cost to the public agency to provide the same or similar service. When viewed in isolation, contracted services may appear highly cost-effective. When the added costs to the public agency for contract oversight functions are calculated as part of the POS overhead expenses, it is less clear that significant savings are realized.

Given the difficulty in controlling the many variables affecting accurate POS cost determination, claims of cost efficiency must thus rely primarily on assumptions and available hard data. The limited information available from empirical studies tends to support the argument that contracted services are less expensive than those provided directly by the public agency. Most such determinations, however, refer to the purchase of concrete services or products, such as fire protection, refuse collection, and municipal services (e.g., water, sewage). These studies are narrow in focus and provide little useful information in relation to the cost of human services, many of which fall into the category of "soft" services—counseling, prevention, and foster care. In these instances the units of measurement are more difficult to identify, and the outcomes often do not lend themselves to easy quantification.

The POS cost-effectiveness studies have been criticized on a number of grounds. First, such studies fail to take into account that a large proportion of contracting occurs between government units, rather than between government and private agents. Is this type of contracting less expensive? If not, what is the rationale for its predominant use? DeHoog (1984) also argues that there is a dearth of hard data on the relative advantages and disadvantages of public versus private delivery, and that comparisons between these two forms are needed in areas in which both types of agencies provide the same service. She further observes that some of the costs associated with contracting out may be underestimated. Before-and-after cost comparisons fail to take into account, according to deHoog, the long-term costs. New contractors, for example, may bid low to get a contract and then negotiate higher rates in succeeding contract years. The costs to the private agency to prepare, negotiate, and administratively operate the contracts are also not always factored into cost studies. Kettner and Martin, however, in this volume (Chapter 7), argue that the more sophisticated application of accountability mechanisms in contracting in recent year has also positively impacted on cost-effectiveness data.

Many public human services organizations require that the private vendors with whom they contract follow budget-planning guidelines similar to those used within the public sector. An object (line) budget is developed, with each item justified. In this approach, all the limitations of and problems associated with public budgeting are then replicated in the private sector. In addition, transfers between object items may be severely limited, resulting in the need for frequent contract revisions. At the other end of the continuum are performance contracts, in which payment is based on what is actually produced or delivered. Measures of service outcomes are identified in the contract as the basis of payment, and incentives and disincentives may also be scheduled. The type of contract budget used may have much to do with public agency regulations and style preferences, but may also be affected by the negotiating ability and influence of the private vendor (Demone & Gibelman, 1989).

There are several methods of calculating payment rates for services. One method is to relate the number of services to an expenditure base; this base may be expanded or contracted, depending on what is included in it (Copeland, 1976). The base almost always includes overhead, depreciation, and other costs of agency operations. Rates of payments may also be negotiated or budget-based. Criteria other than actual costs are used to determine the negotiated rate, whereas budget-based rates are based on actual cost experience, with possible adjustments permitted for any changes in service quality or quantity. Payment rates may also be calculated on the basis of unit cost (the total annual cost of a service divided by the number of treatment/service units) or the proportion of the total cost. Rates may also be variable or fixed. There may be combinations of several types of rate payment methods incorporated into a single contract, for example, a negotiated, unit-cost rate or a closed-ended (fixed) amount (Gibelman & Demone, 1989).

The rate structure established for a contract has important implications for the service program. If the payment rate is determined on the basis of units of service, the contracted provider must ensure that the hours of treatment/service, number of home visits, or weeks of day care agreed upon in advance are actually provided and adequate records maintained. Here, payment is not related to the quality of services or to the sophistication of the services provided, but rather to objective and basic indicators or inputs. To the extent that rates of payment are fixed, budget-based, and have a constant expenditure base, the vendor may have little incentive to go beyond the minimum contract requirements in either quantity or quality. This is consistent with the criticisms of managed health care programs.

Control of line item expenditures may be dysfunctional; when the contracted provider must watch every dollar spent, the goal of POS to provide higher quality services is clearly undermined. The product matters, not the process. However, the specificity with which contracts are written and the often cumbersome financial accounting procedures required may deflect from the product or outcome and focus vendor attention on process. Certainly, contracts for nonhuman services (e.g., garbage collection, fire protection) or goods would not include provisions for the daily management of the provider organization. In the human services, however, there is a tendency to focus as much on *how* budget procedures are managed and *how* services are provided as on how *well* these things are managed and provided.

The "power of the purse" wielded by public agencies does allow substantial latitude in the type and range of demands made upon vendors. The desire of private organizations to successfully bid on contracts may lead them to permit these demands to be made. The result may be the creation of a quasi-public entity with characteristics similar to those of the public agency.

It is precisely because of system weaknesses that the public sector has turned to private vendors to provide selected goods and services. Less encumbered by unnecessary baggage, it is believed that the private sector can perform tasks more effectively and efficiently. However, if we now begin to bureaucratize the private sector through the contracting process, the outcome may be to create two monolithic structural arrangements, one private and one public, in which costs will continue to rise, competition will decrease, and the standard of goods and services will significantly suffer.

OUTCOMES

Given the prevalence of POS, what do we know about the effectiveness of these arrangements? POS can be assessed along a number of dimensions, including the impact of these arrangements on quality of services, access to services, quantity of services, or cost of services.

Typically, when decisions are made to contract services, there is a concomitant decision to decrease or eliminate public provision of that same service. Alternatively, the public agency may decide to provide some components of a service, but contract out other components. For example, in child protective services, the public agency may maintain the investigative function, but purchase family preservation services for substantiated cases of child abuse. Since the public and contracted agencies often do not offer the same service, it is difficult to substantiate the claim that purchased services are qualitatively superior to or more cost-effective than publicly provided services. There is no basis of comparison. A complicating issue is that there is no standard or objective definition of quality; quality is more a relative than an absolute measure (Gibelman, 1995).

The quality issue is most often voiced by those opposed to the breadth of contracting in the arena of domestic programs and services. The concern is that inequities in services among population groups may be increased and that the profit motive serves as a deterrent to quality control and accountability. The debate about cost and quality is likely to continue to reflect ideological and political preferences and beliefs, particularly when little emphasis (or money) is placed on gathering hard data to prove the case either way.

Indices of quality, however, have been identified; these include pro-

fessional qualifications of the staff delivering services, frequency of contacts with clients, types of services provided (concrete vs. soft), and
staff–client ratios. Using such indices, Gibelman (1983) found, in regard
to child protective services, that contracted voluntary agencies offered
more intense, diverse, and frequent services than did the public agency.
However, replication studies using indices of quality are limited by the
lack of available comparative data. Qualitative comparisons between contracted agencies providing the same or similar services to similar client
populations may offer more fruitful findings than comparisons of public
versus private services.

Evaluations of purchase of service have tended to focus more on
process than outcome, in large part due to the difficulty of defining specific performance standards. Judgements about "success" of POS arrangements depend, of course, on the articulation of clear and measurable
outcome expectations. In this respect, POS suffers from the same dearth
of outcome measurements that have characterized most social service
interventions.

POS has been justified and promoted on the basis of cost savings, a variable that may be more amenable to measurement. An earlier study of the
costs of direct delivery versus purchased services raised questions about
actual cost savings (Pacific Consultants, 1979). More recently, Stein (1990)
reported no significant cost savings from POS on the basis of either expenditures or labor force. Savings are more likely to accrue in regard to input
costs such as capital and start-up. But such savings may be negated by the
added transactional costs—the cost of the contracting process itself, including contractor selection, monitoring and enforcement. It is possible that
POS actually costs taxpayers more when contracted overhead rates are
considered. But POS unencumbers government, a benefit factor not easily calculated. Cost benefits include the range of variables that motivate
government to enter contractual relationships, most of which have little
to do with dollars.

PROBLEMS WITH CONTRACTING

By the mid-1980s and well into the 1990s, purchase of service had come
under considerable scrutiny and attack, from which social services contracting has not been immune. Such criticisms range from inadequate
accounting procedures to ineffective services. Frequent and numerous
headlines about allegations, investigations, and outright scandals con-

cerning contracted services appear in major newspapers across the country. Front-page newspaper articles about space program contractors running up a $30 million tab to produce a new space toilet resulted in a perhaps understandable skepticism about contracting run amuck (Sawyer, 1993). Although the volume of defense contracting and the amount of contract dollars involved in the defense and aerospace industries make them more susceptible to public attention, a "ripple" effect has brought all purchase arrangements under increasing scrutiny.

President Clinton's former Chief of Staff, Leon Panetta, urged that a hard look be taken as to whether government does too much contracting out. In a directive to federal agencies to review their contracts with outside organizations and businesses, Panetta said that "these contracts today amount to the staggering sum of $103 billion" (Barr, 1993b, p. A2). He urged a "fresh look" to ensure that these contracts are cost-effective and can be justified.

Unions and politicians protective of civil servants are also calling for close scrutiny of contracting practices, particularly those that replace government workers with contract employees. Representative Eleanor Holmes Norton (D-DC) warned that "the government doesn't have a clue on the billions it is contracting out, or what it is getting" (Causey, 1994, p. B2). It is alleged that, in the zeal to diminish the size of government, a "shadow government" is being created by replacing civil servants with less costly contractees (Causey, 1994). The question of what tasks should be contracted out and what work should be handled in-house by government has intensified within the context of government downsizing goals. Various proposals have been offered to prohibit agencies from replacing federal workers who accept "buyouts" with contracted workers, requiring agencies to compare costs when deciding between contracts, and determining the size of the labor force employed under service contracts (Barr, 1994b).

The problems with purchase of service can be classified into four main categories: waste and fraud; cost inefficiencies; faulty contracting practices and failures in government oversight; and inadequate or ineffective service (Gibelman, 1995). In New Jersey, nine people were indicted for conspiring to steal more than $2 million in a 10-year period by billing Newark city government for supplies and services that were not delivered (Sullivan, 1993). In New York City, it was revealed that almost half of the city's $5 billion in major government contracts are awarded without competitive bidding. A report by the office of the City Comptroller concluded that this lack of competition encourages corruption and increases the city's cost of doing business (Baquet, 1991). In New York, the State

Department of Social Services revoked the license of a group home for the mentally ill after an investigation revealed that, from 1985 to 1992, as much as $4 million in public funds was diverted by the managers for personal use (Raab, 1993). Again in New York, the Giuliani administration, in violation of bidding rules, awarded $43 million in contracts to monitor people on welfare to an agency that submitted the highest bid and did not receive the highest grade from an evaluation committee. Members of the agency's board receiving the contract were reported to have made sizable political contributions (Sexton & Finder, 1996).

Contracting has also been used to build political bases. A Brooklyn New York Assemblyman, Vito J. Lopez, allegedly built a powerful political machine by exploiting contracts. The Ridgewood Bushwick Senior Citizens Council received more than 50 grants totalling more than $33 million annually. As described in the *New York Times*, some of these human service funds have been used for political purposes:

> They have paid for an agglomeration of power that has stunted the neighborhood's political diversity, rewarded a handful of Mr. Lopez's proteges with well-paying jobs, enriched politically connected contractors and produced programs that in several instances have been criticized for accounting and performance. (Gottlieb, 1993, p. B5)

As Gibelman's case study of contracting for child welfare services in the District of Columbia highlights (see companion volume), (Gibelman & Demone, Vol. II, 1998) purchased services are the most likely to be terminated when a city or states faces budget shortfalls. Concerns about the impact on clients, contracted agencies, public–private relationships, and public sector employees who must often pick up the slack are secondary to the realities of balancing budgets. Morality has no place.

These examples illustrate that POS is susceptible to some of the same excesses and inefficiencies that have plagued public service delivery. Fault for the problems in purchasing service has been placed on the government agency, on provider agencies, on both, and/or on the relationship between the public and private sectors. Inevitably, questions about monitoring and accountability, within an environment increasingly concerned about ethics in business practices, have challenged the reputation and legitimacy of purchase of service arrangements.

Criticisms have, not surprisingly, led to some proposals to reform the contracting system. In general, such proposals aim to control discretion, tighten public monitoring, encourage competitive bidding, and ensure that conflict of interest situations are avoided. Recent congressional action has focused on innovative procurement practices and mechanisms to streamline the way government buys goods and services (Barr, 1994a, 1994b). The Clinton Administration has listed procurement reform as one of its top legislative priorities (Barr, 1994a). A frequent side effect of such reform measures is to further complicate contract management for both the already overwhelmed public agency and the contracted service providers. These sometimes burdensome requirements may serve to reduce the likelihood that purchased services will result in more efficient service delivery.

The high expectations for purchase of service and the perception that contracting could and would solve a host of long-standing service delivery problems may have made disillusionment inevitable. So, too, there is a tendency to dwell on the downside of any strategy or program, in part because of the use of public monies. Too often, POS has operated on the basis of poorly articulated assumptions about what taxpayers, clients, government, and voluntary agencies thought could or should be achieved.

LOOKING AHEAD

"Contracting out" for the delivery of services is far from a static phenomenon and may, at times, be viewed within a continuum of a preferred solution or a new type of accountability and administrative problem. Unlike contracting for concrete services (computer services) or products (construction of housing units), the use of purchase arrangements for human services is more complex, and the methods of monitoring, evaluating, and performance standards are more elusive.

Experiences with purchasing human services have shown mixed results. This finding, however, is neither surprising nor unexpected. The implementation of many, if not most, American social policies has been marred by too high expectations, insufficient funding, short time frames, and vague and often competing goals.

Criticisms about purchase of service range from the very general (perpetuation of inadequate service delivery or insufficient steps toward privatization, since POS is based on public funding) to the more specific—lack of standards, lack of long-term planning, inadequate staffing of contracted programs, poor communication and relationships between government and contracted agencies, inadequate rate-setting and/or payment procedures, and so forth.

Despite the general and specific criticisms about POS, it is noteworthy that there remains substantial unanimity about continuing this form of public–private partnership in the delivery of human services. The goal has been to bring about incremental change in the contracting system, rather than to discard it. There may, however, be a lack of real alternatives at a time when public provision is politically unacceptable and total privatization (including funding responsibility) is unrealistic within the human services. On a more optimistic note, POS may satisfy the disparate requirements of a wide segment of the American political and general public.

Cautionary notes are, however, in order. The reliance on government funds has led to substantial changes in the nature of not-for-profit agencies, including primary service focus, types of programs offered, operating mode, and management style. These impacts are clearly seen in the case studies offered in the companion volume by Etta, Gibelman, Kraft and Gibelman, Dukakis, and Johnston (Gibelman & Demone, Vol. II, 1998). The desire to initiate, expand, or supplement existing or new programs may lead voluntary agencies to enter into financially dependent relationships with government with little consideration of the long-term impact. This issue of financial dependence is long-standing. Contracting has become the major means of organizational survival for many not-for-profit agencies.

One of the key advantages to purchasing services, from the point of view of government, is that contracts can be terminated. The general status of the economy, and the consensus among Democrats and Republicans alike that the federal budget deficit must be reduced, suggests that no area of government spending—direct, or through contract—is sacrosanct.

Purchase of service arrangements, although enduring, thus have a tenuous quality. The Personal Responsibility and Work Opportunity Reconciliation Act (P.L. 104-193, 110 Stat 2105) of 1996 suggests a greater role for the private sector as states are authorized and encouraged with new ways of workfare and services that support independence. On the other hand, this same Act, by eliminating welfare as an entitlement, hints that states may opt not to offer a full array of services. Indeed, there is clear evidence that the number of people to be served through traditional mental health and social service programs, at least among those heretofore entitled to and receiving public benefits (the poor, disabled, and disenfranchised), will decrease as states define the parameters of their social welfare programs. Governor Pataki (New York), for example, announced plans to cut benefits for hundreds of thousands of poor families and to end benefits altogether for many legal immigrants and able-bodied child-less adults (Dao, 1996).

Both New York and New Jersey, among other states, are moving toward a managed care system for social services (Blanchard, 1996). In early 1996, New York City ended open-ended payments to contracted agencies pro-viding foster care, and instead provides a lump-sum payment per child. This lump sum does not relate to the length of time a child is in foster care. The goal, of course, is to control costs. The rationale is to provide incentive for contracted agencies to move rapidly toward permanency planning for the child. The outcomes are uncertain, but concerns center on the possibility that children will be returned too quickly to at-risk envi-ronments (McLarin, 1995).

Effective October 1, 1996, a provision of the new welfare law that received relatively little attention went into effect. Fifteen percent, or $420 million out of $2.8 billion distributed by the federal government annu-ally through the Social Services Block Grant Program, is gone (Kilborn, 1996). Services funded under this program range from soup kitchens to homeless shelters. These services are frequently those offered through voluntary agencies under contract. The impetus for opening many shel-ters was the availability of contract funds for such purposes. Such shelters often have little or no other revenue sources. They will go out of business.

The history of American social welfare evidences many swings of the pendulum regarding perceptions of the appropriate relationship between government and the private sector and the respective roles of each sector, including responsibility for what services should be delivered by whom and to whom. Although the volume of contracting may be subject to political currents, the use of POS is now firmly entrenched. These arrangements are no longer idealized, but are generally considered preferable and supe-rior to direct public sector provision. POS now constitutes a viable system of service delivery that links the public and private sectors into a more extensive and far-reaching relationship. As a result, both sectors have changed. It is not likely that the political landscape and societal prefer-ences will support a substantial about-face in these arrangements. The clear preferences of a Democratic president for private sector provision suggests the magnitude of public sentiment in support of privatization.

As Demone discusses in Chapter 8, the fundamental question of where the human services fall or should fall within the privatization movement, although long-standing, still defies simplistic answers. Can the inherently public be clearly differentiated from the inherently private?

Privatization in the near future is to be largely found in the former

Eastern bloc countries. The West has little left to privatize. The purchase of services, as a subtype of privatization, still possesses a worldwide future, including activity by large multinational corporations, whose gross expenditures exceeds that of many small countries.

A major stimulus of these developments is the continuing disenchantment with government throughout much of the world. Certainly governmental favor will cycle back, as the limits of the private sector become more endemic and the overblown promises made on its behalf become more evident, but this is not likely in this generation in western countries.

Monitoring of contracting will become more legitimated, as criticisms of the private sector become more frequent. The private sector may soon be plagued with the same organizational strictures that helped to discredit government, all in the name of controlling misdeeds.

The differences between the public and the private, and the for-profit and the not-for-profit will become less apparent and less meaningful as all are forced to dip into the same trough.

Finally, a gradual growth is likely in understanding that the constant neverending diatribe against all of the essential institutions may be severely counterproductive of stable growth. Constructive criticism and civility may return. The reactions among citizens to the mean-spirited campaigns of 1996 is beginning evidence of an attitude of intolerance toward negativism in this society.

REFERENCES

Adarond Constructors, Inc. v. Federico Pena. (1995). (93-1841), 132 L. Ed. 2d. 158.

Baquet, D. (1991, February 6). Contract study faults awards without bids. *New York Times*, p. B1.

Barr, S. (1993a, September 5). Gore report targets 252,000 federal jobs. *Washington Post*, pp. A1, A18.

Barr, S. (1993b, March 17). Panetta orders review of outside contracting. *Washington Post*, p. A2.

Barr, S. (1994a, June 21). House polishes procurement legislation. *Washington Post*, p. A15.

Barr, S. (1994b, April 27). Key Senate panels pass procurement overhaul. *Washington Post*, p. A21.

Barr, S. (1994c, May 26). Norton targets contract workers "unscathed" by cutbacks. *Washington Post*, p. A21.

Blanchard, C. (1997). *Relationship of services and family reunification in New*

Jersey. Unpublished manuscript. New York: Yeshiva University, Wurzweiler School of Social Work.

Brilliant, E. (1973). Private or public: A model of ambiguities. *Social Service Review, 47,* 384–396.

Burian, W. (1970). *Purchase of service in child welfare: A problem of interorganizational exchange.* Ph.D. dissertation, University of Chicago.

Causey, M. (1994, February 27). Scrutinizing contractors. *Washington Post,* p. B2.

City of Richmond v. J. A. Croson Co. (1989). 488 U. S. 469.

Civil Rights Act of 1964, P. L. 88-352, 78 Stat. 241

Civil Rights Act of 1964, as amended (1991). P. L. 102-166, 105 Stat. 1071.

Clinton, W. (1993). *A vision of change for America.* Washington, DC: U.S. Government Printing Office.

Copeland, W. C. (1976). *Audit-proof contracting for federal money for children's services.* Washington, DC: CWLA Hecht Institute for State Child Welfare Planning.

Council on Accreditation of Services to Families and Children. (1996). *Behavioral healthcare standards.* New York: Author.

Cruthirds, C. T., Jr. (1972). *The community action program agency and voluntary delegate organizations: Issues in interorganizational contracting.* Ph.D. dissertation, Tulane University, New Orleans, LA.

Dao, J. (1996, November 12). Pataki welfare plan would cut payments to families over time. *New York Times,* pp. A1, B5.

DeHoog, R. H. (1984). *Contracting out for human services.* Albany, NY: State University of New York Press.

Demone, H. W., Jr., & Gibelman, M. (1989). In search of a theoretical base for the purchase of services. In H. W. Demone, Jr., & M. Gibelman, (Eds.), *Services for sale: Purchasing health and human services,* (pp. 5–16). New Brunswick, NJ: Rutgers University Press.

Derthick, M. (1975). *Uncontrollable spending for social service grants.* Washington, DC: Brookings Institution.

DiNitto, D. M. (1991). *Social welfare: Politics and public policy,* (3rd ed). New York: Prentice-Hall.

Edwards, R. L. & Yankey, J. A. (1991). Managing effectively in an environment of competing values. In R. L. Edwards, & J. A. Yankey, (Eds.), *Skills for effective human services management,* (pp. 5–43). Silver Spring, MD: NASW Press.

Ferris, J. M. (1993). The double-edged sword of social service contracting: Public accountability versus nonprofit autonomy. *Nonprofit Management & Leadership, 3,* 363–376.

Fullilove v. Klutznick. (1980). 448 U. S. 448.

General Revenue Sharing Act of 1972. (P. L. 92-512). 86 Stat. 20.

Gibelman, M. (1981). Are clients served better when services are purchased? *Public Welfare, 39,* 26–33.

Gibelman, M. (1983). Using public funds to buy private services. In M. Dinerman, (Ed.), *Social work in a turbulent world* (pp. 101–113). Silver Spring, MD: National Association of Social Workers.

Gibelman, M. (1995). Purchasing social services. In R. L. Edwards, (Ed.), *Encyclopedia of social work* (19th ed., pp. 1998–2007). Washington, DC: NASW Press.

Gibelman, M. (1997). *Taking a stand on affirmative action: A social justice perspective.* Manuscript submitted for publication.

Gibelman, M., & Demone, H. W., Jr. (1989). The evolving contract state. In H. W. Demone, Jr. & M. Gibelman, (Eds.), *Services for sale: Purchasing health and human services* (pp. 17–57). New Brunswick, NJ: Rutgers University Press.

Gibelman, M., & Demone, H. W., Jr. (in press). Private solutions to public human service problems: Purchasing services to meet social need. In S. Hakim, G. W. Bowman, & P. Seidenstat, (Eds.), *Privatizing government services.* New York: Praeger.

Goldstein, H. (1993, July 13). Government contracts are emasculating boards and turning charities into agents of the state. *Chronicle of Philanthropy,* p. 41.

Gottlieb, M. (1993, February 7). Growth of a new-age political machine. *New York Times,* p. B5.

Gurin, A., & Friedman, B. (1989). The efficacy of contracting for service. In H. W. Demone, Jr., & M. Gibelman, (Eds.), *Services for sale: Purchasing health and human services* (pp. 310–324). New Brunswick, NJ: Rutgers University Press.

Hasenfeld, Y. (1992). Theoretical approaches to human service organizations. In Y. Hasenfeld, (Ed.), *Human services as complex organizations* (pp 24–44). Newbury Park, CA: Sage.

Henderson, N. (1992, July 19). D.C. out to show pattern of bias in contracting. *Washington Post,* p. B9.

Kahn, A. J. (1973). *Social policy and social services.* New York: Random House.

Karger, H. J., & Stoesz, D. (1994). *American social welfare policy: A pluralistic approach* (2nd ed.) New York: Longman.

Kenworthy, T., & Dewar, H. (1990, January 20). House Republicans push anew for privatization of social security. *Washington Post,* p. A4.

Kilborn, P. T. (1996, September 22). Little-noticed cut imperils safety net for the poor. *New York Times,* pp. A1, A16.

Kramer, R. M. (1964). *An analysis of policy issues in relationships between governmental and voluntary social welfare agencies.* Ph.D. dissertation, University of California at Berkeley.

Leat, D. (1986). Privatization and voluntarization. *Quarterly Journal of Social Affairs, 2,* 285–320.

Lourie, N. V. (1979). Purchase of service contracting: Issues confronting the government-sponsored agency. In K. R. Wedel, A. J. Katz, and A. Weick, (Eds.), *Social services by government contract: A policy analysis* (pp. 18–29). New York: Praeger.

Mathews, J. (1991, April 20). Push to privatize public work reported. *Washington Post,* p. A11.

McLarin, K. J. (1995, October 28). City to pay care agencies 6% less. *New York Times,* pp. B23–24.

McMurtry, S. L., Netting, F. E., & Kettner, P. M. (1990). Critical inputs and strategic choice in non-profit human service organizations. *Administration in Social Work, 14,* 67–82.

Mencher, S. (1967). *Poor law to poverty program.* Pittsburgh, PA: University of Pittsburgh Press.

Mills, J. E. (1985). Moving toward a tripartite marketplace in the human services. *Social Welfare Forum,* 1982–83, 108–116.

National Association of Social Workers. (1996). *Policy statement on affirmative action.* Washington, DC: Author.

National Council of La Raza. (1995). *Fact sheet on affirmative action and Latinos.* Washington, DC: Author.

Pacific Consultants. (1979). *The feasibility of comparing costs between direct delivery and purchased services.* Washington, DC: U.S. Department of Health, Education and Welfare, Administration for Public Services.

Pecora, P. J. (1995). Personnel management. In R. L. Edwards, (Ed.), *Encyclopedia of Social Work* (19th ed. pp. 1828–1836). Washington, DC: NASW Press.

Omnibus Budget Reconciliation Act of 1981. (P. L. 97-35). 95 Stat. 357.

Privatizing city services. (1994, December 19). *New York Times,* p. A18.

Personal Responsibility and Work Opportunity Reconciliation Act of 1996 (P.L. 104-193), 110 Stat. 2105.

Raab, S. (1993, February 4). License of home for mentally ill revoked over fiscal finding. *New York Times,* p. B3.

Randolph, J. L. (1976). *Interagency coordination and purchase of service agreements: A study of public-private dilemmas.* Ph.D. dissertation, University of Utah, Salt Lake City.

Rich, S. (1995, March 1). Medicare voucher idea debated. *Washington Post,*

p. A13.

Robberson, T. (1996, August 25). Fairfax officials fret about rent voucher cluster along Route 1. *Washington Post,* pp. B1, B5.

Rowen, H. (1986, February 9). Privatized priorities. *Washington Post,* pp. F1, F2.

Ruchelman, L. (1989). *Redesigning public services.* Albany, NY: State University of New York Press.

Salamon, L. M. (1984). Nonprofit organizations: The lost opportunity. In J. K. Palmer, & I. V. Sawhill, (Eds.), *The Reagan record* (pp. 261–286). Washington, DC: Urban Institute.

Salamon, L. M. & Abramson, A. J. (1982). The nonprofit sector. In J. K. Palmer, & I. V. Sawhill, (Eds.), *The Reagan experiment* (pp. 219–243). Washington, DC: Urban Institute.

Savas, E. S. (1982). *Privatizing the public sector: How to shrink government.* Chatham, NJ: Chatham House.

Sawyer, K. (1993, January 1). NASA's new space toilet: $30 million up the drain? *Washington Post,* p. A1.

Sexton, J., & Finder, A. (1996, March 26). Giuliani officials broke rules on contract bids with agency. *New York Times,* pp. A1, B7.

Sharkansky, I. (1980). Policymaking and service delivery on the margins of government: The case of contractors. *Public Administration Review, 4,* 116–123.

Slack, I. (1979). *Title XX at the crossroads.* Washington, DC: American Public Welfare Association.

Smith S. R. (1989a). The changing policies of child welfare services: New rules for the government and the nonprofit sectors. *Child Welfare, 68,* 294.

Smith, S. R. (1989b). Federal funding, nonprofit agencies, and victim services. In H. W. Demone, Jr., & M. Gibelman (Eds.), *Services for sale: Purchasing health and human services* (pp. 215–227). New Brunswick, NJ: Rutgers University Press.

Smith, S. R. & Lipsey, M. (1993). *Nonprofits for hire: The welfare state in the age of contracting.* Cambridge, MA: Harvard University Press.

Social Security Act of 1935, as amended (1974). P.L. 97-35, title XX, sec. 2193, 95 Stat 828.

Southerland, D. (1993, May 10). A trickle of U.S. contracts: Procurement process slows with delays in Clinton appointments. *Washington Post,* p. 5.

Stein, R. M. (1990). The budgetary effects of municipal service contracting: A principal-agent explanation. *American Journal of Political Science,*

34, 471–502.

Stoesz, D. (1981). A wake for the welfare state: Social welfare and the neo-conservative challenge. *Social Service Review, 55,* 398–410.

Struyk, R. J. & Bendick, M., Jr. (Eds.) (1982). *Housing vouchers for the poor.* Washington, DC: Urban Institute Press.

Sullivan, J. F. (1993, January 7). Indictments cite corruption in private sanitation service. *New York Times,* p. B8.

Terrell, P. (1987). Purchasing social services. In A. Minahan (Ed.). *Encyclopedia of Social Work* (18th ed., pp. 434–442). Silver Spring, MD: National Association of Social Workers.

Trattner, W. I. (1994). *From poor law to welfare state: A history of social welfare in America* (5th ed). New York: Free Press.

U. S. Commission on Civil Rights. (1995). *The legislative, executive and judicial development of affirmative action.* Washington, DC: Office of General Counsel.

Warner, A. G. (1894). American charities: A study in phllanthropy and economics. New York: Thomas Y. Crowell Company.

Wedel, K. R. (1976). Government contracting for purchase of service. *Social Work, 21,* 101–105.

Wells, R. M., & Idelson, H. (1995, March 18). Panel will examine effects of affirmative action. *Congressional Quarterly, 53,* 819–820.

Wilensky, H. L., & Lebeaux, C. N. (1965). *Industrial society and social welfare* (2nd ed.) New York: Free Press.

2

Evaluating State Mental Health Care Reform: The Case of Privatization of State Mental Services in Massachusetts

Dow A. Wieman and Robert A. Dorwart*

INTRODUCTION:
PRIVATIZATION AND MENTAL
HEALTH CARE REFORM

The collapse of the national health care reform initiative in 1994 marked a lost opportunity for all Americans, but especially for those with chronic conditions who face catastrophic medical costs under the present system. Of all the chronic conditions, serious and persistent mental illness (SPMI) presents the strongest case for reform, because the mentally ill are the most vulnerable to the devastating medical, social, and financial consequences of their illness (Sharfstein & Stoline, 1992). With no further federal initiative on the horizon, the question of how to finance services for

*The authors acknowledge support for work described in this report from the University of Massachusetts Center for Psychosocial and Forensic Mental Health Services Research.

the SPMI is now one of the most pressing "inescapable decisions" of health care reform (Mechanic, 1994).

Like other unresolved health care issues, this question of financing will now most likely be addressed at the state level ("State officials strive," 1994). In fact, the process of reexamining existing methods is already underway in a number of states, prompted by two concerns. One is the burden on state budgets due to the increasing cost of the Medicaid program, which finances a growing proportion of mental health services. The other is a recognition that expensive state-operated inpatient facilities continue to drive up mental health care costs, even after decades of deinstitutionalization.

Massachusetts is one of the states currently confronting these issues. The state is proceeding with a reorganization of the financing of mental health services through two somewhat independent initiatives. The first is an initiative of the Division of Medical Assistance involving a reorganization of Medicaid into a system of managed care wherein all persons, including the mentally ill, are enrolled, and for whom Medicaid is the primary payor. The second, spearheaded by the administration of Republican Governor William Weld, is a plan known as "facilities consolidation" aimed at downsizing the system of state institutions for the mentally retarded, mentally ill, and chronically ill.

Privatization, as an instrument of public policy, figures prominently in both of the Massachusetts initiatives. In the Medicaid reorganization, privatization takes the form of a "carve-out" of mental health and substance abuse benefits. This relates to privatization in two primary ways: first, it is a model that originated with the private sector; and second, the state has contracted with a private health care provider (Mental Health Management of America, now owned by First Health, Inc. and doing business in Massachusetts as MHMA) to set up and manage the network of mental health services for Medicaid recipients.

The facilities consolidation initiative involves privatization in three respects. First, the Department of Mental Health has contracted with general and private psychiatric hospitals to develop "replacement units" as substitutes for state hospitals that are being closed. Second, many of the patients in state facilities being downsized or closed were transferred to privately managed community placements, such as nursing homes or residential programs contracting with the state. Finally, the Department of Mental Health has also sought to emulate the private sector by developing a system of "public managed care" known as the Comprehensive Community Support System (CCSS).

BACKGROUND: MEDICAID AND FACILITIES CONSOLIDATION INITIATIVES

The process of privatization and emulation of the private sector by public agencies reflects a nationwide trend in the delivery of services for persons with severe and persistent mental illness (Dorwart & Epstein, 1993). More specifically, it represents Massachusetts Governor William Weld's promotion of "entrepreneurial government," a term that refers explicitly to Osborne and Gaebler's influential book, *Reinventing Government* (1992), which discusses privatization as a means of creating incentives for the effective and efficient management of public services.

From a longer term perspective, these two initiatives represent a continuation in the historical development of the system of care for the SPMI. This had its beginnings in the mid-19th century, when the state assumed responsibility for providing services through the system of state mental hospitals. A century later, the deinstitutionalization movement was prompted in part by the states' efforts to alleviate the costs of these services by developing community alternatives. Purchase of service contracting was often the means of shifting resources from hospitals and quickly developing community-based programs.

The federal government also contributed to deinstitutionalization, both with the Community Mental Health Centers Act of 1965 (Public Law 89-108, U.S. Statutes at large, 79:427-430 [1965]) and with the creation of the public insurance programs of Medicaid and Medicare, which created additional incentives for private sector alternatives to the state hospital. These factors combined to reduce the census of state hospitals dramatically, and the federal initiatives relieved the states of a part of the responsibility of caring for the SPMI. None of these initiatives was sufficient to produce the alternative of a comprehensive and fully integrated system of community-based care, however (Grob, 1991). The states failed to provide adequate funding for community-based programs. The community mental health centers established by the federal government did not adequately target services for the SPMI. Medicare and Medicaid, with their focus on inpatient medical treatment, did not provide the necessary incentives for the private sector to provide needed community-based social services. Moreover, the fee-for-service structure of Medicare and Medicaid did not provide for the coordination and continuity of care required by the SPMI.

Without an adequate community-based system of care, many states, including Massachusetts, were forced to continue relying on the state hospitals to meet the needs of the mentally ill, especially the most severely impaired. Because of the high fixed costs involved in the operation of these facilities, even with significantly lower census, the cost per patient has remained very high.

Given this background, Massachusetts' Medicaid and facilities consolidation initiatives may be perceived as an effort to address the unfinished business of the deinstitutionalization movement. The parallel course of the two initiatives reflects the bipartite structure that currently prevails in financing services for the SPMI. The federal government funds some mental health services through Medicare, Medicaid, and Social Security Disability Insurance. The state, as payor of last resort, pays for needed services not reimbursed by public insurance (such as social services, housing, and long-term hospitalization) and provides all services for the uninsured. The state's contribution of approximately 50% of Medicaid costs represents a rather unstable link between the two systems, in which cost-sharing often shades into cost-shifting.

Although privatization has a long history in Massachusetts as a policy tool for developing the outpatient services required by deinstitutionalization, the privatization of inpatient services is more than just another step in the continuing shift in the locus of care from state hospitals to the community. In fact, it represents a basic redefinition of DMH's mission and of the relationship between the state and the SPMI population. The Governor's Commission, which developed the consolidation plan, specifically acknowledges this point with a prominent statement in its report:

> The fundamental recommendation of the Special Commission is to promote a change in how the state operates, shifting from the provider of last resort to the payor and guarantor of last resort. (Governor's Commission 1991, p. V)

THE MEDICAID MANAGED CARE PROGRAM (MassHealth)

Between 1988 and 1990, rapid expansion of the Massachusetts Medicaid program during a period of fiscal crisis threatened to crowd out spending for other essential social programs. In its eligibility criteria and benefits, Massachusetts has offered one of the nation's most generous plans, and one consideration was to make it more restrictive. The Division of Medical Assistance eventually decided against this approach on political and humanitarian grounds, however, and instead applied for a waiver of federal regulations that would allow the state to reorganize the program to be more cost-effective.

The waiver process was established by the Omnibus Reconciliation Act of 1981, when federal officials recognized the need for modification of the Medicaid program. Because the solution was far from clear, however, instead of settling on a uniform reorganization, they chose to encourage experimentation at the state level. Congress thus approved a process whereby states could apply to the Health Care Financing Administration (HCFA) for a waiver allowing them to modify federally mandated rules in order to test out innovative cost-saving alternatives. The waiver required states to obtain an independent evaluation of the program after 1 year, with renewal for another 2 years contingent on the outcome.

Since 1981, a number of states in addition to Massachusetts have taken advantage of this opportunity to develop some form of managed care system for Medicaid enrollees, including Oregon, Tennessee, Hawaii, Rhode Island, and Florida (Hurley, & Paul, 1993). A Medicaid managed care plan had been considered in the early 1980s in Massachusetts, when a provider consortium known as the Commonwealth Corporation proposed it as an alternative to reducing the level of reimbursements to providers. It was the state's fiscal crisis at the beginning of the 1990s that finally resulted in action by the administration and legislature, however.

The plan approved by HCFA and implemented in January 1, 1992 was called MassHealth. Among other provisions, the waiver allowed the state to (1) enroll Medicare recipients in a primary care case management system, (2) require recipients to choose between an HMO or single Primary Care Clinician, (3) restrict recipients of mental health and substance abuse services to designated providers, and (4) use cost savings to provide additional types of services (Callahan, Shepard, Beinecke, Larson & Cavanaugh, 1994).

The Medicaid managed care system consists of three components. The first is a state-run Independent Practice Association called the Primary Care Clinician (PCC) Program, which provides health services through a network of primary care providers. PCCs serve as gatekeepers for all specialty services except mental health and substance abuse treatment. The second component is the HMO program, consisting of 14 HMOs (subsequently reduced to 12 after two withdrew) contracting with the state to provide services for Medicaid recipients. Medicaid enrollees are required to choose between any PCC or any of these HMOs; those who do not indicate a choice are assigned to a PCC. The third component is a "carve-out" of mental health and substance abuse (MH/SA) benefits managed separately under a contract with a proprietary health provider, MHMA. The MHMA network provides mental health and substance abuse services to everyone in the managed care program except those belonging to an HMO.

Eligibility for Medicaid is based on two mandatory categories established by the federal government—people receiving Aid to Families with Dependent Children (AFDC) or Supplemental Security Income (SSI) for the blind, aged and disabled, with most SPMI belonging to the latter category. In addition, states are allowed to establish other optional categories of eligibility. Thus, Massachusetts' managed care program includes people in the following eligibility categories: AFDC, Medical Assistance/Aid to Families with Dependent Children (MA/AFDC), Supplemental Security Income for the Disabled (SSI/Disabled), Medical Assistance for Disabled (MA/Disabled), Medical Assistance for recipients under 21 not enrolled through AFDC (MA/Under 21), and Refugee programs.

Importantly, the managed care program excludes any Medicaid recipient who is covered by any additional insurance, for which Medicaid is by government regulations a secondary payor. For the mentally ill, this is most relevant in the case of persons who qualify for Social Security Disability Insurance (SSDI), which is a program for disabled workers, including those disabled by mental illness. As opposed to SSI, which is a means-tested assistance program for the needy aged, blind, and disabled, SSDI makes a person eligible for Medicare after 24 months, which consequently excludes him or her from the managed care program.

In March 1993, approximately 650,000 people were eligible for Medicaid. Of these, 90,000 were excluded from the managed care program because they were also covered by Medicare or some other insurance, and another 85,000 were excluded because they were enrolled in HMOs. The enrollment process for the PCC program was staggered, and in March 1993 there were 200,000 enrollees. During the course of implementation, DMA decided to slow the enrollment process for various categories of eligibility with special needs, such as the disabled. Consequently, a year later, enrollment had increased only to 242,000, primarily through the addition of persons in the AFDC category and considerably fewer than the 405,000 estimated in the waiver application (Grant et al., 1994).

THE MEDICAID MENTAL HEALTH/SUBSTANCE ABUSE PROGRAM

The Division of Medical Assistance initially considered following the model of many HMOs by having the Primary Care Clinicians (PCC) manage mental health and substance abuse services. DMA administrators decided that providers in the PCC network would be less receptive or effective in this role than their counterparts in HMOs, however, and that a social model would be preferable to a medical model (Executive Office of Health and Human Services, 1993a). Moreover, a carve-out of mental health benefits, as a model emulating the private-sector approach to managing health care benefits, presented an opportunity for furthering the privatization agenda of Governor Weld's administration. Accordingly, the final plan was to contract out for the management of Medicaid mental health and substance abuse benefits as a separate program.

In January 1992, the month the HCFA waiver became effective, the state signed a contract with MHMA. The stated purpose of the MH/SA Program is to ensure that eligible Medicaid recipients receive medically necessary mental health and substance abuse services in the most clinically appropriate, accessible, and cost-effective settings (Callahan et al., 1994). The contract with MHMA specifies that it perform a range of managed care functions including management of a subcontracted service network, claims processing and payment, service authorization, utilization management, quality management, information system operation, and interagency service coordination.

MHMA implemented the MH\SA program in phases through 1992, beginning with utilization review of inpatient services in April and of outpatient services in July. Also in July, MHMA assumed responsibility for Medicaid claims processing and payment and began developing a network of diversionary services, such as acute residential care for adolescent mental health and substance abuse, partial hospitalization, and family stabilization teams, which Medicaid previously had not reimbursed. MHMA completed contracting for the inpatient services network by October and in January 1993 began contracting for outpatient services.

By June 1993, the MHMA inpatient network consisted of 55 inpatient units in 46 hospitals, 25 level III detoxification units, 16 acute residential substance abuse units, and 17 child/adolescent residential programs (including two for adolescent substance abuse). Outpatient services included 129 mental health clinics, 56 hospital clinics, 79 substance abuse clinics, 516 individual psychiatrists, and 471 psychologists. In July 1993, MHMA also contracted for screening teams in conjunction with DMH. These contracts included crisis stabilization beds for short-term treatment.

Enrollees include all Medicaid recipients except two kinds: those who are enrolled in an HMO instead, and those who are excluded from MassHealth managed care programs because they are also covered by Medicare or some other health insurance. As of July 1993, the MH/SA program covered about 374,000 people, or about 57% of the 650,000 total Medicaid population.

Most important for the purposes of understanding the impact of managed care on the SPMI is the distinction between disabled beneficiaries, most of whom belong to the SSDI category, and the nondisabled, who are distributed among the other categories. The two groups have very different utilization patterns, with the disabled representing only 16% of the population but accounting for 34% of the cost. In recognition of this difference, the state provides a different capitation rate for the two groups.

FACILITIES CONSOLIDATION AND THE COMPREHENSIVE COMMUNITY SUPPORT SYSTEM

Concurrent with the Medicaid reorganization but quite separate from it, the state undertook a second cost-containment initiative that affected the mentally ill, among other populations. This was aimed at controlling the rising per-patient cost of care provided in the 34 state-owned facilities for the mentally ill, chronically ill, and mentally retarded operated, respectively, by the Department of Mental Health, Department of Public Health, and Department of Mental Retardation. As their census had steadily declined to the current level of about 6,200 patients, these facilities, with their high fixed operating costs, absorbed an increasingly disproportionate share of their agencies' budgets. DMH facilities, with about 6,400 adult admissions a year, were serving only about 6% of DMH clients annually, but absorbing more than 40% of the Department's resource allocation.

The plan for the consolidation of state facilities was developed by the Governor's Special Commission on Consolidation of Health and Human Services Institutional Facilities, convened by the newly elected Republican governor William Weld in 1991. The Department of Mental Health then followed with a plan of its own for reorganizing services into a system of "public sector managed care" based on a model termed the "Comprehensive Community Care System" (Executive Office of Health and Human Services, 1993a).

When the Commission convened, the system of state institutions consisted of 34 facilities: seven long-term care hospitals for the chronically ill, operated under the auspices of the Department of Public Health; 10 facilities for the mentally retarded, under the Department of Mental Retardation; and 17 mental hospitals, including a 91-bed facility for children and adolescents and eight Community Mental Health Centers (CMHCs). At its peak, the system had accommodated over 35,000 patients; at the time of the Commission's study, the census had declined to 6,200. DMH facilities accounted for about one-third of the census—1,648 in the state hospitals and 373 in CMHCs.

The Commission concluded that the system of state institutions should be and could be reduced. Accordingly, the Governor's Commission recommended further reducing the inpatient census by developing more appropriate and lower cost alternatives for various categories of patients, either in the community or elsewhere in the inpatient health care system. Transferring a third of the 6,200 patients to alternative settings would enable the state to close 12 facilities, including four mental hospitals and one (CMHC) inpatient service.

Privatization of DMH Facilities

Although the plan for reducing the census and consolidating facilities was not limited to the DMH population, it had the greatest effect on the configuration of services for that group. This is because the population served by DMH and the services provided were particularly amenable to the principal policy tool recommended by the Commission, namely, privatization. Privatization was especially attractive at this point because of the incentives and opportunities presented by a surplus capacity in the inpatient system throughout the state, including general hospitals, private psychiatric hospitals, and nursing homes. Privatizing inpatient services offered cost savings in a variety of ways, including reducing capital expenditures and the public work force. However, its greatest utility, especially for the DMH population, was in maximizing leverage of third-party reimbursement, especially Medicaid, of which the federal government shares about one-half the cost. Many of the state's mental hospitals and community mental health centers were ineligible for Medicaid reimbursement on two counts: (1) without prohibitory capital investments, they could not meet the standards for certification by HCFA and accreditation by JCAHO; and, (2) they exceeded the maximum size of 16 beds, which under HCFA regulations classifies them as Institutions of Mental Disease, which are ineligible for Medicaid reimbursement.

A second consideration for privatization, though one that figured less prominently in the Commission's report, was to allow the Department of Mental Health to take advantage of the Free Care Pool, the state's formula for reimbursing general hospitals that care for a disproportionate number of indigent patients.

The Commission's recommendations for DMH facilities essentially consisted of four privatization models, each appropriate for a particular set of institutions, but all effective as mechanisms for leveraging Medicaid reimbursement:

1. The direct transfer of certain categories of patients from state to private facilities (e.g., the medically ill/mentally ill to nursing homes.
2. Privately owned and managed "replacement units" through purchase of service contracting (e.g., acute and long-term care services from general and psychiatric hospitals).
3. Affiliation agreements whereby general hospitals provide "wraparound" licenses for state-owned and operated facilities.
4. Management contracts, whereby private entities operate state-owned facilities.

For the DMH population, this strategy produced alternative placements for five categories of patients:

1. Those requiring acute care would be redirected to general hospitals with psychiatric units, either under contract with DMH or as part of the Medicaid managed care network.
2. Medically ill/mentally ill patients would be transferred to nursing homes and chronic care hospitals.
3. Mentally retarded patients with secondary psychiatric diagnoses would be transferred to DMR facilities.
4. Patients awaiting discharge would be placed in new community residences to be developed with funds redirected from hospitals.
5. The 91 children in Gaebler, a specialized children's unit, would be served in a privatized system to be developed, which would include 21 acute intermediate-care beds, 14 long-term-care beds, and 14 Intensive Residential Treatment beds.

The Commission estimated that to meet present and future needs, DMH would need to contract for 700 community beds (in addition to the 3,255 already in existence), 300 beds in general hospitals to replace the state's acute care capacity, and 200 nursing home beds for the medically ill/mentally ill. The state would continue to provide approximately 300 beds for intermediate and long-term care in several of the remaining state hospitals and through a contract with a municipal hospital.

To emphasize the community-based nature of the new system, the Department replaced the existing statewide organizational structure, which was based on catchment areas, each served by a state hospital. The new structure, based on DMH-identified "natural service areas" and developed after a statewide needs assessment, survey of consumers, and public meetings, was designated the Comprehensive Community Service System. Utilizing case managers to coordinate services, the new organization was promoted by DMH as a system of "public sector managed care" (Executive Office of Health and Human Services, 1993a).

CHALLENGES IN ASSESSING THE IMPACT OF CONSOLIDATION AND MEDICAID MANAGED MENTAL HEALTH CARE

Researchers and policymakers typically seek to determine how initiatives such as the two described here affect the cost, quality, availability, and accessibility of services for the SPMI. In this case, assessment is considerably complicated by the nature of these policies and the manner in which they were implemented.

Specifically, there are three primary challenges for assessment. First, because the two policies were initiated separately by different agencies of the state government, they have many overlapping and interacting effects that are difficult to identify. For example, Medicaid managed care practices may require DMH community programs to deal with more acute problems at a correspondingly higher cost. The reverse of this effect is also possible. A provision for the managed care program to transfer patients in need of long-term hospitalization to the Department of Mental Health—a sanctioned form of "dumping"—might drive up costs overall.

Much of the anticipated cost savings in the DMH plan are predicated on leveraging federal reimbursement by maximizing Medicaid eligibility for DMH consumers, who will now be treated in the reimbursable privatized units. However, this initiative by DMH will substantially alter utilization patterns and, consequently, costs in the MH/SA program. Much of the Division of Medical Assistance's strategy for controlling Medicaid costs, before and after the implementation of managed care, is based on discounting, that is, reducing payments to providers. How this practice affects provider behavior with regard to the SPMI, especially over the long term, has yet to be fully assessed. The difficulty of accounting for confounding factors such as this has been a major limitation of evaluations of Medicaid managed care programs, especially when the analysis is based on projecting trends (Hurley et al., 1993).

The second difficulty in assessing the impact of these initiatives on the SPMI is that both target broader, more heterogeneous populations, in which the SPMI are included as subgroups, making it difficult to disentangle effects specific to the mentally ill. Facilities consolidation involves not only the mentally ill, but also the mentally retarded clients of the Department of Mental Retardation and chronically ill clients of the Department of Public Health. The total census of state facilities prior to consolidation was 6,500, of whom less than one-third, or approximately 2,000, were mentally ill. Similarly, the Medicaid managed care program affects not only the SPMI, but all persons with Medicaid as their primary insurance, approximately 375,000 persons. The proportion of this group who are SPMI is unknown but may be estimated crudely based on the fact that only 16%, or about 60,000 persons, are eligible by reason of disability, with mental illness being the most frequent, but not the only, form of disability.

At the same time, in both initiatives, the group of mentally ill that is affected does not represent the state's entire SPMI population. Perhaps 30% of the Department of Mental Health's clients who are assigned case managers (an indication of being the most ill) are unaffected by the managed care program because they are not enrolled in Medicaid or have Medicaid only as secondary insurance. Likewise, many DMH clients are not affected by the facilities consolidation initiative because they have never received treatment in the facilities being closed or privatized.

Thus, the third challenge is to detect the possible indirect effects of either initiative on the mentally ill who are not targeted. For example, the option to transfer problematic patients out of the managed care program into the state system creates the potential for "creaming." Disenrolling these patients prevents them from obtaining services available to other Medicaid enrollees and removes incentives to develop programs appropriate to their needs. Likewise, with regard to facilities consolidation, a major concern among advocates was that patients already settled in community residences would be displaced by those being discharged from hospitals scheduled for closure.

Given the objectives of these two initiatives, unless they are carefully coordinated, the situation is inherently inimical to the interests of the SPMI. The Department of Mental Health aims to achieve savings by closing state facilities and shifting the locus of inpatient care to private Medicaid-reimbursable units. The Division of Medical Assistance intends to achieve savings by limiting the frequency and duration of treatment to that which is "appropriate and medically necessary." The risk is that many of the mentally ill will be caught between these two trends, and will be worse off than ever before.

ASSESSMENTS OF THE FACILITIES CONSOLIDATION AND MANAGED MENTAL HEALTH CARE INITIATIVES

Because of the controversial nature of these initiatives and the highly politicized environment in which they occurred, both have attracted considerable attention from diverse sources, resulting in a variety of evaluations and studies. These include planning studies by government agencies, evaluations mandated by state and federal government, and assessments by a variety of interest groups, legislative oversight bodies, and public policy research organizations.

The Statewide Needs Assessment

A statewide needs assessment was carried out as part of the planning for the CCSS, the new organizational structure to be implemented following consolidation of state facilities. To determine the proper allocation of resources within this system, the Department contracted with Human Services Research Institute to conduct a needs assessment for DMH clients throughout the state. The study, consisting of a provider survey and consumer interviews, the latter administered by DMH consumers, was completed in August of 1993 (Massachusetts Department of Mental Health [DMH], 1993a).

The provider survey covered a random sample of 7,140 clients drawn from a total population of 26,589 currently active DMH clients. It involved an assessment of clinical status and a comparison of the amount of services the provider considered to be ideal, versus what was actually provided. Clinical status was measured according to a scale devised by HSRI entitled the Resource Associated Functional Level Scale (RAFLS). Based on the providers' assessment of actual and ideal services, the Department then calculated for each service type an aggregate "percentage of needs met" in each service area. This approach was intended to provide information for making decisions about the allocation of resources by allowing for comparison of resources allotted to different service types and to different areas—an important and complex consideration in Massachusetts, where the patient population and therefore the need varies considerably between metropolitan Boston and the rural Western part of the state.

The RAFLS divides clients into seven levels of functioning. The first six describe various degrees of treatment needs ranging from level 1 (dangerous) to level 6 (needs support/treatment to cope with extreme stress or seeks treatment to maintain or enhance personal development). A person at level 7 is "system-independent." The provider survey found that 57% of DMH clients were at functional levels of 5 or 6, another 36% were at levels 3 and 4, and the remaining 7% were at levels 1 and 2.

The "percentage of needs met," which the Department calculated from these data, generally showed an excess of resources committed to inpatient care and a shortage of community services. For example, 5% more acute inpatient care and 20% more extended inpatient care was provided than was required; however, only 40% of clients in need of day hospital and partial hospitalization received these services. DMH officials interpreted these findings of the study as providing strong support for facilities consolidation (DMH, 1993b).

However, other interpretations of the aggregate patient-level data are possible. For example, it may be that some clients receive too little inpatient care at the same time that others receive more than needed. In that case, the problem is not an imbalance in the service system, but a lack of efficiency in delivering the services, and the solution is not to reallocate resources, but to improve discharge planning or case management.

The second limitation of a cross-sectional study of this type is that, as a description of the client population, it does not accommodate the difference between census and admissions resulting from differing lengths of stay. A longitudinal survey of admissions might show, for example, a much higher proportion of substance abusers and a lower proportion of chronic schizophrenics, which would alter the ratio between various service types and also, if there are differences in case mix, between different areas of the state.

Mandated Assessments of Facilities Consolidation

The Governor's Special Commission recommended an evaluation of the consolidation initiative, which was subsequently conducted by the University of Massachusetts at Boston. The evaluation consisted of a series of studies intended "to document the short-term impacts of facility consolidation on consumers and families, assess whether the process of consolidation was carried out as promised, assess the cost-effectiveness of the changes, and develop recommendations for future research" (Benson, Clemons, Fisher, Leff, & Schutt, 1994, p. 1).

The studies included a follow-up of patients placed in the community following closure of a DMH facility, Metropolitan State Hospital, and a follow-up of mentally ill patients transferred from a DMH facility, Danvers State, to a long-term Department of Public Health chronic care facility, Tewksbury State Hospital, and a cost analysis of community placement.

In general, the evaluation identified few negative consequences from hospital consolidation and found many positives. The strongest finding, perhaps, was the patients' evaluation of their quality of life following discharge from the state hospital: none considered the overall experience in the community to be worse than the hospital. Sixty-nine percent judged it to be "better" and 31% considered it "equal." Long-term patients transferred from the DMH facility to a chronic care facility were likewise generally satisfied, with 30% preferring the new placement.

The cost analysis focused on a group of ten discharged consumers, five of whom were high users and five low users of services. The study compared the costs of their care in the community for a 1-month period with a 30-day hospitalization. For all but one, community care was considerably less expensive—in some cases, by as much as 200 to 300%.

A major shortcoming of these studies, however, which their authors frankly acknowledge, is the limitation of the follow-up data. Despite the prospective design of the studies and the relative accessibility of at least those patients transferred between facilities, many patients could not be located or refused to be interviewed. Similarly, the cost analysis data was not sufficiently comprehensive and systematic to allow for generalization about the comparative cost of community care. Although the researchers employed a variety of statistical methods to compensate for these limitations, the problems they encountered raise questions about the state's capacity to monitor the well-being of patients and the costs of caring for them outside the state hospital.

Reports by Interest Groups and Legislative Oversight Bodies

Three other reports, which preceded the U-Mass evaluation, indicate the variety of problems that can be anticipated, at least in the implementation phase of privatizing acute care services. The first is the report conducted for the Pioneer Institute by students at the Kennedy School (Gow et al., 1993). The second is the report by a legislative oversight body, the House Post Audit and Oversight Bureau (HPAOB), on one of DMH's contracted replacement units (House Post Audit and Oversight Bureau [HPAOB], 1993). The third is an evaluation of another replacement unit, the Secure Assessment Unit at Cambridge Hospital, conducted by the Partnership for Quality Care and published in May, 1992 (Krasner, 1992).

The Kennedy School report conducted for the Pioneer Institute analyzes a number of privatization initiatives, one of which is DMH inpatient care. The authors focus on two issues in contracting for mental health services: The difficulty of measuring and ensuring quality, and the problem of maintaining a competitive environment without negatively affecting quality. They found that DMH has made progress in developing the necessary management mechanisms to address these issues, but the scale and complexity of the change still challenges DMH's capacity to monitor quality and costs.

In an effort to ensure the quality of services, the Department has imposed many stipulations, resulting in a contracting process so burdensome that it threatens to stifle competition. In the year previous to the report (Fiscal Year [FY] 93), the department received fewer than two bids per contract on average, suggesting the possibility of an oligopoly, which could demand higher contract prices.

Charles River Hospital—West

The House Post Audit and Oversight Bureau report on Charles River Hospital—West (HPAOB, 1993) cites a number of serious problems both in costs and in quality of care at that facility. These stem primarily from the fact that the hospital's parent company, Community Care Systems, Inc. was in financial difficulty at the time they submitted the bid for the $10.7 million contract, which led in turn to a series of managerial and clinical problems. Many of these problems stemmed from the strategy for financing, which required CRHW to obtain a "wraparound license" from a community hospital in order to qualify for Medicaid reimbursement.

The initial licensing agreement fell apart when the partner, Holyoke Hospital, backed out following considerable managerial conflicts between the two institutions. These were apparently related to Holyoke's concern about CRHW's failure to address various safety and quality issues due to their cash-flow problems. CRHW subsequently reached an agreement with another partner, Providence Hospital, which, however, had no experience in providing mental health services.

The report criticizes this wrap-around arrangement as a mechanism for privatizing acute services. In the first place, the relationship between Holyoke and CRHW was strained by the CRHW resistance to Holyoke's effort to maintain administrative control as required by law. The replacement of Holyoke by Providence Hospital created an additional cause for concern in the latter's lack of experience with treating the seriously mentally ill. Moreover, similar managerial conflicts ensued in this arrangement as well. Subsequently, Charles River Hospital—West did close due to financial problems, requiring DMH to develop alternative arrangements for acute services in that area.

The Cambridge Hospital Secure Assessment Unit

This 17-bed replacement unit, the first developed by DMH, was assessed by an advocacy organization known as The Partnership for Quality Care (Krasner, 1992). The evaluation concluded that Cambridge Hospital, in contrast to CRHW, is a financially secure, well-managed institution with strong ties to the community and extensive experience in providing high-quality services to persons with serious mental illness. Although the facility itself thus justifies the privatization policy, because of a "systemic problem" of inadequate resources, it is unable to meet the needs of the population fully. This has resulted in continuous use of overflow beds in state facilities, with negative consequences for both costs and quality of care.

The report also expressed concerns about the uncertainty of funding sources, especially Medicaid and the Free Care Pool, which are vulnerable to policy changes that would undermine the fiscal stability of the venture.

MEDICAID MANAGED CARE

Planning

No planning studies for the Medicaid reorganization comparable to the Department of Mental Health's Statewide Needs Assessment are publicly available. However, the state's rationale and expectations for the program are presented in the Division of Medical Assistance's waiver application submitted to HCFA, as is required of any state seeking to modify the Medicaid program as defined by federal regulations. In the 3-year period from FY 88 to 90, the Massachusetts Medicaid Program had grown by 80%, from $1.5 billion in FY 88 to nearly $2.7 billion in FY 90. Mental health services accounted for 4.5% of the total expenditures in 1990 and substance abuse treatment for 0.9%. This increase in the Medicaid program overall had occurred despite a variety of strenuous cost-containment efforts by the state, including third-party recovery programs, rate-setting, and hospital financing laws. The Division attributed this growth primarily to expansion of eligibility for children and pregnant women and to growth in the category of the disabled, especially due to AIDS.

The Division estimated that the PCC program would result in a first-year net aggregate savings of $14.5 million, or 1.4% of the projected costs without such a program. Savings predicted for the mental health and substance abuse program were $23.2 million, or 10.2% of the expenditures projected in the absence of managed care.

Evaluations of the Medicaid Managed Care Programs

As a condition of granting a waiver, HCFA requires any state modifying its welfare program to conduct an independent evaluation after 1 year, with continuation of the waiver dependent on the outcome. The evaluation of the Primary Care Clinician program was conducted by the John W. McCormack Institute of Public Affairs and published in June 1994 (Grant et al., 1994). The Mental Health and Substance Abuse plan required by HCFA was evaluated by the Heller School at Brandeis University.

The Primary Care Clinician Program: Unlike the Mental Health and Substance Abuse Program, which enrolled all eligible recipients simultaneously, PCC enrollment was planned to be gradual. Even so, the Division of Medical Assistance had to slow the process when it encountered problems, especially with enrollment of recipients in the disabled category. Consequently, at the time of the evaluation, enrollment was much lower than anticipated and included primarily the AFDC category. Thus, most of the Medicaid-eligible SPMI were not included.

The study found overall that the PCC program had achieved its goals as defined by the waiver, specifically, to improve the cost-effectiveness of care for Medicaid enrollees without creating barriers to services or reducing the quality of care. The evaluators estimated that the program achieved an aggregate net savings of 7.4% per enrollee, as compared to projected costs if there were no program. As noted, this considerably exceeded the expectations stated in the waiver application.

The magnitude of the savings was not the only unexpected finding; the source of savings differed as well. The waiver application had anticipated that much of the savings would come from a projected 6.2% reduction in inpatient hospital utilization rates, with a secondary savings from a 1.6% reduction in the use of hospital emergency services. Instead, inpatient utilization rates actually increased by some 10%. This increased cost was more than offset by a reduction in emergency services that was much greater than expected, however, about 22%. In short, the program achieved the hoped-for savings, but its impact on service utilization patterns was very different from what was expected.

With some qualifications and reservations, the authors found no direct evidence that savings were achieved either by restricting access or reducing the quality of care. However, their findings do raise some concern about the program's effect on access to mental health services. The Mental Health/Substance Abuse program was differentiated from the PCC program, based on two assumptions: first, that primary care clinicians lack adequate knowledge of MH/SA problems and resources to serve effectively as gatekeepers; and second, that removing MH/SA services from the referral process would provide a necessary safeguard for patient confidentiality in the use of these services.

In the Managed Care Program, the PCC is not informed about the use of MH/SA services unless the patient specifically authorizes a release of information. Critics of mental health carve-outs have pointed out that a drawback in this kind of arrangement is the lack of coordination of care. This is particularly problematic with SPMI, for whom comorbidities are highly prevalent. This aspect of the program could not be evaluated directly, as Medicaid recipients were not yet enrolled and, in any case, the database does not record referrals to specialists. However, interviews with providers are cause for concern, as the evaluators note: "PCC's lack of information about the mental health/substance abuse program was striking" (Grant et al., 1995, p. 68).

The Mental Health/Substance Abuse Program. Like the PCC component of the Medicaid managed care plan, this program was evaluated to determine whether it had reduced costs without significantly reducing either the quality of services or enrollees' access to them. This evaluation was conducted by a team of researchers at the Heller School, Brandeis University (Callahan et al., 1994). The evaluation defined cost-effectiveness to mean that Medicaid costs are lower than what they would have been without the program, taking into account enrollment trends and inflation. Access meant that the program provided an "adequate amount of services during reasonable time periods and within reasonable geographic distance" of enrollees. HCFA also required documentation of access to emergency services. HCFA apparently did not specify standards of quality, beyond saying that it should be "adequate" and should not be reduced as a consequence of the waiver.

Cost. The Brandeis team calculated that the program reduced costs by $47 million dollars, 22% less than costs projected without a program.

Access. Measured by penetration rates (total number of users per 1,000 enrollees), utilization of all services increased by 4.6%. Consistent with the goals of managed care, which seeks to substitute less costly outpatient services for inpatient care, the penetration rate for outpatient services rose about 6%, although it declined slightly for inpatient care.

Quality. Noting the difficulty of measuring quality generally, and especially changes in quality, without a baseline from the previous fee-for-service system, the Brandeis team's conclusions were generally positive, with some important qualifications. The quality assessment consisted of analyzing readmission rates (percentage of discharges followed by a readmission within 30 days), surveying providers, and meeting with focus groups of DMH consumers enrolled in Medicaid. Although readmission rates did not change for the Medicaid population as a whole under managed care, they did (in different directions) for specific subgroups. Specifically, for adults in the eligibility category of "disabled" the rate fell slightly, offsetting a corresponding slight increase for adults in other categories of eligibility. A more substantial change occurred for children, with the readmission rate increasing from 7.5 to 10.1%.

The results of the provider survey regarding quality yielded a mean score that was positive but with negative opinions expressed by a substantial subgroup, especially among providers of children's services.

The evaluators' discussions with DMH consumers revealed a high level of concern about the effect of managed care. The team did not survey consumers themselves, and perhaps their strongest criticism of the managed care program was its delay in implementing a required consumer survey process.

The evaluators found that persons in the disabled category, which includes most of the SPMI, had nine times the admission rate of other Medicaid enrollees (18.37% versus 2.06%); used seven times as many days of care per person per year (1.885 versus 0.264); and incurred five times as much direct service costs ($1595 versus $301). This difference is all the more significant as the proportion of disabled in the Medicaid population increased during the study period, from 14.4 to 16.1%.

Clearly those in the disabled group have distinctly different characteristics and needs. This raises the question of whether and how managed care practices might affect them differently. For example, given these utilization patterns, any strategy that targets "high users" is likely to have a disproportionate impact on the disabled for better or for worse, whether or not that is the specific intention. Because the disabled represent a relatively small proportion of the total, any such negative effect might disappear in the aggregate statistics.

The Brandeis evaluation did attempt to differentiate between the disabled and nondisabled whenever possible in their analyses. However, in several key areas, notably the analysis of penetration rates, the data provided to them did not differentiate the disabled group. Despite these limitations, it is possible to see in the data presented some of the ways in which managed care affected the disabled group differently.

Enrollment. Although the number of persons enrolled in Medicaid declined slightly (0.8 percent) from FY92 to FY93, the proportion of disabled increased by 1.7%.

Savings. As noted, the per-enrollee costs for the disabled was some five times that of the nondisabled prior to managed care. Likewise, the reduction of the per-enrollee cost (from what was predicted without managed care) for the disabled was proportionately much greater than the reduction for the nondisabled.

Utilization. The length of stay in all forms of 24-hour care was reduced less for the disabled than for the nondisabled, 7.5% versus 21.8%. The disabled did not have more admissions after managed care; presumably, therefore, annual days of care did not change. The nondisabled, in contrast, had a slight increase in the number of admissions; however, this was more than offset by the reduced length of stay, resulting in a 21.8% reduction in annual days of care.

The lack of data related to the adequacy of services in the baseline fee-for-service period makes it difficult to interpret these statistics. If it were known that, prior to managed care, expenditures for the disabled were disproportionately high even when their greater need was taken into account, then the disproportionate reduction in expenditures for this group in managed care disabled would be appropriate. This is hardly a safe assumption, however. In short, more research is required to understand the implications of these differences in the effects of managed care on the disabled and nondisabled population.

The Kennedy School Mental Health Policy Working Group. The Mental Health Policy Working Group (MHPWG) of the Kennedy School at Harvard University recently conducted a series of preliminary studies exploring the joint impact of the privatization and managed care initiatives on service utilization by the mentally ill (Jacobson, 1994; Shi, 1994; Stroup & Dorwart, 1994). The group examined a number of factors related to managed care, including penetration rates (number of admissions per 1,000 enrollees); length of stay (probability of rapid discharge and survival functions); readmission rates (recidivism); use of alternative services, such as emergency wards and diversionary beds; and the extent of cost-shifting, i.e., "dumping". These studies used data from a joint Medicaid-DMH claims dataset provided by DMH and a DMH database known as the Client Tracking System. These data covered a time period that allowed for before and after comparisons of both initiatives. The studies employed regression analysis to control for clinical and demographic differences between the Medicaid and DMH groups. In studying length of stay, survival analysis was also used.

In general, this research showed length of stay decreasing in both the privatized DMH units in general hospitals (replacement units) and in the managed care network units, but more so for the latter. Among different patient groups, the decrease was particularly dramatic for children and adolescents in network hospitals. At the same time, both the utilization rate (the proportion of enrollees admitted) and the rapid readmission rate (proportion of discharges readmitted within 30 days) increased following the implementation of managed care.

To measure quality of care, the group also examined emergency room utilization and found that ER visits increased for Medicaid enrollees but remained stable for DMH beneficiaries. Disposition from the emergency room was also examined. The proportion of emergency room visits resulting in admissions to the hospital declined for both the DMH and the managed care group, but the proportion sent home remained the same for both groups. Both groups had increases in alternative outcomes (e.g., referral to 24-hour diversionary beds), with the managed care group having the greater percentage increase.

The increase in the admission rate for Medicaid enrollees suggests that managed care did not reduce access. As the Brandeis report noted, however, (Callahan et al., 1994), at least some of this increase may be attributed to a proportionate increase in the category of the disabled (whose utilization rates are higher) during the period. The increase in emergency room utilization and rapid readmissions raises questions about whether the managed care system has yet developed adequate substitutes for reduced inpatient care.

THE FUTURE OF MENTAL HEALTH CARE REFORM

The clearest finding of research conducted to date is that the hospital consolidation and Medicaid managed care initiatives did achieve cost savings in the first 2 years. The consolidation of underutilized facilities represents significant savings. Managed care of mental health and substance abuse treatment has reduced costs in Massachusetts consistent with comparable programs elsewhere. The difficult but necessary task for further research is to determine whether these savings primarily represent ongoing cost reductions or one-time effects, whether they will be offset by increased costs elsewhere, and whether they came at the expense of quality, access, and availability of services.

Evaluating costs for mental health services and determining the impact of factors such as privatization and managed care is very difficult (Dorwart & Epstein, 1993). The limitations of purchase of service contracting for mental health care have been widely noted (Dangerfield & Betit, 1993; Schlesinger, Dorwart, et al. 1986; Smith & Lipsky, 1992). Similarly, the practice of managed mental health care is so recent that little research exists to substantiate its claims, and many have suggested that initial cost savings may be negated in the long run by unmet need and pent-up demand (Tischler, 1990).

The Massachusetts initiatives may have long-term consequences that are not captured by assessments of the type described here. For example, a significant part of the Department of Mental Health's projected savings through privatization was based on gaining access to the Free Care Pool; however, changes in the allocation of those funds shortly afterward resulted in an unanticipated additional expenditure of over $3 million, causing a significant deficit in the Department's budget and prompting consideration of additional, controversial hospital closures ("Mental health shifts," 1994).

The privatization and managed care initiatives in Massachusetts, like many comparable efforts throughout the country, are largely unproven innovations carried out in the real world of constraints and exigencies by administrators who do not have the luxury of being able to obtain all possible evidence before taking action (Mechanic & Surles, 1992). To gain that understanding will require further study of how large-scale trends such as privatization and managed care initiatives affect the cost, quality, and accessibility of mental health services, the structure and behavior of provider organizations, and the management functions of government.

To achieve this more comprehensive understanding, researchers must overcome formidable problems of research design and data analysis. The issue of inadequate baseline data is one example. Another, on the conceptual level, is the lack of generally shared definitions of quality. More comprehensive evaluation will require a clearer understanding of what taxpayers, government officials, providers, and consumers of mental health services can and should expect from the mental health system. The increasing attention to outcomes assessment indicates a widespread recognition of this need (Dorwart et al., 1995). Progress in these areas will be a major contribution to the goal of improving the quality and reducing the costs of care for persons with serious and persistent mental illness within the larger framework of national health care reform.

REFERENCES

Benson P., Clemens, E., et al. (1994). *Overview: Findings of University of Massachusetts studies of Department of Mental Health facility consolidation.* Boston, MA: Center for the Study of Social Acceptance, University of Massachusetts.

Callahan, J., Shepard, D., et al. (1994). *Evaluation of the Massachusetts Medicaid Mental Health/Substance Abuse Program. Report submitted to Massachusetts Division of Medical Assistance.* Waltham, MA: Heller School of Advanced Studies in Social Welfare, Brandeis University.

Dangerfield, D., & Betit, R. (1993). Managed mental health care in the public sector. *New Directions for Mental Health Services, 59,* 67–79.

Department of Mental Health. (1993a, September 16). *DMH statewide needs assessment executive summary of statewide findings.* DMH memorandum.

Department of Mental Health. (1993b, August 9). *Department of Mental Health needs assessment.*

Dorwart, R., et al. (1996). Outcomes assessment and psychiatric services. *Hospital and Community Psychiatry, 45,* 1165.

Dorwart, R., & Epstein, S. (1993). *Privatization and mental health care.* Westport, CT: Greenwood.

Executive Office of Health and Human Services, Commonwealth of Massachusetts. (1993a). *Public managed behavioral healthcare in Massachusetts: The first two years.* Unpublished manuscript.

Executive Office of Health and Human Services, Commonwealth of Massachusetts. (1993b). *Developing a system of public managed care.* Unpublished manuscript.

Governor's Special Commission on Consolidation of Health and Human Services Institutional Facilities. (1991). *Actions for quality care: A plan for the consolidation of state institutions and for the provision of appropriate care services.*

Gow, D., & Jovovich, C., et al. (1993). *From public to private: The Massachusetts experience, 1991–1993.* Cambridge, MA: John F. Kennedy School of Government, Harvard University, for Pioneer Institute for Public Policy Research.

Grant, M., Wagner, L., Porel, F., et al. (1994). *A report to the Massachusetts Division of Medical Assistance: Evaluation of the Primary Care Clinician Program.* Boston, MA: John W. McCormack Institute of Public Affairs, University of Massachusetts.

Grob, G. (1991). *From asylum to community.* Princeton, NJ: Princeton University Press.

House Post Audit Bureau. (1993). *Charles River Hospital-West: Preliminary report.* Unpublished manuscript.

Hurley, R., Freund, D., & Paul, J. (1993). *Managed care in medicaid.* Ann Arbor, MI: Health Administration Press.

Jacobson, K. (1994). *Evaluating medicaid managed care for Massachusetts mental health services: An analysis of effects on inpatient service use in two state agencies.* Unpublished master's thesis, John F. Kennedy School of Government, Harvard University.

Krasner, S. (1992). *The Cambridge Hospital secure assessment unit: A good try for a flawed concept.* Unpublished manuscript.

Massachusetts Department of Mental Health. (1993a, September 16). DMH statewide needs assessment. Executive summary of statewide findings. DMH Memorandum.

Mechanic, D. (1994). *Inescapable decisions.* New Brunswick, NJ: Transaction Books

Mechanic, D., & Surles, R. (1992, Fall). Challenges in state mental health policy and administration. *Health Affairs,* 34–49.

Mental health shift costs state $3.3m. (1994, December 20), *Boston Globe.*

Osborne, D., & Gaebler, T. (1992). *Reinventing government.* Reading,MA: Addison-Wesley.

Schlesinger, M., Dorwart, R., et al. (1986). Competitive bidding and state's purchase of services: The case of mental health care in Massachusetts. *Journal of Policy Analysis and Management, 5,* 245–263.

Sharfstein, S., & Stoline, M. (1992, Fall). Reform issues for insuring mental health care. *Health Affairs,* 84–7.

Shi, J. (1994). *Patient utilization analysis of medicaid managed care for Massachusetts mental health services.* Unpublished master's thesis. Harvard University School of Public Health.

Smith, S., & Lipsky, M. (1992). Privatization in health and human services: A critique. *Journal of Health Politics, Policy and Law, 17,* 233–252.

State officials strive to bring the healthcare debate home. (1994, September 25). *New York Times.* p. B1.

Stroup, S., & Dorwart, R. (1995). The impact of a medicaid mental health managed care program on the severely mentally ill. *Psychiatric Services, 56,* 885–889.

Tischler, G. (1990). Utilization management and the quality of care. *Hospital and Community Psychiatry, 41,* 1099–1102.

3

Purchase of Service and Fostered Failure: A Massachusetts Case Study

Paul S. Regan

INTRODUCTION

The root of failure in a system as complex and multifaceted as a state-run purchase of service (POS) system is often difficult to determine. When things run well, government administration is quick to claim credit. But when the agencies providing needed human services are plagued by organizational failure and bankruptcy, a mad scramble ensues to determine where the blame should lie.

Some accuse state government of poor contracting and monitoring practices; others condemn the providers for poor management and fiscal accountability. Perhaps, however, neither the purchasing authority nor the provider agencies are at fault. The POS system itself may foster poor performance and organizational decline.

PROVIDERS IN DECLINE

Unfortunately, such organizational decline is all too common in POS delivery systems across the nation. This chapter provides an example of one such system failure. An overview of provider organizations operating within the Massachusetts Department of Mental Retardation during a recent 3-year period highlights some striking indicators of organizational morbidity and mortality (Regan, 1991). The findings reported below are indicative of serious organizational hardship experienced by provider organizations, both for-profit and nonprofit, operating within the Massachusetts system.

If the reason for this high rate of organizational morbidity and mortality among provider agencies in the Massachusetts POS system is the system itself, then surely organizational theories and case studies exist to provide some illumination. This would seem to be the case.

The organizational theory that speaks most directly to the matter is the theory of "permanently failing organizations" (PFO) proposed by Marshall Meyer and Lynne Zucker (1989). The Commonwealth of Massachusetts' POS system is a case study that is especially illustrative of how and why organizations fail. This examination sheds some light on the pitfalls of a typical state-run POS system and offers insights into how the best of intentions can give rise to an environment that fosters failure and jeopardizes the delivery of care.

THEORIES OF ORGANIZATIONAL PERFORMANCE

Early models of organization were based on mainstream economic theory. Accordingly, organizations were viewed as economic entities—as players in the marketplace. Admittedly, not all organizations sold products; some existed to sell services. But in true economic fashion, it was assumed by early theorists that organizations that could sell their services in the most efficient and cost-effective manner would excel and displace less efficient, less effective organizations (DiMaggio, 1989). For purposes of definition, "efficiency" was understood as the ability to provide a service at the lowest possible cost to the organization. Effectiveness was defined as the ability to produce and deliver the service promised.

According to these early models, marketplace forces would weed out low-performance (inefficient, ineffective) organizations, resulting in their eventual demise. High-performance (efficient, effective) organizations would thrive, displaying greater organizational persistence—that is, a longer organizational life span.

Like economic models of organization, early sociological models also stressed the significance of efficiency and effectiveness and their effect on overall organizational performance and persistence (Weber, 1946). More recent sociological models, however, have identified additional factors affecting performance and persistence. These models maintain that an organization must be viewed in its environmental context and emphasize that performance and persistence are more properly understood as functions of an organization's ability to survive in its own unique environment (Pfeffer & Salancik, 1978).

Different theorists have stressed various components of the organization–environment nexus. Some have defined organizational performance as the organization's ability to access necessary resources (Pfeffer & Salancik, 1978). Others have focused on the organization's ability to weather periods of economic downturn and diminishing support (Hannan & Freeman, 1977). Zald (1970) offered a theory of "political economy," in which organizational performance is viewed as a function of how well an organization controls its own internal and external political economies, both of which contain fiscal and human elements.

Although most of these sociological models acknowledge financial efficiency and effectiveness as measures of organizational performance, these are only two of many measures. Other measures and indicators also need to be considered. For example, some long-lived organizations may in fact be relatively inefficient and/or unable to meet their own programming goals. In these cases, performance may best be measured by the organization's ability to stabilize within its own environment in response to the contextual demands placed upon it (Meyer & Zucker, 1989).

Traditional economic measures of efficiency, effectiveness, and attainment of stated goals may be inadequate to assess survival ability. According to Meyer and Zucker (1989), some organizations may survive for years as a result of their ability to stabilize within the environment, the whole time evidencing complete failure in terms of efficiency, effectiveness, and goal attainment.

The theory of "permanently failing organizations,"[1] as proposed by Meyer and Zucker in 1989, describes how low-performance (inefficient, ineffective) organizations can successfully stabilize within their environments and demonstrate a high degree of organizational persistence. This concept of an organization which is both low performance and high persistence clearly runs contrary to most of the existing economic models of organization. According to Meyer and Zucker (1989), certain environments actually foster this particular performance/persistence scenario. These authors describe the environmental constraints that not only make such a scenario possible, but an expected outcome for some

---

1. Though referred to as "permanently failing organizations," they are only so in the economic sense. In terms of organizational persistence and performance, as measured by the ability to stabilize in their environments, they are remarkably successful.

organizations.

According to PFO theory, two environmental constraints bear on an organization's persistence and performance: *owner* interests and *dependent actor* interests. *Owners* are those individuals or powers able to shift or control resources and commitments in relation to the organization and who are motivated to do so by consideration of profits or other benefits of organizational performance. *Dependent actors* are those individuals or powers lacking ownership or sovereignty interests in the performance of an organization as owners or shareholders do, but who are nevertheless dependent on the organization for some form of benefit.

Meyer and Zucker (1989) state that an organization's *owners* will want to maintain the organization if it is profitable. If it is not profitable, then they will want to discontinue it, unless they are vested in the continuance of the organization for other, noneconomic reasons. Also, if the organization's goals are ambiguous or unclear, then owners will tend to perpetuate it regardless of its performance.

The organization's *dependent actors* will also want to maintain the organization if it is performing well, because they receive benefits from it in some form or other. Should organizational performance decline significantly, then they may look for other organizations to provide them with the benefit they seek. The exception is when a monopoly situation exists and there are no other organizations from which to select, or when the differences between organizations are not significant. In such a situation, *dependent actors* will work toward maintaining the existing organization, regardless of its performance or stability.

An organization that is maintained over an extended period of time through the convergent interests of *owners* and *dependent actors*, even though it is unprofitable and ineffective, is, according to Meyer and Zucker's criteria (1989), a permanently failing organization.

APPLICATION OF THEORY

Understanding sociological models of organization, particularly the PFO model of Meyer and Zucker (1989), is of particular importance when dealing with nonprofit human service providers in a purchase-of-service environment. The reason for this is that economic models of organizational performance just don't work well when applied to nonprofits (Kanter & Summers, 1987) and the vast majority of providers operating within POS systems in the United States are nonprofit organizations.

Nonprofit service providers, by their very nature, aren't driven by economic considerations. Their primary goal is to deliver a service, not to make a profit. As a result, the economic dynamic of efficiency and effectiveness referenced by DiMaggio (1989) and others has little explanatory power for understanding organizational performance and viability among them.

On the other hand, many of the sociological models of organizations do offer some explanations. The PFO theory in particular not only offers some explanatory power, but some predictive power as well. For if environmental constraints do indeed exist within a typical POS system, then it is reasonable to assume that an increased incidence of "permanently failing organizations" will be observed as well. And they will be easy to identify, because they will evidence significant levels of low performance in terms of the traditional measures of efficiency and effectiveness, while at the same time displaying a high degree of organizational persistence.

CASE STUDY

It is useful to step outside the realm of the theoretical and into the concrete world of the case study. One study that is particularly helpful in illustrating the application of PFO theory to a purchase-of-service system is the historical development of the Commonwealth of Massachusetts' POS system for the delivery of services for the mentally retarded.

The Massachusetts POS system was one of the first large-scale POS systems to evolve. As a result, it is richly illustrative, because it has experienced many of the legal and economic forces that have come to bear on POS systems across the nation. And within the Massachusetts POS system, the Department of Mental Retardation (DMR) tends to be the best source of comparative statistics, thanks to a concerted effort over the past several years to collect quantitative data on provider organizations.

Although the case study to follow focuses on the Massachusetts' Department of Mental Retardation's POS delivery system, the truths gleaned from the study are easily generalizable. The developmental history of the system and the forces that come to bear can be seen in other states and other POS systems as well.

Early Programming for the Mentally Retarded

Throughout much of the 17th, 18th, and the first half of the 19th centuries, mental retardation was viewed throughout the United States in a decidedly negative light. The popular conception, born of general ignorance, was that mental retardation was shameful and that mentally retarded individuals were to be hidden away if at all possible. During that time period, the medical profession understood mental retardation as a hopelessly irreversible medical condition. There was no treatment to be provided, only custodial maintenance. Consequently, the societal response to mental retardation at that time consisted of isolating mentally retarded individuals in almshouses, institutions, and correctional facilities for the criminally insane and mentally ill. This was the case in Massachusetts, as well as throughout the rest of the United States.

As the 19th century progressed, several Massachusetts individuals rose to prominence who pioneered humanitarian efforts in dealing with the mentally retarded. Samuel Gridley Howe, a physician educated at Harvard Medical School, began employing some of the more recent medical advances of the day in his dealings with children with mental retardation and other disabling conditions. Horace Mann, a prominent educator and close friend of Dr. Howe, also began working with individual school districts to modernize their educational approach to working with retarded children. Meanwhile, Senator Charles Sumner and his brother George began working through the Massachusetts political system to improve conditions for mentally retarded individuals in the Commonwealth.

As Samuel Gridley Howe's efforts on behalf of the mentally retarded were beginning to earn recognition in Massachusetts, Dorothea Lynde Dix was crusading nationally and internationally for the rights of the mentally ill. Dix, a close friend of Dr. Howe, shared with him figures she had gathered on the national incidence and prevalence of mental retardation. The two began to work together more closely, and through his association with Dix, a Howe was able to bring the plight of the mentally retarded before a national audience.

Massachusetts House of Representatives member Judge Horatio Boyington, an avid follower of Howe's work, made a successful motion on January 22, 1846 to appoint a committee to investigate establishing a commission to "inquire into the condition of the idiots of the Commonwealth, to ascertain their number and whether anything can be done for their relief" (Kanner, 1964, p. 41). On March 25, 1846, the appointed committee recommended establishing a commission of three individuals to oversee such work.

In addition to the creation of the three-member commission, the Massachusetts legislature also appropriated $2,500 in 1848 for the establishment of a school for the mentally retarded to be operated by the Perkins School for the Blind. This was the first legislative action in

Massachusetts appropriating funds for services for the retarded, and allowed for the care of ten children. The school that was established later separated from the Perkins School for the Blind and became known as the Massachusetts School for Idiotic and Feeble-Minded Youth. In 1887 it relocated to Waltham and was renamed the Walter E. Fernald State School in honor of one of its early superintendents.

In 1848, the first private school for retarded children was established by Dr. Harvey Wilbur of Barre, Massachusetts. It was so successful that Dr. Wilbur received national recognition and later went on to become one of the founders of the American Association on Mental Deficiency.

By all appearances, Massachusetts was becoming a national leader in terms of services for the mentally retarded. An historical analysis of the period, however, indicates that early advocates for the retarded remarked that they had to fight a "constant struggle to overcome the indifference of the Massachusetts legislature" (Massachusetts Department of Mental Health, 1966, p. 138). Although Massachusetts had set precedents among the states for its initial treatment of the retarded, other states such as New York, Pennsylvania, and Ohio advanced more quickly in the development of facilities and resources for the care of greater numbers of individuals.

The Move Toward Institutions

Slowly but surely, Massachusetts moved forward in its plans for the retarded. In 1905, an extension of the Massachusetts Act of 1851 established that the Commonwealth had responsibility for the care and treatment of all mentally retarded individuals in the state. This legislation resulted in the establishment of several of the state institutions for the retarded: Wrentham State School in 1907, Belchertown State School in 1929, and the Dever State School in 1947. In all, five state schools were established. In addition, the Hogan Regional Center was established, which also functioned as a state school, bringing the total number of such institutions for the mentally retarded in Massachusetts to six (Rubenstein, 1977).

During that time period, community-based clinics were also established for the proper diagnosis of children with mental retardation. Child guidance clinics were established in East Boston, Boston, Lawrence, Lowell, Reading, Springfield, and Worcester. As these community-based clinics became more firmly established, a successful model of public–private partnership developed. The state, local mental health associations, and advocates for mentally retarded children worked together to provide services and programs, although a formal arrangement by which the state purchased services did not exist at the time.

To a large extent, it was this preexisting network of public–private partnerships that allowed for Massachusetts' ready implementation of federally sponsored community mental health centers in the mid-1960s. But in spite of a growing understanding of mental retardation, its causes, and its treatment, societal opinion regarding individuals with mental retardation rose to new heights of public alarm.

> Writers talked of the social menace of feeble-minded persons and how the multiplication of children of these families threatened to overwhelm the civilizations of the future. There was minimal legislative interest in providing adequate facilities and equipment. (Massachusetts Department of Mental Health, 1966, p. 136)

Contributing to this attitude was early research in genetics conducted during the first half of the 20th century. Advocates of eugenics called for the reproductive control of mentally retarded individuals. Publicly sanctioned purging of retarded individuals took place in Germany from 1930 to 1945. Elsewhere around the world, numerous countries and states adopted legal statutes that deprived mentally retarded individuals of their basic human rights, including such atrocities as forced sterilizations.

The Rise of State Schools for the Mentally Retarded

Although Massachusetts never instituted a practice of systematic sterilization, it did promote laws that allowed for the lifetime institutionalization of the retarded, effectively stripping them of any self-determinism or legal standing. And regardless of the availability of community-based services and the growing body of knowledge regarding mental retardation and its treatment, increasing numbers of referrals for care in state schools were made. This growth continued to be based, in part, on archaic beliefs that the mentally retarded should be hidden away or warehoused. It was also based, in part, on the fact that Massachusetts had increased its capacity for such care, and referrals were being made to fill that capacity.

The inadequacy of care provided for mentally retarded individuals in Massachusetts state schools, however, became apparent in the early 1950s. At that time, a Special Commission on Mental Retardation established in 1952 noted that there were still large numbers of mentally retarded individuals who were not receiving adequate care. The Special

Commission also noted that mentally retarded individuals were being placed in state schools at an earlier age than ever before and that a growing number of severely and profoundly retarded individuals were being housed there.

This growing demand on state schools, both in terms of the numbers served and the extent of the services needed, created an untenable situation. The Special Commission documented dangerous conditions in some of the state schools. Specifically, staff coverage of some of the wards within the schools was shamefully low. In fact, "it was not uncommon to find one person on night duty in a dormitory containing more than 100 boys and girls" (Massachusetts Department of Mental Health, 1966, p. 140). The state, however, failed to respond to these warnings.

Not only was staffing a problem in the state schools, but the physical condition of the schools themselves was also an issue. In 1964, the Special Commission conducted an in-depth examination of four of the state schools. The ensuing report condemned Massachusetts for the inhumane treatment mentally retarded individuals were receiving there. The report cited several reasons why such deplorable conditions had developed within the state schools. Social and economic upheaval related to the Great Depression of the 1930s and the two World Wars was listed, as well as the diversion of state monies to other public projects. But, whatever the reason, the fact remained that in 1964, overcrowding in at least two of Massachusetts' state schools ran as high as 20% (Massachusetts Department of Mental Health, 1966).

A Growing Emphasis on Community-Based Care

Concurrent with the decaying situation in Massachusetts' state schools came a new national agenda under President John F. Kennedy to provide services to the mentally retarded in the context of the community, rather than within state institutions. Effectively dealing with disadvantaged people such as the mentally retarded became community and governmental issues, and, as President Kennedy stated, would

> require both selected specific programs directed especially at known causes, and the general strengthening of our fundamental communities, social welfare, and education programs which can do much to eliminate or correct the harsh environmental conditions which often are associated with mental retardation and mental illness. (Kennedy, 1963, p. 2)

This emphasis on the "general strengthening of our fundamental communities" shifted the focus of the delivery of services for these populations from state-run institutions to the local communities and the available support services these communities could muster. Financial backing behind the concept of community-based services came in the form of the Title XIX and Title XX Amendments to the Social Security Act of 1935.

These amendments allowed the federal government to reimburse states for services provided to mentally retarded individuals in the community. As a result, services did not have to be provided by state agencies, but could be provided by approved private agencies as well. Prior to this, the individual states were directly responsible for funding and providing care. The emphasis on community-based services, together with new provisions to pay for these services, paved the way for a general move from institutional care to community-based care.

The Role of Litigation

During the early 1970s, the movement toward community-based services for the mentally retarded was hastened by a series of landmark lawsuits filed on behalf of mentally retarded individuals in state institutions.

The first of these suits, *Wyatt v. Stickney*, was filed in 1971 in Alabama. It concerned the involuntary confinement of mentally retarded individuals in a decrepit state institution known as Partlow State School. Citing violations of the Fourteenth Amendment's due-process clause, federal district court Judge Frank Johnson ruled that improved standards of institutional operations needed to be established, that a humane environment with sufficient staffing needed to be maintained, and that every attempt needed to be made to move residents of Partlow State School to less restrictive environments.

This constitutional right to "less restrictive environments" became known as the "right to habilitation." It was the most potent precedent established by *Wyatt v. Stickney* in that it began to force a transition from institution-based care to community-based care (Braddock, 1981). In the next 9 years, at least 38 more right-to-habilitation lawsuits were filed in 27 states and the District of Columbia.

As the 1970s progressed, the focus of legal policy began to turn from the *improvement* of existing state institutions to the *abolition* of institutions. In 1977, another landmark legal case, *Halderman v. Pennhurst*, ordered the closing of Pennhurst, a state institution for the mentally retarded in

Pennsylvania. This was the first time in which the Courts had mandated the closing of an entire state facility for the mentally retarded. Judge Broderick based his decision on equal protection principles inherent in the Constitution, which prohibit segregation of individuals, such as the mentally retarded, in isolated institutions.

The federal district court's decision was immediately appealed by Pennsylvania, and continued to be appealed throughout the 1970s in a series of legal maneuvers. The eventual resolution of the case was the legal determination that state institutions for the mentally retarded do not necessarily deprive *all* individuals of their rights to least restrictive environments. But it also acknowledged that the rights of *some* individuals may indeed be very much denied. The decision emphasized that such determinations need to be made on a case-by-case basis.

Across the nation, legal battles regarding the right of mentally retarded individuals to receive needed services in least restrictive environments raged throughout the 1970s. Although litigation didn't always prove effective in achieving specific results, the *threat* of litigation definitely served to focus the attention of federal, state, and local officials on the quality of care being offered. According to Braddock, litigation (both actual and threatened) "significantly increased federal and state spending, heightened levels of community awareness, improved staffing of facilities, renovated physical environments, and resulted in the significant expansion of community residential services" (1981, p. 610).

Class Action Suits in Massachusetts

By the early 1970s, conditions at the state schools for the mentally retarded in Massachusetts were characterized by "overcrowding, understaffing, crumbling physical plants, and inhumane environments. There was little or no service being provided beyond minimal custodial care" (Massachusetts Department of Mental Retardation, 1989, p. 4).

In 1971, a class action suit was filed on behalf of the residents of Belchertown State School. Over the next 3 years, similar suits were brought against the Dever, Fernald, Monson, and Wrentham state schools. The lawsuits were brought by parents of state school residents and the Association for Retarded Citizens of Massachusetts. The lawsuits sought the improvement of the state facilities in order to comply with minimal constitutional requirements.

The Commonwealth of Massachusetts never contested the lawsuits, choosing instead to enter into consent decrees with the plaintiffs. These consent decrees guaranteed the improvement of staffing and physical facilities in all of the state schools mentioned in the suits and adopted as compliance standards the federal government's Title XIX criteria for Medicaid reimbursement (Massachusetts Department of Mental Retardation, 1989).

The consent decrees also guaranteed that all of the class-action suit members (all of the residents of the state schools at the time the lawsuits were filed) would live in appropriate housing by 1990. This housing could be in community-based settings, or in the to-be-renovated state schools. Because of the incredible expense involved in renovating and staffing the state schools in accordance with the consent decrees and because of the growing national agenda of deinstitutionalization, vast numbers of class members were released to community-based residences. Some of these community residences were state-owned, and in fact run by the state schools. Most of the community residences, though, were owned and operated by various private, nonprofit providers operating in local communities.

The trend toward decreasing the number of residents in the state schools and increasing placements in community-based settings is clearly reflected in the statistics. From 1969 to 1988, the number of mentally retarded individuals in the Massachusetts state schools dropped from 8,200 to 3,320, representing a 60% reduction in the number of state school residents. In contrast, the number of mentally retarded individuals placed in community-based residences rose from virtually none in 1969 to 13,500 in 1988 (Massachusetts Developmental Disability Council, 1990).

Unfortunately, Massachusetts was slow in responding to all of the conditions of the consent decrees (Moscovitch, 1991). By the time the final court decision was handed down in the case of *Ricci v. Okin* (1982), an atmosphere of mistrust and even hostility had developed between the plaintiffs (represented by federal district court Judge Joseph L. Tauro as court-appointed monitor of the consent decrees) and the Commonwealth of Massachusetts.

In response to the state's delays in moving ahead with the provisions of the consent decrees, Judge Tauro adopted a rigid stand on state school renovations and the maintenance of institutional staff. Heeding the advice of parents of mentally retarded individuals in the state schools, Judge Tauro was vehement in requiring the state to upgrade the state schools. Unfortunately, due to the realities of limited state funding, this also resulted in decreased financial support for community-based services. The ironic result was that Judge Tauro's rigid handling of the consent decrees may in fact have lowered the quality of services received by mentally retarded individuals in community settings, while perpetuating an antiquated system of state schools.

Massachusetts in the 1990s

The consent decrees accomplished two very important things in regard to the provision of services for the mentally retarded in Massachusetts. First, they allowed for the continuance of the state schools, mandating wholesale improvements in physical facilities, staffing, and quality of care. Second, the consent decrees dramatically accelerated the move to community-based care in Massachusetts, as evidenced by the statistics previously cited.

The move to community-based care was beneficial in terms of normalized living and "right to habilitation" for many mentally retarded individuals. Community-based care may not be appropriate for every individual with mental retardation, however. Depending on the severity of mental retardation, it is conceivable that some individuals may best be served in what would be termed "institutions." As a result, a dual system of state school and community-based care was established and is currently being maintained in Massachusetts.

The state schools are perpetuated because the consent decrees mandate it. Community-based services are developed and used with greater frequency because of the national agenda toward deinstitutionalization, their cost-effectiveness as compared to institutionalization, and because the consent decrees also mandate it.

The present controversy in Massachusetts in regard to mental retardation services is how to balance the two effectively: improving services and quality of care in the state schools, while fostering the concurrent development of effective community-based services. Because both of these systems are being maintained at the same time, state spending for human services is growing increasingly limited.

Applying Theory to the Case Study

The Massachusetts Department of Mental Retardation case study provides ample material for the application of PFO theory. The environmental constraint forces of *owner interests* and *dependent actor* interests can be so easily identified and examined in context.

In the case of nonprofit providers of mental retardation services in Massachusetts, the state exists and operates as *owner* (Nessen, 1990) and it is within the best interests of the state to maintain the existing system of community-based, typically nonprofit, providers. Without them, the state would be morally and legally obligated to provide services directly for its disadvantaged populations. Consequently, the state is invested in the perpetuation of these organizations, apart from organizational performance. It doesn't matter whether the community-based human service provider is performing well as an organization, as long as the needed services are being provided. At the same time, the state is forced to be restrictive in terms of licensing and reimbursement for services because of the mandates of the consent decrees. The dual system of state schools and community-based providers forces competition for limited financial resources and levels of care are established that are increasingly costly to maintain. As a result, the community-based nonprofit provider operating under the Massachusetts POS system is typically underfunded and unable to stabilize itself financially. Organizational performance is less than optimal, and in many cases the provider is rendered technically insolvent (Nessen, 1990). The nonprofit, community-based service provider is perpetuated and constrained by *owner interests*, consistent with Meyer and Zucker's premises (1989).

Although the state in its role as *owner* contributes to the continuance of the human service provider, regardless of organizational performance, recipients of service and/or their legal and legislative advocates, functioning as *dependent actors*, also serve to perpetuate the agency. In essence, the state has a monopoly in regard to the provision of these services; the state pays for the actual delivery of services, and the state "plugs" the individual consumer into the service provider that it deems most appropriate. PFO theory asserts that in this type of monopoly situation, dependent actors are motivated to maintain the organization as it exists, apart from performance. Dependent actors, therefore, perpetuate the existing delivery of services and the existing system of provider agencies, just as the state perpetuates the continued existence of the insolvent nonprofit provider.

An Analysis of the Data

It is clear that community-based service providers operating within the Massachusetts Department of Mental Retardation POS system are subject to the environmental constraints outlined in PFO theory.

The history of the system's development in Massachusetts shows the vested interest of the state in a dual system of state schools and private, typically nonprofit, community-based providers. Out of necessity, limited tax dollars are spread increasingly thinly, with a disproportionate amount going to the state schools as a result of the consent decrees. The nonprofit, community-based provider operating with less than adequate funding finds itself in a spiral of declining organizational performance, often to the point of technical insolvency or bankruptcy. The convergence of *owner interests* (the state) and *dependent actor interests* (the recipients of care) perpetuates this network of crippled providers.

Having identified the environmental forces that constrain organizational performance among POS providers, it is necessary to establish whether the two outcome variables of PFO theory are confirmed by data. In fact, they are. The 3-year data analysis of organizational statistics for Massachusetts' Department of Mental Retardation providers highlights that reality quite well.

Organizational persistence for the typically nonprofit providers is very high, with an average lifespan of 225 months for those agencies operating within the POS system. Organizational performance, as measured by traditional financial indicators, is quite low and of a sustained nature. Year-end fund balance figures, year-end working capital figures, and overall solvency figures were dangerously low and showed no signs of improving. Overall organizational performance as measured by the state's prequalification process is declining (Regan, 1991).

SUMMARY

The theory of permanently failing organizations provides real and valuable explanatory power for understanding why the Massachusetts Department of Mental Retardation's POS providers are experiencing organizational hardships.

An historical review of the development of the system allows for easy identification of the *owner interests* and *dependent actor interests* outlined by Meyer and Zucker (1989). It also provides a base for understanding the intense budgetary stresses behind funding for services. These environmental forces, in turn, are constraining the organizational performance of provider agencies in a way specifically prescribed by PFO theory. Organizational data for a recent 3 year period confirms that fact.

Though this case study has focused on just one POS delivery system, the principles are clear and generalizable. Most of the POS systems operating within the United States came into being during roughly the same period and in response to roughly the same issues and forces. It can safely be assumed that many POS systems across the nation are providing the same environment-constraining forces as are evidenced in Massachusetts.

Assuming that a POS environment can foster organizational failure, the logical solution is to alter the environment to break the relationship. Either the owner interests of the state or the dependent actor interests of the service recipients should be examined for opportunities to break the environmental scenario of fostered failure.

What clearly isn't appropriate is the blaming of provider agencies, which typically occurs in election years. Elected officials need to work together toward refining the entire delivery system if substantive and beneficial change is to come to human service providers and the recipients of their services.

REFERENCES

Braddock, D. (1981). Deinstitutionalization of the retarded: Trends in public policy. *Hospital and Community Psychiatry, 32*, 607–615.

DiMaggio, P. (1989). Foreword. In M. W. Meyer, & L. G. Zuckcer, *Permanently failing organizations.* Newbury Park, CA: Sage Publications.

Halderman v. Pennhurst State School and Hospital, 466 F.Supp. 1295 (East District Court, PA, 1977), 612 F.2d 84 (3rd Circuit Court, 1979), 49 U.S.L.W. 4363 (Superior Court, April 20, 1981).

Hannan, M. T., & Freeman, J. H. (1977). The population ecology of organizations. *American Journal of Sociology, 82*, 929–964.

Kanner, L. (1964). *History of the care and study of the mentally retarded.* Springfield, IL: Thomas Books.

Kanter, R. M., & Summers, D. V. (1987). Doing well while doing good: Dilemmas of performance measurement in nonprofit organizations and the need for a multiple-constituency approach. In W. W. Powell (Ed.), *The nonprofit sector: A research handbook* (pp. 154–166). New Haven, CT: Yale University Press.

Kennedy, J. F. (1963). *Message from the President of the United States relative to mental illness and mental retardation.* 88th Congress, First Session, U.S. House of Representatives, Document No. 58. Washington, DC: U.S. Government Printing Office.

Massachusetts Department of Mental Health. (1966). *Massachusetts plans for its retarded.* The Report of the Mental Retardation Planning Project. Boston, MA: Author.

Massachusetts Department of Mental Retardation. (1989). *A study of the feasibility of consolidating certain retardation facilities in the commonwealth.* Boston, MA: Author.

Massachusetts Developmental Disabilities Council. (1990). *Creating open communities.* Boston, MA: Author.

Meyer, M. W., & Zucker, L. G. (1989). *Permanently failing organizations.* Newbury Park, CA: Sage Publications.

Moscovitch, E. (1991). *Mental retardation programs: How does Massachusetts compare?* Boston: Pioneer Institute for Public Policy Research.

Nessen, P. (1990). *Purchase of service reform: final report.* Commonwealth of Massachusetts, Executive Office of Administration and Finance. (Publication #16, 174–25–3000–1–90–CR.)

Pfeffer, J., & Salancik, G. R. (1978). *The external control of organizations: A resource dependence perspective.* New York: Harper & Row.

Regan, P. S. (1991). Organizational performance of nonprofit providers of mental retardation services in a purchase of service economy. *Dissertation Abstracts International, 53,* 0039A.

Ricci v. Okin, 537 F. Supp. 817 (Federal District Court, MA, 1982).

Rubenstein, S. (1977). *Toward independent living, state schools to community programs,* Unpublished manuscript.

Weber, M. (1946). Bureaucracy. In H. H. Gerth & C. W. Mills (Eds.), *From Max Weber: Essays in sociology* (pp. 196–244). New York: Oxford University Press.

Wyatt v. Stickney, 325 F. Supp. 781 (M.D., AL, 1971), 334 F. Supp. 1341 (M.D., AL, 1971), 344 F. Supp. 373 (M.D., AL, 1972).

Zald, M. N. (1970). Political economy: A framework for comparative analysis. In M. N. Zald (Ed.), *Power in organizations* (pp. 221–265). Nashville, TN: Vanderbilt University Press.

4

Contracting for Alcohol and Drug Treatment: Implications for Public Management

*Steven Rathgeb Smith**

INTRODUCTION AND OVERVIEW

This chapter examines contracting for substance abuse services in North Carolina. Drug abuse is one of the more serious social problems of the late 20th century. Its links with crime, mental illness, and family stress are well documented, and governments across the globe devote substantial resources to prevent and counteract the effects of drug abuse.

Drug abuse is a relatively recent social problem, and government programs to tackle it are also relatively new. Many service programs for drug abuse clients are provided by the state authority through contracts with private nonprofit and for-profit agencies. Recent and pending changes in public policy are a particular threat to these services provided by private agencies. Indeed, contrary to public expectation, drug programs are more financially vulnerable than many other service programs, due to the high number of indigent clients ineligible for Medicaid or private insurance, undercapitalization, and their relatively small scale.

* The author is especially indebted to Judith Smyth for comments on earlier versions of this paper. Financial support was provided by the Arts and Sciences Research Council and the Center for the Study of Philanthropy and Voluntarism at Duke University.

Since the 1960s, America has relied extensively on government contracting with private nonprofit and for-profit organizations to provide key social and health services, including child welfare, hospice care, home care, residential programs for the disabled, drug and alcohol treatment, and services to AIDS patients, to name just a few. In many states, state government agencies rely entirely on contracted services with nonprofit agencies (Smith & Lipsky, 1993). The growth of contracted services was spurred by the sharp growth in federal social and health spending in the 1960s and 1970s. Federal spending has declined since 1980 in selected areas of social policy. Contracting with nonprofit organizations has continued to rise, however, due to state and local government substitution for federal cuts and the shifting of program costs to other sources of revenue.

Purchase-of-service contracting with private agencies is in the midst of unprecedented change and uncertainty. The managed care revolution in health care means that many nonprofit and for-profit agencies cannot shift rising costs to private and public health insurance programs. The widespread enthusiasm for reinventing government means that private contract agencies are facing new demands for accountability, including more rigorous outcome evaluations. And the federal cutbacks in social and health programs will result in millions of dollars of lost federal revenue for nonprofit and for-profit service agencies. In addition, state and local governments will be forced to assume more responsibility for the provision of public services, creating additional ripple effects in locally delivered contract services. Competition between for-profit and nonprofit agencies for government contracts is likely to increase significantly.

North Carolina is a good state in which to examine the impact of current trends on contracted services. Contracting for social and health services in North Carolina occurs within a decentralized structure lacking strong centralized control at the state level. Contracting decisions are made by 41 area authorities with jurisdiction over local services. These area authorities are supervised by area boards comprised of appointed volunteers from the community. This chapter focuses on contracting for alcohol and drug services by these local area authorities.

The broader relevance of this North Carolina case is as an illustration of the policy trade-offs of the decentralized program structure favored by many policymakers around the country. The public management challenges currently faced by public officials and private contract agencies will be experienced to varying degrees by local governing bodies around the country in the coming years.

Moreover, the basic argument of this chapter runs counter to many prevailing assumptions of backers of a sharply reduced federal role in social and health policy. During the last 25 years, federal funding has been crucial to improved access to services, the expansion of contracted services, and the promotion of policy innovation, particularly for the treatment and prevention of drug and alcohol abuse. The lack of public funds for service provision, oversight, evaluation, and training presents a serious long-term problem for the service system at variance to public pressures and expectation that the prevention of drug abuse remains a priority for government funding.

Data Sources

This chapter is based on research undertaken in 1994–95 on contracting for substance abuse services in North Carolina. (See also Smith & Smythe, 1996.) As part of this research project, a representative sample of 13 area authorities in North Carolina was selected. All major urban areas were included: Charlotte, Winston-Salem, Durham, Raleigh, Greensboro, and Wilmington. In addition, several rural jurisdictions were investigated.

Interviews were conducted with key personnel in these areas responsible for substance abuse services and relevant state officials and individuals within the nonprofit advocacy community. A standard list of questions was asked of each area authority interviewee. In addition, interviews were conducted with key contract agencies in the nonprofit and for-profit sectors. Where feasible and appropriate, documents from the area authorities, contract agencies, and state division of substance abuse were reviewed and analyzed. Comparative data on the experience of contracting for mental health and substance abuse services in other states was also undertaken.

The next section provides an in-depth discussion of the contracting situation in North Carolina with particular reference to substance abuse services. Next, the challenges facing the contracted services are examined, including: declining funding and a weak private provider infrastructure; scant competition for contracts; insufficient incentives for innovation; and inadequate political support. The concluding section discusses the implications for contract management and practice as these relate to the current issues facing policymakers and private providers. Recommendations are offered for balancing state and local management of contracting, enhancing citizen review and oversight, and improving the provider infrastructure.

CONTRACTING IN NORTH CAROLINA

Prior to the 1970s, publicly funded substance abuse services around the country were scarce. The few programs in existence tended to be small private nonprofit and for-profit programs dependent on client fee income and public institutional programs. In North Carolina, a handful of private residential programs for alcoholics were about the only services available. Drug addicts were sometimes sent to a federal institutional program in Lexington, Kentucky. In the 1970s, the National Institute of Alcohol Abuse (NIAAA) and the National Institute of Drug Abuse (NIDA) were established. These federal agencies used their rapidly rising budgets to create a drug and alcohol treatment system through direct contracting with local public and private service providers and grants to state governments, which were, in turn, distributed to local government and private nonprofit service providers. The effect of expanded federal funding varied. Some states, localities, and service providers aggressively tapped federal funds. In Massachusetts, for example, an existing system of contracted services administered by the state was expanded. In contrast, in North Carolina, federal funds were used selectively to establish new programs in major urban areas such as Charlotte, Winston-Salem, and Greensboro. The state public institutions remained important as residual providers for alcohol and drug treatment services. And in North Carolina, unlike other states, a substantial portion of the new monies for drug and alcohol services was spent by public area authorities, rather than through the creation and development of private contract agencies.

Federal funds for substance abuse declined after the imposition of cuts by the Reagan administration in the early 1980s. Since the mid–1980s, federal funding has risen through the refinancing of services and the addition of new monies and programs. The service system established in North Carolina in the 1970s through federal grants has been left largely intact: selective contracting in the urban areas and limited substantial contracting in rural areas.

The decision-making structure for mental health and substance abuse services in North Carolina is quite different from that in other states— even other states in the region. In North Carolina, the state legislature is very powerful and the governor relatively weak compared with other states. (The governor of North Carolina is the only governor in the country without veto authority.) The state mental health and substance abuse agency is relatively small in size, in relation to its scope of responsibilities, compared with other states. Its main functions are oversight and monitoring, rather than direct provision of services or extensive funding of contracted services. The direct service role is limited to the operation of large public institutional facilities in different regions of the state.

The 41 local area authorities responsible for the delivery of public services receive their funding from the state on the basis of a formula. Area authorities vary in population considerably. North Carolina has 100 counties; some populous area authorities represent a single county (e.g. Wake, Durham, and Mecklenburg), whereas the authorities in rural areas represent three or four counties.

Area authorities are governed by volunteer area boards whose members are appointed by local county commissioners. Board members serve time-limited terms, which are often renewed. These boards hire the area director who is responsible for the provision of publicly subsidized services to the mentally ill, developmentally disabled, and persons with substance abuse problems. These services can be provided directly by the area authority staff or through contracts with nonprofit and for-profit service providers.

Unlike some local government entities across the country, these authorities face little pressure to contract out services to private agencies. These authorities also lack any rules or regulations requiring them to take bids for services. As a result, contracting tends to be used as a niche service for specialized programs. The area programs are primarily oriented to outpatient counseling and detoxification services. For example, in FY94, area programs received $3.6 million in public funds for social-setting detoxification, whereas contract agencies received only $300,000. Area programs received $4.6 million in nonhospital detoxification, whereas contract agencies received $3.1 million. In contrast, two-thirds of all public funds for halfway houses and residential programs such as 28–day treatment programs are spent by private nonprofit and for-profit contract agencies. In FY94, private contract halfway houses received $3.3 million in public funds, whereas public area programs received only $1.4 million. More intensive private contract residential programs received $3.7 million, whereas area programs received only $1.4 million. Only five methadone programs operate in the state and all of these programs are operated on a purchase-of-service contracting basis.

A positive correlation exists between the extent of contracting and federal financing. In cities such as Charlotte, Winston-Salem, Greensboro, Raleigh, and Wilmington, the federal government provided extensive grants to establish private, nonprofit drug and alcohol agencies during the 1970s. Thus, in these communities, the area authorities have long-standing contracts with these nonprofit agencies, with some contracts dating back 20 years or more. Contracting in these communities tends to comprise a much bigger part of the total area budget than in the localities without nonprofit organizations created through federal funds. Charlotte spends almost 40% of its budget on contracts. Greensboro spends its entire substance abuse budget on contracts. Cities without sizable nonprofit agencies created with federal grants such as Fayetteville, Rocky Mount, and Gastonia spent 10% or less of their substance abuse budgets on contracts.

Incremental growth in contracting has been the norm during the last 15 years. New contracts are costly, and often require a commitment of funds beyond the reach of many area authorities. Further, area authorities have a large investment in their own staff and facilities; they are understandably reluctant to contract out existing services because of the disruptive effects on staff and clients. Consequently, contracting tends to expand through the addition of new monies, especially federal grants for research-and-demonstration purposes. These grants are crucial for innovation and the development of additional services.

Overall, area programs are heavily dependent upon federal dollars. For non-Medicaid services, the federal government contributed about $22 million in 1994, while the state contributed $25 million. Some area programs receive funding from private insurance and county funds, although both sources have been declining in the last few years.

Data on the breakdown between nonprofit and for-profit contract agencies is unavailable. Most contracting is done by nonprofit agencies, however, for-profit contracting tends to be confined to residential programs such as 28-day treatment and detoxification. Usually, client slots in these programs are purchased on a per-day basis, rather than on a block contract basis, where the area authority guarantees to buy a certain number of slots per year.

The state of North Carolina maintains three state-run institutional facilities for substance abusers. The continued prominence of these three regional institutions stands in the way of program innovation, absorbs resources inappropriately, and frustrates the development of an infrastructure of public and private service providers. The area authority uses the institutions as a "safety valve" for the area authorities; absent sufficient services to meet demand, the area authorities refer patients to the institutions. Most clients then wait several weeks to be admitted.

In short, the structure of contracting for services is highly decentralized, with an unusually strong role for public authorities and institutions compared with other states. For instance, substance abuse services in states such as New York and Massachusetts are entirely contracted with an extremely limited role for public institutions. Nonetheless, the current state of contract services in North Carolina for substance abuse raises a number of very important policy issues and concerns for the future of contracting, the role of the public sector, and the future of government's response to citizens in need.

The next section addresses the key program issues facing purchase-of-service contracting for substance abuse in North Carolina and, indeed, for the future of drug treatment and prevention in general. The concluding section discusses the implications of the North Carolina case for contracting management and practice.

CHALLENGES TO CONTRACTING FOR SUBSTANCE ABUSE SERVICES

Policymakers, advocates, area authorities, and private service providers are confronted with several key issues: funding (and, relatedly, a collapsing service infrastructure), the market for contracts, accountability, insufficient incentives for innovation, and a weak constituency base for contract programs.

Funding

The current fiscal problems of local area authorities and their contract agencies are directly related to shifts in public finance and the private health insurance market in the last 25 years. Federal funding for the substance abuse services block grant to the states rose only slightly in the 1980s and then increased at a hefty rate during the late 1980s and early 1990s due to the Bush Administration's War on Drugs (Office of National Drug Control Policy [ONDCP], 1995).

The recent increase in public funding tends to be channeled through research and demonstration monies for specialized categorical programs. For example, the Drug-Free Schools Program of the U.S. Department of Education and the Community Partnership Program of the federal Center for Substance Abuse Prevention (CSAP) provide funding for community drug and alcohol prevention programs. The Justice Department offers financial support for drug prevention and treatment programs, especially programs with linkages to the criminal justice system. Many of these programs have been operated by nonprofit contract agencies.

Funding is in decline for these programs, and CSAP is fighting for its life in Congress. (The Drug-Free Schools program may be eliminated entirely.) The future of the substance abuse block grant—a major source of support for local public and private contract agencies—is unclear, but it is almost certainly slated for reductions.

Drug and alcohol services will also be affected by proposals to restructure the Medicaid program, which are already underway in some states. At the federal level, proposals to alter the program include transforming Medicaid into a block grant program administered by the states. Many states are placing their Medicaid program in managed care systems for at least part of Medicaid eligible services. Because many drug abuse clients are Medicaid-eligible, the shift to managed care or block grants will affect service delivery and most likely reduce available funding.

Also, private health insurance money for substance abuse is being drastically curtailed by managed care firms, health maintenance programs, and regular fee-for-service plans. In the 1980s, the expansion of private health insurance to include drug and alcohol abuse fueled a rapid increase in private for-profit and nonprofit inpatient programs. By the late 1980s, private insurance programs reversed course and severely limited their funding of substance abuse programs, especially inpatient programs. Program closures and bankruptcies are common in the wake of these new restrictions. Within a span of a few years, many programs in North Carolina were forced out of business.

Arguably, the rise in private for-profit inpatient programs led to an over-investment in expensive inpatient programs. Thus, part of the resulting shake-out may be desirable from a public policy perspective. However, the reductions in private insurance coverage combined with declining federal dollars poses tremendous funding problems for many private contract agencies. Despite the growth of contract substance abuse services in the 1970s and 1980s, many private agencies are woefully undercapitalized, leaving them financially vulnerable. For instance, a nonprofit residential program in Winston-Salem, ARCA, prospered in the 1980s, but is currently financially precarious. In recent years, the agency has received financial help from the local area authority to stay open. Agencies in Charlotte and Greensboro have experienced similar problems.

When federal cutbacks initially hit nonprofit contract agencies in the early to mid-1980s, many agencies tried to use private insurance money to cross-subsidize money-losing programs. (See James [1982] for further discussion of the incentive to cross-subsidize by nonprofit organizations.) For a time, some agencies were successful, but the drop in insurance money in recent years has severely squeezed many substance abuse programs, forcing cutbacks in service and program closures.

Funding problems for contract agencies are further exacerbated by changes in state and local public finance. Federal program devolution and opposition to tax increases at the state level limit the capacity of state and local government to substitute for cutbacks in federal funding or private insurance. In North Carolina, counties are retrenching at a rapid rate in their funding commitment to substance abuse, even in counties with a long tradition of supporting health and social services.

The cumulative effect of these shifts in public and private financing is to seriously weaken the infrastructure of contract agencies providing substance abuse services. Many agencies are tottering on the brink of failure. Many jurisdictions around the state have a very limited number of private agencies available to provide services. The market for for-profit service organizations—which concentrated on residential programs—has collapsed, with few for-profit residential programs still in existence. Many of the high-end nonprofit residential programs have also closed or retrenched severely.

The result is significantly diminished options for residential substance abuse programs. Remaining are a few for-profit programs, some long-standing nonprofit programs, usually with ties to public authorities, and public residential services usually in the three large state institutions. Individuals without adequate public or private insurance have few service options, as local area authorities have very little, if any, discretionary money for these patients.

Public authorities responsible for finding placement for these individuals can sometimes bargain with for-profit and nonprofit programs to gain admittance of a person without insurance. For example, some residential facilities will admit a nonpaying patient on referral from public authorities, but only on the condition that the public authorities agree to refer future paying clients with insurance to the facility. This option is only useful for a very limited number of cases. The result is that public authorities responsible for clients without adequate insurance are left with few available options: nonprofit programs based in part in religious communities, which usually require work as part of the treatment program, thus reducing the cost of placement; self-help residential therapeutic community programs; and public institutional programs. None of these options involve contracting per se, because little public money from the local public authorities is involved. The self-help residential therapeutic communities in North Carolina, such as Delancey Street, a nationally renowned therapeutic community based in San Francisco with a program in Greensboro, generally avoid taking public funds, especially on a contract basis. In contrast to other states, such as New York, North Carolina does not provide direct public funding of therapeutic communities through contracts.

In sum, insufficient funding for substance abuse in general produces a weak private provider infrastructure which then sharply reduces the service options for individuals with substance abuse problems. In a sense, the service system is returning to a status comparable to the big buildup in federal funds in the 1970s: individuals in need of inpatient services without adequate funds are forced to rely upon the public institutions (with their long waiting lists) or on a few private programs. Contracting can be a strategy to increase access, but it requires adequate public funding, as demonstrated by the North Carolina experience.

Lack of Competition

At present, private agencies providing contracted substance abuse services generally face little formal competition for their contracts, except in very specialized service niches. Few contracts are competitively bid and once created, a contract tends to be renewed routinely. This lack of competition reflects several factors: funding deficiencies, an inadequate supplier network, and the difficulties of evaluating social and health services. Formal competition entails the use of competitive bidding or requests for proposals, either on a planned cycle or as required.

Formal competition requires the purchaser (e.g., the public agency) to define in detail what it is seeking to buy so that it can be priced by the provider and then monitored. In human services and community-based services, this specification is very difficult and controversial. Moreover, formal competition requires an ample supply of providers. Yet, in North Carolina, public authorities often have little choice in the selection of providers due to supply problems. Scarce funding discourages providers from seeking funds and contributes to provider instability and inadequate supply.

Another factor exacerbating the supply problem is the fragmented, decentralized governance structure of social and health services. Large private substance abuse providers such as Step One in Winston-Salem, Southlight in Raleigh, or Substance Abuse Services of Guilford County in Greensboro do not compete statewide or even in their region for contract services. Part of the explanation lies with the perception by area authorities that the transaction costs of contracting with an out-of-area provider are much higher than using a locally based provider. The area authorities typically have long-standing relationships with these large providers, building a bond of trust and dependence that helps facilitate cooperation. Over time, these large providers become extensions of the local area authority, in whose view out-of-area providers tend to be seen as potentially more costly in terms of monitoring and evaluation. As a result, outside contractors are only used for special services, which cannot be provided locally, such as methadone and certain residential programs.

The decentralized service structure is evident in the absence of a statewide policy to impose methods of service procurement. There is no requirement to subject all services to formal competitive bidding. Consequently, formal competitive bidding is only used sporadically, with little sustained commitment. Although formal competition is rare, informal competition between government agencies and between private service providers for contracts is quite prevalent. Informal competition occurs between organizations with similar goals for resources or contract work, staff, and capital investment. For example, informal competition between area authorities exists in the search for good providers. Within the area authority, mental health departments and substance abuse departments may informally compete for patients and lead agency roles.

Informal competition between providers also occurs, but it is unevenly distributed across the state. It was found to be most common in communities with an excess of supply over demand. In these areas, a strong forward-looking and growing private agency can push an aggressive strategy to garner more contract dollars, forcing smaller, less assertive organizations to adapt. Smaller, less dynamic agencies tended not to compete with each other.

Informal competition between residential providers—both for-profit and nonprofit—is quite common. Providers were conscious of the pricing strategy and admission and programmatic policies of other providers, adjusting their policies if it appeared feasible. The high cost structure of some for-profit programs prevents them from lowering prices to a level where they can compete in the new, more austere funding environment. The consequence has been that many for-profit programs have closed.

The market for providers—and levels of competition—can be artificially stimulated. However, this action requires area authorities or the state and federal government to invest resources in the development of a service infrastructure to allow greater diversity of programming and more choices for local government. In North Carolina, this commitment of resources, which requires a sustained commitment on the part of state government, has been lacking.

Fostering Innovation

Prevailing political wisdom suggests that innovation in services is most likely to flourish in decentralized systems with volunteer governance—exactly the structure of North Carolina's substance abuse services. However, innovation in publicly financed substance abuse services in North Carolina tends to be externally driven—primarily through federal research and demonstration grants and, to a lesser extent, private foundation grants. Most of the current community drug programs, especially those run by the nonprofit agencies, owe their existence to the federal grants of the early to mid-1970s. More recently, innovative programs such as services for pregnant women at risk for substance abuse, community drug prevention, and services for drug abusers at risk for HIV infection have been financed almost entirely by federal grants. Most of these innovative, grant-funded programs are developed as purchase-of-service contracts with private service agencies.

The financial pressures on state and local governments create problems in sustaining innovation. In the 1970s, many contract agencies with research and demonstration grants to develop new pilot programs transferred to state and local funding on the expiration of their federal or foundation grants. State and local governments are no longer in a position to substitute for federal funds once they are withdrawn, however. As a result, many programs closed at the end of the grant.

Although most innovation is externally driven through outside grants, some exceptions exist. During the 1970s and 1980s, many residential programs grew and prospered with a 28-day program model. Individuals seeking treatment would enter a program and leave after 28 days, although occasionally longer stays were possible. But the cutbacks in public and private insurance have forced these programs to develop new shorter stay program models. Whether or not these new models are effective remains to be determined.

Accountability

Maintaining accountability for the expenditure of public funds by non-profit agencies is a major source of concern (Kettl, 1993; Smith & Lipsky, 1993). Government administrators will always face the challenge of overseeing private contractors who control, at least in part, key information of interest to administrators (Donahue, 1989).

The example of substance abuse services in North Carolina raises several specific issues regarding accountability that are especially timely given the push for program devolution and reduced government funding. First, overall statewide information on the provision of publicly supported substance abuse services is inadequate. The state does not have the resources or personpower to devote to collecting data, and the area authorities currently lack the incentive to cooperate with themselves or the state in developing a comprehensive data system. Some statewide data are collected by a private nonprofit watchdog group, the Alcohol and Drug Council of North Carolina. But specific data on important issues such as agency expenditures, number of clients seen by public and private contract agencies, and mix of revenue sources remain unavailable.

Second, the local area board system needs reform if it is to be an effective monitoring body. Area boards govern a combined mental health, developmental disabilities and substance abuse agency. Thus, the number of advocates or representatives knowledgeable about substance abuse on the area board at any one time is limited to usually less than five. Then, too, overlap may exist between the mental health and substance abuse representatives. Moreover, many area board members, even members with a specific interest in substance abuse, are not familiar with the research on substance abuse and the various program models in substance abuse treatment and prevention. Area board members face a further complication in that they are volunteers, often with other volunteer responsibilities, and may not have the time to oversee the operation of the local area authority.

Training programs for area board members are underway across the state with the goal of helping board members exercise their responsibilities. Although this training is important, area board members will still face significant obstacles to effective oversight and evaluation of area board programs, especially contract agencies.

Third, substance abuse treatment and prevention is notoriously difficult to evaluate. Area authority staff tend to evaluate contract agencies through process measures, such as the number of clients and program expenditures according to contract stipulations. Outcome evaluation procedures are in early stages due to the limited supply of contract agencies, so switching agencies is unrealistic; resources to conduct outcome evaluations are unavailable; and controversy exists on the proper measures to use for outcome evaluation purposes. In addition, many area authority staff are personal friends of the staff and volunteers of a contract agency, thus complicating rigorous implementation of outcome evaluations with the uncertainty of the results and the potential threat to a contract agency.

The obstacles to outcome evaluation leave public and contract agencies vulnerable in this era of managed care. An inability to demonstrate convincing results may provide an opening to managed care firms eager to obtain contracts to operate substance abuse and mental health programs for government, or offer ammunition to state and county legislators interested in shrinking government and shifting services to self-help groups and organizations which do not depend upon public funds. Although state administrators, in cooperation with private providers and local area personnel, are now developing outcome measures to guide the provision of public and private substance abuse services, these measures are unlikely to be extensively adopted unless there is a resurgence of political interest and popular support for new expenditures on substance abuse services.

The Politics of Contracting for Substance Abuse Services

The decentralized contracting system directly affects the politics of contracting. As noted, area authorities use contracting relatively selectively, except in a few larger urban areas, such as Charlotte. Until recently, the politics of contracting for substance abuse services were also decentralized. Because contracting decisions were made locally, private agencies and their supporters focused their attention on the area authority staff and the area boards. Also, in some jurisdictions, contracting was so limited that the politics around contractor selection and, more broadly, the extent of contracting was muted.

The downturn in private insurance reimbursement for private inpatient substance abuse programs and the reluctance of area authorities to expand their contracting has spurred a loose group of private, primarily for-profit facilities to push for direct contracting between the state and private residential facilities. These private programs argue that they have unused capacity that could be filled with publicly supported clients. These larger agencies also find it difficult to work with many different local boards, each with their own requirements and expectations. Charter Northridge Hospital (recently merged with Holy Hill Hospital), is a good example of a for-profit program with this perspective. To date, no substantive changes in contracting policy have occurred, although political pressure for a state contracting role continues to build. Devolution is strongly entrenched.

In states with extensive contracting for substance abuse, such as Florida and New York, private agencies are mobilized politically to advocate for service funding. In North Carolina, this mobilization has not been as cohesive or sustained. The North Carolina Substance Abuse Federation is a statewide association founded with encouragement of state officials. The Federation's purpose is to advocate for resources for substance abuse treatment and prevention. Membership of the federation is comprised of representatives of public area authorities and private nonprofit and for-profit agencies. Leaders of the federation have also participated in Coalition 2000, a multiagency, statewide lobbying effort for mental health, developmental disabilities, and substance abuse services. Although the impact of the coalition's political efforts is difficult to evaluate, state funding for these three service categories has risen during the past 5 years, although substance abuse funding has lagged behind the other two service categories.

Overall, the federation has yet to emerge as a major political force, reflecting the decentralization of substance abuse services and the relatively limited contracting for services. The federation is also affected by the unique character of the substance abuse field. Unlike some services, such as child welfare, substance abuse services have many different program models—from highly professionalized and expensive inpatient hospital programs to voluntary self-help. The federation's work is itself handicapped by the fragmentation of the substance abuse services system. Consequently, the federation has not chosen to develop more uniform practice guidelines or widespread dissemination of best practice program models.

IMPLICATIONS FOR CONTRACTING MANAGEMENT AND PRACTICE

Balancing State and Local Responsibility

The North Carolina experience with contracting for substance abuse services suggests that the proper management and development of contracted services requires an investment in effective state and local administrative capacity. At present, the state substance abuse agency is relatively small. More resources and authority would allow the state agency to collect important data and monitor the performance of local area authorities and their contract agencies. The state agency could then use this data to push for greater emphasis on outcome evaluation and to foster good practice and new program innovations. The development of state capacity for policy development, data collection, and monitoring capacity would require a new investment, and should be undertaken in consultation with the local area authorities, private agencies and the state legislature.

The overall delivery of public and private services would also be improved by two new initiatives. First, direct state contracting with private agencies can play a useful role for specific niche services. Currently, many area authorities do not offer certain services because of insufficient demand. This is particularly the case in rural regions of the state. The state could overcome this problem by directly contracting with private agencies for services available to a specified population of individuals in need of service. A state contracting capability would also allow the state to fund experimental and innovative programs that are too controversial or too narrow in focus for area authorities to undertake.

Second, greater use of regional contracting would be valuable. At present, limited regional contracting exists, primarily for methadone services and specialized children's programs. Trends in public finance, including federal cutbacks, are squeezing local governments and forcing them to retrench in their commitment to social and health services. Many area authorities seek the fiscal capacity to fund needed services; pooling of resources through regional contracting is a viable strategy to partially overcome this local fiscal problem. Regional contracting would have to be undertaken with care in order to avoid a shift in the market of services toward a few larger providers.

Voluntarism and Community Oversight

Area authorities are governed by citizen volunteers. This phenonmenon is in line with the reigning vision of governance problems and consistent with the push for program devolution across the country and the prevailing emphasis on community responsibility for social problems. The area board system is predicated on the assumption that local community members can effectively oversee publicly supported social and health services. These volunteers are supposed to be "above politics," assessing community needs and developing appropriate programs. In practice, however, area boards—whose members are appointed by the elected county commissioners—are often enmeshed in local politics and have strong ties to various local politicians. Due to political considerations and time constraints, area boards tend to favor policies that do not radically disturb the existing service system. Consequently, they do not generally push for contracting policies even when it is advisable.

The absence of strong advocates for substance abuse programs on area boards, combined with the restricted use of contracting in most jurisdictions, means that the area board does not serve as a vehicle for cultivating a local constituency for substance abuse treatment and prevention programs. Two possible strategies to build this constituency are: (a) to create specific slots for advocates on the area boards, and (b) to develop new linkages between the community and the area boards. The first option has been pushed by some advocacy groups such as the Alcohol and Drug Council of North Carolina. However, the proposal is opposed by the area authorities and their statewide advocacy organization out of fear that creating a quota for advocates on the area board might compromise their own legitimacy, power, and independence.

The second option would require more fundamental change in the local area board and authority structure. At present, the area board is comprised of individuals from around the community. However, the area board does not play a proactive role in creating broad-based community involvement in the area board affairs. One model for the area boards to contemplate is to borrow from current efforts to "reinvent government" in municipalities across the country (Osborne & Gaebler, 1993). Many of these communities, such as Portland, Oregon, have established citizen oversight bodies and structured methods of achieving citizen input which go well beyond conventional elected or appointed municipal entities. These entities vary in their membership, but they can be comprised of representatives of private contract agencies, businesses, the United Way, and local foundations.

This restructuring would seem to depend on a revival of popular concern about substance abuse services and political leadership, but the potential advantages for the effective delivery of public and private services could be substantial. The creation of new linkages and network ties in the community could help build support for more local funding of services, provide more effective oversight for local services, and stimulate cooperation among diverse segments of the substance abuse community.

Developing a Provider Infrastructure

An effective contracting system depends upon an adequate supply of contractors. But a sufficient supply of contractors for publicly supported social and health services does not just happen. It requires an ongoing commitment by government. Private substance abuse agencies in North Carolina, with a few exceptions, tend to be relatively small, undercapitalized, and financially fragile. Many programs have closed or merged in recent years. (Overcapacity of inpatient substance abuse services was a genuine problem in the mid-1980s, so some contraction was both necessary and understandable.) Without available contractors, area authorities are in a weak position to develop good practices, including comprehensive outcome measures.

The state could help nurture local providers through funding and technical assistance. It could also help in connecting providers across the state with each other as a way of helping providers learn from each other. It could contract with a private organization to provide the needed functions. These connections between providers will be especially important in the coming years with the continued devolution of federal programs.

CONCLUSION

Public management is in the midst of dramatic restructuring reflected by the growth of contracting for public services and program devolution. However, the experience of contracting for substance abuse services in North Carolina indicates that contracting as a policy strategy is unsustainable without affirmative, effective government. This is especially important given the current push for outcome evaluation.

More broadly, this case illustrates the interconnections between government and the private sector. Much of contemporary policy discourse makes sharp and misleading distinctions between the public and private sectors. Assumptions suggest that the private sector can develop in a policy vacuum, when in fact, government policy shapes the private sector through funding, its regulatory power, its oversight, and the participation of government officials in the management of private agencies. The conceptual separation of the sectors encourages an underinvestment in government management capacity and a lack of attention to ways in which government can help strengthen private contract agencies. In the coming years, government agencies will need to work closely with nonprofit and for-profit service agencies in order to deliver effective, quality substance abuse services to citizens in need.

REFERENCES

Donahue, J. D. (1989). *The privatization decision.* New York: Basic.

James, E. (1982). How nonprofits grow: A model. *Journal of Public Policy Analysis and Management, 2,* 350–365.

Kettl, D. F. (1993). *Sharing power: Public governance and private markets.* Washington, DC: Brookings.

Office of National Drug Control Policy (ONDCP). (1995). *National drug control strategy: Budget summary.* Washington, DC: Author.

Osborne, D., & Gaebler, T. (1993). *Reinventing government.* New York: Plume.

Smith, S. R., & Lipsky, M. (1993). *Nonprofits for hire: The welfare state in the age of contracting.* Cambridge, MA: Harvard University Press.

Smith, S. R., & Smyth, J. (1996). Contracting for services in a decentralized system. *Journal of Public Administration Research and Theory, 6,* 277–296.

5

Church, State, and Social Welfare: Purchase of Service and the Sectarian Agency*

Eric M. Levine

INTRODUCTION

Social service agencies under religious or sectarian auspices have a well-established and distinguished role in the history of American social welfare. They have made important contributions toward improving the quality of life for their clientele, thereby enhancing societal well-being overall. Often created to serve specific populations and to offer particular kinds of services, in recent decades these sectarian providers have been recipients of government funds to support their ongoing programs or to expand into new areas of service delivery. These purchase-of-service arrangements with all levels of government introduce a number of ethical and practical issues that can potentially have a significant impact on sectarian agency policy and functioning, as well as on the professional

* A number of scholar-practitioners were very helpful at various stages in the preparation of this chapter. I would like to express thanks to Dr. Jeffrey Solomon, Chief Operating Officer for Program Services at UJA–Federation of New York, who provided valuable insights and extensive background on the experience of the UJA–Federation network and purchase of service contracts. Dr. Margaret Gibelman provided friendly advice and sound editorial direction and guidance for this writer.

practice of individuals employed by such agencies.

This chapter examines the range of issues that affect the sectarian agency involved in purchase-of-service (POS) contracts with government. It will highlight the main issues confronting all sectarian agencies, and in addition, will examine those issues that specifically affect the Jewish purpose agency. Case examples will also be drawn from the experience of one agency to further explore the meaning of purchase-of-service for the sectarian domain.

The receipt of government funds by religious institutions and service agencies is very much a current and serious issue. It takes on particular importance in the contemporary American context, where the role of religion and its relation to societal values has been the subject of much public debate. Some commentators have observed that society today has less of a shared, religiously grounded moral basis and a weaker religious culture. The unity of religious and cultural values has dissolved. Consequently, American society lacks a commonly accepted faith and morality.

Religious groups now find themselves contending with one another to become the shaping cultural influences, within a context of a broader pluralism of religious and secular ideologies. This environment has produced an ever-increasing incidence of religious themes being debated in the public arena, leading to greater open conflict over the definitions and boundaries of societal morality, lifestyle and culture, and the role of religion in relation to public policy (Roof & McKinney, 1987).

As just one example, in a recent case, a major educational institution under religious Jewish auspices has become embroiled in a conflict over the funding of gay student clubs on campus. The issue has raised a host of legal, religious, moral, and financial issues potentially affecting not only the university's future, but perhaps even challenging the core purpose for its existence (Rosenblatt, 1995). Officially, the school considers itself to be nonsectarian, and is therefore eligible to receive government funds and tax exemptions. Furthermore, the university does not want to be seen as intolerant, discriminatory, or denying free speech to segments of the student population. But, to sanction some such groups is perceived by various camps within the university as a blatant affront to traditional interpretation of Jewish religious law (Jolkovsky, 1995).

This case, however dramatic, represents only the surface of a very complex issue. It is symbolic of the tensions and value conflicts confronting most sectarian agencies on a recurring basis.

THE EMERGENCE OF SECTARIAN SOCIAL WELFARE AND GOVERNMENT CONTRACTING

A Brief History of Sectarian Social Welfare

The religious basis for social action and social work are well-documented, as are the historical and religious roots of sectarian service agencies in 20th-century America (Ortiz, 1995; Reid & Stimpson, 1987). The values of charity are cornerstones of the Jewish and Christian faiths and have provided the basis for American social work.

> Whether practice is based on religious conviction or on scientific humanism, social work's fundamental commitment to help those in need is rooted in Judeo-Christian precepts. More specifically, most modern forms of social work have essentially religious origins; in a church program, a religiously inspired social movement, or the individual acts of the Christian and Jewish clergy and laity following the dictates of their consciences. (Reid & Stimpson, 1987, p. 546)

Sectarian social welfare efforts have been part of the fabric of American society since the nation's founding, and have remained central to the country's social welfare enterprise. The development of modern social welfare has generally followed two patterns: the maintenance or even growth of sectarian service organizations; and the secularization of organizations and programs originated under religious auspices or inspired by religious motives (Reid & Stimpson, 1987).

Nonprofit organizations have been in existence and have been the recipients of government funds since colonial times. During the antebellum period, the young nation witnessed an explosion in the number of nonprofit groups established to serve the needs of the poor. Many of these new organizations were under the auspices of evangelical Protestant and Catholic groups (Smith & Lipsky, 1993). The origins of contemporary sectarian social welfare systems can be traced back to efforts from the latter part of the 19th century taken under Protestant sponsorship. As Protestantism was the dominant religious form in America at the time, these endeavors accounted for nearly all of the organized social welfare activity.

Catholic social welfare systems grew in response to the increasing tide of Catholic immigration that began in the mid-19th century. Due to the nature of the Catholic religious tradition, the social welfare system that evolved operated very clearly under church auspices, in contrast to the rather decentralized and autonomous, noncohesive nature of Protestant efforts.

The first cases of formal purchase-of-service arrangements appeared toward the end of the 19th century. In general, this government funding was limited, except in a few states and cities. Most of these funds were allocated to the sectarian agencies established by Catholic and Protestant immigrant groups to serve their own clientele, their coreligionists. The Catholic system particularly emphasized the development of residential care facilities for dependent children, and public dollars were used to reimburse these institutions for child care (Smith & Lipsky, 1993).

Historically, resistance to government funding of the voluntary sector for the delivery of social services has been strong, both within government circles and the nonprofit sphere. This opposition began to weaken during the Depression, however. After World War II, federal outlays for social welfare increased slowly, with most of the public support for such programs coming from state and local governments. This pattern continued through the 1950s into the mid–1960s. But, as public involvement in the funding of relief programs and social security increased, starting in the 1930s, government turned to the sectarian sector to provide an array of social welfare services. Such funding to sectarian organizations dramatically increased in the 1960s, as it did for all voluntary agencies (Blum & Naparstek, 1987; Gibelman, 1995; Ortiz, 1995; Smith & Lipsky, 1993; Wernet, 1994). It was in the 1960s and 1970s that the attitude of government substantially changed to permit contracting with nonprofit organizations as an option (Terrell, 1987). Thus, the issues related to purchase-of-service and the sectarian agency emerged with full force in the post–1960s period.

Sectarian organizations have been eligible for, and have been the recipients of funds made available through various pieces of legislation, such as Model Cities funding in the 1960s (Demonstration Cities and Metropolitan Development Act of 1966, P. L. 89-754, 80 Stat. 1255); the Social Security Act (see the Public Welfare Amendments of 1962, P. L. 87-543, 76 Stat. 172, the 1967 Social Security Act Amendments, P. L. 90-248, 81 Stat. 821, and the Social Security Act Amendments of 1974, P. L. 93-647, 88 Stat. 2337); the Comprehensive Employment and Training Act (CETA) of 1973 (P. L. 03-203, 87 Stat. 839); the Older Americans Act of 1965 (P. L. 89-73, 79 Stat. 218), for which it has been estimated that over 50% of all aging funds were contracted out; the 1963 Community Mental Health Centers Act (P. L. 88-164, 77 Stat. 290); and the Economic Opportunity Act of 1964 (P. L. 88-452, 78 Stat. 508). These funding streams cover the full range of human service needs: mental health, emergency shelters for homeless people, group homes, day care, child protective services, foster care, residential care, mental retardation services, services to pregnant and parenting teenagers, substance abuse, pupil personnel services, psychiatric hospital care, senior citizens centers and services for the elderly, anti-poverty programs, probation and juvenile services, and more (Gibelman, 1995; Hartogs & Weber, 1978; "Shadowed by budget cuts," 1995; Smith & Lipsky, 1993; Terrell, 1987).

The forms of purchased service can be separated into two categories: those payments that are patient- or client-based; that is, where payments are tied to services received by eligible individuals (i.e., third-party reimbursements, such as Medicaid, State Office of Mental Health funds, vouchers for day care, etc.); and program-based funds, where government funds are granted to an agency to provide the best, lowest-cost service. Sectarian agencies have participated extensively in both types of purchase-of-service arrangements. Funds in the form of direct dollars, low interest loans, or subsidy have also been made available for building programs to expand sectarian hospitals, housing for the elderly, homes for the elderly, and other institutional developments (Bernstein, 1991; Blum & Naparstek, 1987).

The Organizational Structure of Sectarian Social Welfare Systems

The organizational structures of sectarian social welfare systems differ from religion to religion and from denomination to denomination. Protestant service agencies today exhibit the greatest variation in their relation to religious bodies, running from the extreme of complete independence from a denomination (i.e., an independent Protestant agency with no formal ties to a denomination or church, such as Methodist, Episcopalian, or Lutheran) to formal denominational recognition of an agency through control of the budget and board membership. According to Reid & Stimpson (1987, p. 548): "Most Protestant denominations provide national structures for the organization of social work carried out under their auspices." Catholic social services are more closely aligned to the church hierarchy, especially at the local diocesan level. The National Conference of Catholic Charities (established in 1910) provides a structure for 545 diocesan agencies and 200 member institutions in the United States.

The Jewish social welfare network emerged as a result of the rising levels of immigration to the United States.

The pattern of Jewish welfare organizations differed distinctively, however, from that of other sectarian groups. For the most part Jewish social services developed apart from the synagogue. . . . Although the beginnings of American Jewish philanthropy took place in the synagogue, the sudden and massive influx of Jewish immigrants created needs for which the synagogue alone could not provide. (Reid & Stimpson, 1987, p. 548)

Jewish agencies were not necessarily secular in origin, and the institutions that emerged were not under religious sponsorship, per se. Still, these institutions were closely aligned with the religious sphere and the community at large. Jewish agencies today exhibit the greatest degree of autonomy from religious authority. Jewish social service agencies are typically locally organized and community-based and are normally members of a local Jewish federation, of which there are almost 200 nationally. These local federations are affiliated with the national Council of Jewish Federations (CJF), which provides consulting, planning, and information services (Reid & Stimpson, 1987). The New York UJA (United Jewish Appeal)-Federation, treated as a case study below, is the New York affiliate of this national system.

PRACTICE ISSUES AND MORAL DILEMMAS[1]

The Extent of Purchase of Service in the Sectarian Sector

It is clear that as purchase of service contracting became a common practice, a relationship of mutual dependence between the government and

---

[1] The reader will note that many of the articles cited in the literature dealing with the issue of purchase of service and the Jewish community date primarily from the 1960s and 1970s. This author did not conduct an exhaustive content analysis of the material on the subject. However, it appears that from a cursory review of the principal sources in the field of Jewish social welfare—i.e., the annual *American Jewish Year Book* and the *Journal of Jewish Communal Service*—the number of articles in this area of inquiry dwindled by the late 1970s and for the most part had disappeared by the 1980s. Although concern regarding government funding certainly continued and received periodic treatment, writing on the tensions of accepting public contracts and grants was virtually absent. Other issues emerged in the forefront of communal concern. One could only surmise that the various issues discussed in this chapter were either resolved in practice, left to benign neglect, or just tacitly ignored.

the nonprofit agency evolved. In the eyes of some scholars, the "rise of contract income in the support of nonprofit organizations has transformed nonprofit organizations, literally, into agents of the state" (Smith & Lipsky, 1993, p. 72). Gibelman (1995, p. 1998) reported that "POS presently is the dominant means of delivering social services." Indeed, Smith and Lipsky (1993) indicate that, by the early 1990s, contracting for social services with nonprofit organizations had become a $15 billion-a-year business.

In terms of all revenue streams flowing into nonprofit organizations, government funding accounted for 31% of income, private donations 18%, and fees/charges for services 51% (Solomon, 1995). Similar trends also characterize the experiences of sectarian agencies. Ortiz (1995) maintains that government and sectarian agencies are increasingly dependent on each other to provide both services and funding for those services, claiming that sectarian agencies rely heavily on government funding and government, in turn, relies heavily on the private sector, including sectarian agencies, to fulfill its service mandate.

In the case of the Jewish community, one observer, writing in 1977, implied the extent to which purchase of service dominated the agency funding picture. Even at that relatively early date, it was noted that a long-term objective was to work off the excessive reliance of noninstitutional Jewish agencies on government funds, as well as to resist the temptation to seek a disproportionate amount of such funding (Horowitz, 1977). Other writers noted that the expansion of agencies and programs in the Jewish community resulted largely from increases in government funding at all levels (Blum & Naparstek, 1987). Indeed, government payments to Jewish-sponsored agencies increased 20-fold from 1962 to 1973, from $27 million to $561 million (Gilbert, 1983; Ortiz, 1995). In one decade, "government payments as a proportion of the total income received by Jewish-sponsored agencies rose from 11 to 51%" (Gilbert, 1983, p. 7). For 1977, it was reported that Jewish-sponsored agencies affiliated with the federation system received more than $125 million from government sources, excluding "huge" government funds for hospitals (Zibbell, 1978).

Comparable patterns are found among other American religious groups. As early as the 1930s, the National Catholic Welfare Conference formally endorsed massive federal aid to alleviate the suffering brought about by the Depression. By the end of the decade, "most diocesan charitable bureaus were actively pursuing opportunities to collaborate with all levels of government in social welfare programs" (Oates, 1995, p. 113). By the 1960s a higher percentage of diocesan agency budgets came from government funding than was the case for Jewish or Protestant agencies, and by the 1980s, government funding constituted the major proportion of charity agency budgets in large and small dioceses across America.

In the experience of Boston, one of the large archdioceses, public funds represented some 70% of Catholic charity agency budgets throughout the decade of the 1970s. The National Conference of Catholic Charities reported an overall income growth from 1981 to 1982 of $75 million to $565 million, with government funding constituting half of the income (Reid & Stimpson, 1987). Similarly, Catholic Charities U.S.A. estimated that government funding accounted for 44% of affiliate agency revenues for fiscal year 1988 (Ortiz, 1995; Smith & Lipsky, 1993). A 1991 national study of diocesan charities revealed that government funding accounted for 63% of their collective income of more than $1.8 billion (Oates, 1995). Finally, a 1982 analysis of the funding sources of Episcopal, Lutheran Church-Missouri Synod, and Salvation Army agencies found the same pattern of government providing approximately half of their funding (Reid & Stimpson, 1987).

In a recent study of 45 Jewish federations conducted by the Council of Jewish Federations (CJF), it was estimated that Jewish communal agencies receive more than $3.67 billion from federal, state, and local government sources (Council of Jewish Federations, 1995). That figure represents some 41% of their total budgets, substantially higher than the average of 35% for all nonprofits. More than two-thirds of the $3.67 billion is provided to Jewish-supported hospitals in the form of Medicaid and Medicare payments. Still, the 45 federations and their beneficiary agencies receive $1.08 billion a year for services and programs outside of hospitals, and about half of the funds support Jewish nursing homes, with the rest for agencies serving individuals and families. Federation-supported Jewish vocational service agencies receive $135 million in government funding, representing 77% of their budgets, and Jewish family service agencies receive 61% of their budgets from government sources, amounting to $134 million a year.

UJA–Federation of New York is the largest recipient of government funds in the Jewish community. According to the study, the New York federation and its 130-beneficiary-agency network receive $2.45 billion a year, approximately 62% of the network budget. To illustrate the kind of funding obtained, in 1993–1994 five UJA–Federation beneficiary network agencies received $30.3 million in federal grants to build 441 subsidized housing units in New York City (UJA–Federation, 1994a). The New York-based

Jewish Board of Family and Children's Services, also a New York UJA–Federation network agency and reputed to be the largest nonprofit mental health and social service organization in the nation, receives some 82% of its annual $80 million budget from government funds.

In the wake of a mid–1990s national fiscal conservatism driven by Congress (as exemplified in the 1994 Republican "Contract with America"), nonprofit organizations have begun to estimate the potential loss of government revenue. Internal communications at New York UJA–Federation placed the extent of anticipated budget cuts in stark relief. UJA–Federation funds 130 beneficiary agencies in the eight-county area of Greater New York (Manhattan, Brooklyn, Staten Island, the Bronx, and Queens, as well as the three suburban counties of Westchester, Suffolk, and Nassau). After reviewing the projected 1995–1996 budgets, staff estimated that the network would lose $40 million as a result of state and city cuts. Only $2.5 million was expected to come as a result of the projected cuts in the New York City budget, with the rest from the State budget (UJA–Federation, 1995a, 1995b).

The Mayor's office and the City Council were given credit for protecting most of the programs important to the network agencies. Ballpark estimates projected losses at $14 million for child welfare services (i.e., foster care, homemaking), $12.5 for nursing homes, $5 million for community-based health services, $6 million for home care for seniors, $1 million in state member items affecting a variety of programs (i.e., senior transportation, youth recreation), and $.5 million affecting youth services. It was further anticipated that the number would jump substantially if the proposed federal cuts were approved (personal communication, July 19, 1995).

The devastating effect of funding cuts is, of course, not limited to New York. The Jewish Federation in Chicago estimated that, not including Medicaid and Medicare payments to its hospital, it would suffer a $7.3 million deficit if proposed congressional spending cuts were approved (Dorf, 1995).

The Risks of Dependence on Government Funding

The fact has been bemoaned that as more and more public dollars became available, those entities providing the funding determined the direction of agency and program expansion (Miller, 1992). Following the dollar potentially causes the bending of policy and philosophy in order to attract more income or to meet the criteria of funding sources (Hart, 1988; Horowitz, 1977; Selig, 1973). Such a practice potentially places agency autonomy at risk. From the perspective of strategic planning, chasing after available dollars for its own sake undermines any legitimate attempt at conducting rational planning for the agency and shaping a long-term approach that leads the agency into its future. Zibbell (1978) makes the case with a particularly poignant comment. His focus was on Jewish purpose agencies but aptly informs the sectarian agency of whatever stripe, exhorting that agencies need "to make sure that the sectarian goals of our communal programs are not sacrificed on the altar of government funding" (p. 143).

Similarly, an overreliance on public funding also undercuts an agency's ability to conduct independent fund-raising. Alternative sources of funds are often not explored and developed, whether they derive from foundations, private citizens, or corporations. In addition, agencies tend to turn to the same potential private sector sources of funds (Reid & Stimpson, 1987).

Fortunately, the more resilient agencies are becoming more attuned to government priorities, changing legislation, public values, and shifting funding emphases. As cuts in government funding have affected older programs, these agencies have been innovative in developing new programs and services (Reid & Stimpson, 1987).

Precisely because nonprofits, including sectarian service agencies, have become so dependent on government money, a real challenge emerges when these funds dwindle or disappear totally. In most cases, the level of funding was never sufficient in the first place to cover all needs. As government money declines, major cuts create enormous problems in budgeting for the agency, provoking the question of who picks up the tab for continuing services that have come to be expected and relied on by people in need. To illustrate, the impact of budget cuts on Catholic social welfare systems during the Reagan era was serious:

> And since federal funds were accounting for such a high proportion of the income of Catholic Charities nationally, cuts in federal appropriations for social programs in the 1980s were immediately reflected, not only in their own agency budgets, but also in an increase in applications for help from people whom other private agencies could no longer assist. Since state appropriations to compensate for reductions in federal funding have not been forthcoming, dioceses are now asking grassroots parishioners to make up the shortfalls. (Oates, 1995, p. 170)

In sectarian communities with a limited resource pool for alternative funding, such as the relatively small American Jewish community, similar difficult choices are presented: close the programs; raise more money; or divert funds, which in the end may harm all other programs or services. Another danger is the possibility that agencies will be forced to provide services only to populations that can afford to pay or where government reimbursements are likely, thus creating or reinforcing a dual-tier service system between those who are able to pay and those who are not, with the latter the real and usual victims (Blum & Naparstek, 1987; Boeko, 1992; Selig 1973).

A related concern emerges if an agency must scale back due to funding shortfalls and thus enters into a situation where it must (or chooses to) deny services to nonpaying clients. Such a withdrawal of service raises important ethical questions about a sectarian agency's supposed religious value of helping people (Blum & Naparstek, 1987).

Sadly, the ability of nonprofit organizations to replace lost grant dollars is quite dubious. According to the Lilly Endowment's "American Congregational Giving Study," conducted in 1994 ("Catholics report they lack, 1995"), charitable giving among Roman Catholics nationally has lagged far behind that of other religious groups. For example, the average Catholic household contributed $386 to church organizations. Presbyterian households averaged $1,106 and homes affiliated with the Assemblies of God contributed $1,696. Although the report was not conducted in any way related to the Contract with America or to projected funding cuts, it places into stark relief the prospects for some sectarian groups to replace contract funds. The evidence demonstrates the fiscal vulnerability of the nonprofit sectarian sector and raises the question of whether such groups will be able to mobilize sufficient resources and systems to fund not only "core" activities, but programs formerly funded through purchase-of-service contracts.

Organizational Competition

Increased competition for funding commonly occurs within similar geographic or service areas. Interagency competition in the not-for-profit marketplace may be useful, stimulating organizations to improve their product and operate more efficiently. However, some competition in the family may not be healthy, as when two Jewish social service organizations in New York City were contending with each other for the same government funding.[2] These were agencies with previous close ties, planning to serve similar constituencies and communities. Both appealed to local elected officials as well as UJA–Federation for moral and political support, producing a situation of influence trading at its worst and leading to great tension between two heretofore sister organizations.

Personnel Practices

Another implication of receiving funds is the effect on the hiring practices of the agency. Sectarian organizations commonly require staff to accept their mission. Such support can take the form of a verbal affirmation, the signing of statements of faith, or an agreement to adhere to formalized codes to work within the framework of the identity of the church, to be committed to the mission of the agency, and to act according to the church's basic values and principles as they relate to the agency (Ortiz, 1995; Reid & Stimpson, 1987). Lutheran Social Services includes in its criteria for church affiliation of a social agency the integration of Christian theology in its programs and professional practice (Reid & Stimpson, 1987).

With the acceptance of public funds, equal opportunity hiring guidelines apply, including, at least at the time of this writing, such rules as affirmative action, selecting personnel who are broadly representative of the community, and administering personnel practices without discrimination, including religion (Reid & Stimpson, 1987). Such rules may be in conflict with sectarian philosophy. For example, "Catholic agencies oppose being compelled to pledge not to discriminate against homosexuals in hiring as a condition for receiving contract support" (Terrell, 1987, p. 441). However, there may be a thin line between showing preference for candidates for employment who demonstrate commitment to the sectarian agency's cause and mission, and religious or other forms of discrimination.

A related matter concerns the qualifications agencies seek in their candidates for employment. Should the sectarian agency hire someone with professional credentials (i.e., a social work degree) or religious credentials (i.e., clergy)? In the Jewish community, an ongoing debate has revolved

---

[2] This interagency conflict was reported in a series of confidential communications between the author and colleagues at UJA–Federation during July and August 1995. The agency names were disguised to protect their confidentiality.

around which degree should take precedence in hiring: the Master's of Social Work degree, or the Master's degree in Jewish Communal Service offered by various prestigious schools. The question goes to the heart of another issue: what field of practice takes precedence in Jewish agencies, social work or a related discipline, or Jewish communal service? Which code of ethics takes priority: that of the National Association of Social Workers, or the Jewish Communal Service Association?

If the agency carries a sectarian mission and its staff are expected to promulgate it and perform in certain ways that are compatible with that mission, equal employment can present potential barriers to hiring desired candidates. Levine (1985) has made the case that in the UJA–Federation network, the role of the fund-raising executive is manifold but its primary purposes are promoting Jewish identity and securing financial resources. As discussed below, a current and major concern in Jewish communal circles is the promotion of Jewish continuity and strengthening of positive Jewish identity in the community. Levine emphatically supports the notion that the sectarian agency should be an equal opportunity employer, and acknowledges that the caring and skilled non-Jewish professional can make real contributions to the agency. But, he writes:

> I would venture the opinion that it is dependent upon the exact role the employee plays and the nature and extent of contact with the client and community. In theory, it is not inconceivable for a non-Jew to be a Jewish communal worker, but I would maintain that practically it would be unfeasible. Despite any legal or moral reasons why we might not be comfortable with excluding non-Jews, it would be extremely difficult at best for such an employee to fulfil the mandate. A sincere, competent, dedicated non-Jewish professional can make real contributions to the short term goals of the Jewish organization, but I doubt whether the employee could play a meaningful and effective part in the broader mission of community building, consciousness-raising and providing informed Jewish leadership. (Levine, 1985, p. 48)

Board Composition

Similar to the discussion regarding hiring practices, the sectarian nature of an agency's lay structure can come into question. Government sources increasingly seek diversification of agency boards as a condition of funding (Solomon, 1995). Such a mandate raises implications for the ethnic, religious, or racial mix of board members. Questions of leadership succession become palpable. Can a Catholic become president of an agency that advances a Protestant or Jewish mission and function effectively in that role? Can or should a Jew preside over the local Catholic Charities? Given the high rate of ethnic and religious intermarriage in America today, the issue becomes even further accentuated. Can the non-Jewish spouse of a Jewish person take on leadership portfolios for a Jewish agency? Should the agency even consider such a person for these roles? What messages does an agency send to the community and its constituency in either scenario? Once again, the moral, practical, and even aesthetic conflicts create challenges for the sectarian entity contracting with government.

Funding, Philosophy, and Values: Conflicts and Challenges

The issue of how a sectarian agency's mission is altered when it accepts government funding has been the subject of debate. In general, church–state concerns come into play when sectarian groups enter into contracts with government agencies, either from the standpoint of whether government is funding religious activity, or if the funding is imposing a threat to the sectarian agency's mission (Ortiz, 1995). Inevitably, value conflicts occur, and the integrity of the mission can be placed in doubt. Most sectarian agencies now "deliver a multitude of direct services, responding to community needs as they are able, and are no longer bound to their historic clientele or field of service" (Ortiz, 1995, p. 2112).

The first question relates to organizational mission. Can an agency remain distinctively Catholic, Jewish, Moslem, Protestant, African American, Asian, Hispanic, etc., if it serves diverse ethnic, religious, racial, or cultural groups? Once the organization accepts government money, it must provide for all who apply for and are eligible to receive service. If so, what remains special, and has the agency's core purpose changed? Can the agency remain loyal to its sponsoring traditions, or is it just becoming another non-profit agency? (Levin, 1978; Ortiz, 1995).

Church-related agencies can be placed on a sectarian-secular continuum. Thus, for the sectarian agency, "the dominant question is what should be the position of the agency in relation to the religion and the religious bodies with which it is identified" (Reid & Stimpson, 1987, p. 553). As Horowitz correctly notes (1977, p. 16), "it can be safely assumed that securing a disproportionate amount of government funds for Jewish agencies will lead to a disproportionate amount of effort for causes unrelated to our private sectarian purposes." Indeed, he argues that agencies need to follow the needs of people and communities and not chase after available dollars, or the latter may compromise the basic mission of the agency. In parallel fashion, Catholic leaders echoed the concern that although government funding enabled agencies to expand the scale, quality, and scope of services offered, uncritical acceptance of public dollars, policies, and goals would weaken the foundations of Catholic philanthropy and raise serious question about the religious character of these agencies (Oates, 1995).

The second consideration relates to the challenges that confront the staff of sectarian programs. Often, they face difficult religious and moral dilemmas when they are called on to provide service on issues that offend traditional religious teachings: that is, abortion referral and Christian teachings, or sexual practices and Jewish law (Ortiz, 1995). Does the agency permit the staff person the right to decline to serve the client? If so, what are the implications for the client's right to self-determination? Are there repercussions in terms of the relationship of the client to the staff and agency, affecting the trust, confidence, and comfort that client may hold for either? Does the agency run the risk of forfeiting its contract, either by supporting staff decisions not to serve, or if the agency overall refuses to provide the "scorned" service?

In a positive sense, government money may allow a sectarian group to divert its privately raised money more to sectarian concerns, while public money may allow the agency to fulfil its universal responsibilities to the community (Horowitz, 1977). The freedom to be flexible and to redeploy these other funds enables the agency to maintain a balance of service (Selig, 1973). Horowitz makes a dual argument to support the point. Jewish agencies should not turn inward but have a responsibility to assist the general community. However,

> It is reasonable in the context of our present service delivery system to expect that some of these funds (money from governmental sources generated by taxes) should return to the Jewish community through the Jewish communal service sector which is a most natural entry point for many Jews needing services. It is therefore appropriate in the selective pursuit of government funds by representatives of the Jewish community, to do so with an attitude of entitlement and in the context of our rights, rather than seeming to plead for funds belonging to "someone else." (Horowitz, 1977, p.16)

For Horowitz, the agency would be remiss in not seeking and securing funds to help Jews in need. He adds that in purchase-of-service contracts, the Jewish agency should insist on reimbursement for full cost and on upholding the Jewish nature of the program. He challenges agencies to seek and to accept only those public funds which can be spent on service where there is an unmistakable and clear coincidence between the goals of the Jewish agency and the public purchaser. Solender (1978) argues that the Jewish community should go as far as the courts to safeguard its right to receive public funds without compromising its position as an institutional system dedicated to serving the Jewish community. An agency's right to a sectarian preference in intake or to sectarian emphasis in government-funded programs should not be questioned (Eskenazi, 1973).

The counter-argument is that once government funds are accepted, an agency must serve all people without respect to ethnic or religious origin. Indeed, it can be argued that as a condition of contracting, all expectations of serving a unitary clientele must be relinquished. In practice, most Jewish federation supported agencies serve Jews as well as non-Jews to varying degrees. Federations calculate that the overwhelming number of recipients of their services are Jews. Some communities report a service population that is over 70% Jewish, while it rises to as high as 90% in other communities. However, these are only estimates, since government regulations prohibit some programs from tracking clients on the basis of religion or ethnicity (Dorf, 1995).

In New York, despite the Jewish mission of many of the 130 UJA–Federation agencies, their clientele is substantially nonsectarian in character, due to legal requirements as well as sheer demand and the diverse New York area demographic profile. For these agencies, the challenge is to maintain the distinctive Jewish nature of the agency while serving a quite multicultural population.

Creating a comfortable, appropriate, and legal balance of service is always a common practical and philosophical consideration for sectarian organizations. The tension between a universal and particular service orientation can be a source of conflict (Weinberger & Weinberger, 1974). Addressing himself to the philosophical implications of the problem, Levine (1990) advocates on behalf of the position that concern with sectarian groups' needs does not preclude concern and action on behalf of other groups. Indeed, there is a Jewish religious obligation to assist non-Jews. In terms of priority setting, a prior action obligation to serve one's own group does exist. But, such an understanding does not minimize universal commitment and action on behalf of others, within a broad vision of seeking to create peace and to repair the world.

These value clashes are very much apparent in the case of a Jewish family service agency in Los Angeles. Saltzman reported that since 1975, the agency budget has grown from approximately $2 million to $10 million:

> This dramatic growth can be directly attributed to government support—principally for senior service programs, in part for the homeless and chronically mentally ill. Our acceptance of this funding has resulted in some significant trade-offs. We no longer refer to ourselves as a sectarian agency. Today, the agency's mission statement should read: A Jewish agency with an open-door policy. (Saltzman, 1987, p. 79)

Clearly, sectarian agencies were established, for the most part, to serve the needs of distinctive clienteles or to promulgate specific goals. On a very simple level, people are often just more comfortable in a familiar setting. Jewish organizations are aware that "many of our Jewish people are far more comfortable in seeking and receiving help in a Jewish place than in a public or non-sectarian voluntary place and therefore are more willing to seek the needed service" (Horowitz, 1977, p. 14). It would be necessary to know more about the case of the family service agency to understand how agency policy and professional practice have been affected by the restatement of the agency mission. Taken at face value, unless the agency has carved out a balance of service with a prior action obligation for the Jewish community, it would seem that it is no longer loyal to a specific sectarian mission or to the support of Jewish identity within a broader social service mandate. This appears to be a case where government funds have undermined the sectarian mission of an agency.

The Jewish community harbored serious reservations regarding government funding requirements during the 1960s and 1970s, especially antipoverty funding. Social targeting as a policy of anti-poverty programs attempted to focus services on especially needy or underserved racial, ethnic or disability groups (Terrell, 1987). However, it was feared that these new developments in policy would threaten the identity and integrity of the sectarian Jewish agency. The new funding requirements, revolving around community control, maximum feasible participation, "catchmentizing," and preferences for the disadvantaged and minorities, seemed to imply that many clients, even if needy, could not be served because they did not fit into various geographic or other eligibility guidelines, all in the guise of participatory democracy.

Selig (1973) maintained that Jewish agencies needed public funds and had a right to secure such funds. Furthermore, she defended the sovereignty of agencies and their right to serve a specific clientele, and claimed that the predetermination of geographic areas of service was discriminatory. In New York, the Jewish community was able to secure a change in the ruling, which preserved the right of an agency to serve clientele on a city-wide basis; the right to give priority to Jewish applicants, or to serve only Jews; the right of each eligible person to choose the qualified service agency, regardless of its location; and the right of any minority, including Jews, within a catchment area to have their needs considered and provided.

Selig (1973) also offered a set of guidelines for action for the Jewish agency as it relates to seeking and entering into contractual arrangements with government for the provision of social services. She argued that there must be a commitment to the preservation of the Jewish group; that assimilation is not an acceptable orientation. In her view, a "melting pot" dilutes individual values and destroys the unique character of all cultures. Jewish health and welfare organizations are or should be instruments to preserve and strengthen the Jewish community. Furthermore, all sectarian groups have the right and responsibility to take care of members of their own groups. Sectarian groups should acknowledge the need for public funds and their right to secure them, and that government has an obligation to fund the health and welfare aspects of an agency under sectarian auspices. Indeed, both public and private, sectarian and nonsectarian agencies are essential to provide the optimum in social welfare programs. Government is enjoined to recognize the sovereignty of agencies and their right to serve a specific clientele, and that predetermination of geographic service areas as was common in anti-poverty funding is in itself a form of discrimination.

In practice, federation agencies that received public funding tended to relinquish the secular character of their service as a *quid pro quo* for the acceptance of this funding. There were exceptions. The nature of the agency's location and its outreach to the community often resulted in programs and services that were overwhelmingly Jewish in subscription, although in virtually no case was this exclusively true. For example, public housing programs had a very specific set of guidelines regarding the process to be used in the placement of tenants. However, due to the priority given to families at risk, such as the homeless, Jewish refugees from the former Soviet Union disproportionately received vacant slots, because multigenerational extended families were doubling up in apartments. Similarly, the availability of kosher food often increased the tendency for clients to be Jewish at many senior citizen centers. While some funding sources continued the emphasis toward maximum feasible participation, community control and social targeting of clients, some 20 or 30 years down the road, little has changed in reality. Agencies often responded to these requirements by diversifying board membership and creating advisory committees. In many cases, a situation of benign neglect eventuated, because there was often little in the way of effective enforcement of these guidelines. Ultimately, ensuring compliance with these rules in such a culturally diverse location as New York City proved to be impracticable due to the intense nature of ethnic politics and intergroup relations (Solomon-Levine, personal communication, October 31, 1995).

The existence of the sectarian social welfare agency represents an ongoing, inherent tension between pluralism and democracy, compounded further when public funds and their use are at stake. Government funds, with their various regulatory requirements, threaten the parochial quality of the sectarian agency, potentially undermining the sectarian goals of its programs (Zibbell, 1978). Indeed, agency directors posed the core question to the National Conference of Catholic Charities in 1975: "How do you Christianize your services when your funding source (particularly government) is constantly trying to secularize the institutions?" (Oates, 1995, p. 171).

From the vantage point of the Jewish community relations field, always vigilant in protecting the First Amendment, the community is confronted with the dilemma of how to provide vital and costly human services while avoiding the entanglement of church and state (Dawidowicz, 1966; Elazar & Goldstein, 1972).

> Government support means government involvement, and government involvement is inherently coercive, however benign. Government involvement either will lead the state to insist that sectarian agencies provide non-sectarian services and maintain an open intake policy or will cause the state to become an instrument of promoting religion. Neither is in the interest of the Jewish community. Throughout history Jews have suffered when church and state were co-mingled. (Chernin, 1991, p. 168)

Wickenden (1976, p. 159) offered a sobering commentary on the debate:

> But what of the traditional role of voluntary agencies in creating particular facilities and services for particular groups? If elderly Jews or Methodists or Greeks wish to spend their last years with their own fellows, is this discriminatory or pluralistic? Perhaps when we get over the terrible prison walls imposed by years of racial segregation we can afford to look on this question of particularization with a wider perspective.

Steinberg (1989, p. 258) summarized the problem well in explaining that

> our society in principle sanctions the right of ethnic groups to maintain their separate cultures and communities, but it also guarantees individual freedoms and specifically proscribes various forms of discrimination. The problem is that these two sets of rights are often in conflict. This is because ethnic groups in a position of social and economic advantage, when exercising their prerogatives of associating with their own ethnic kind, deprive outsiders of rights and opportunities protected by democratic norms.

As a result, laws protecting the rights of minorities and enhancing democracy function to narrowly circumscribe the areas in which ethnic exclusivity is possible, making it difficult for ethnic groups to maintain the institutions that are essential to their collective survival.

In sum, herein lies the dilemma. Nonprofit and sectarian agencies do not have to accept government contracts, especially if they wish to preserve their predominant ethnic or religious nature. But, sectarian agencies commonly seek out and receive government funding for a variety of reasons (i.e., recognition of emerging needs in their catchment area, desire to extend service or expand agency, increased demand for current services, desire to increase bases of support). They know in advance that the probable trade-off for agreeing to a purchase-of-service arrangement is the surrendering of a closed door policy or ethnic/religious preference, or at best, a constant juggling act among deeply held but conflicting values.

All options bear costs and benefits. The choice to refuse funding preserves sectarian interests, although added potential resources are sacrificed. A decision to accept funding means one of two outcomes: foregoing agency distinctiveness (such as it appears in the case of the Los Angeles family service agency, noted above), or living with the often difficult tensions inherent in trying to maintain a sectarian mission while serving a universal clientele.

CASES FROM THE LITERATURE AND THE FIELD

Nackman (1984) presents an honest and engaging account of one agency's experience in receiving state funds for the first time for a new service. Responding to the availability of funds from the Maryland Division for

Mental Retardation and other Developmental Disabilities (MRDD), the Jewish Family and Children's Services of Baltimore submitted a proposal and was funded to open an Alternative Living Unit (ALU) to house higher functioning individuals previously living in two state institutions. The agency had not served the long-term needs of the mentally retarded previously, having viewed such services as the responsibility of the state and because long-term care required enormous sums of money.

The funds were used to set up a supervised residence. Nackman admits that her account omits any discussion of the struggle involved in the up-and-down process of being a partner with a state agency and, especially from the perspective of a sectarian entity, "whether we would be willing to serve a non-Jew under prevailing Federation policy" (p. 188). But, it was clear that the agency would adhere to the sectarian nature of its mission.

> The home was set up for observance of the Kashruth (dietary laws). Candles are lit and blessings over washing of hands, wine and bread are observed on Friday nights. Our consulting rabbi affixed the mezuzah at the apartment with the residents present. Synagogue services on Friday evening or Saturday morning are attended by one resident faithfully.
> Though the State early raised questions about our offering a sectarian service, our lawyers researched the state law governing discrimination in provision of services. Race and national origin are mentioned, but not religion. Technically, we are within the law. (p. 189)

After the first 6 months of operation, the opportunity to apply to open additional ALU residences presented itself. Nackman reports that the state changed its method of funding and application procedures, however.

> The procedure involves a Request for Proposal and the state personnel preparing a list of residents in the institutions with a little information on them, and holding a "bidder's" conference in which one reviews the information on the clients and submits a proposal based on the needs of these individuals. Then the bidder waits to see if they have been awarded the contract. The sectarian issue remained a somewhat difficult one. We did not feel completely comfortable in saying outright that we would prefer to serve only Jewish residents, so, instead, in reviewing the list we searched for Jewish names, tried to find the religious designation in the record which was not always there and generally felt surreptitious in our search. The expansion of the program became more of the state's prerogative than ours; a reverse situation. (p. 190)

A similar experience was reported by the Jewish Family Service Association in Cleveland (Sheriff & Hulewat, 1990). Here, too, the agency maintained a strong sectarian mission of promoting a Jewish identity dimension in its services. As a result of a study undertaken by the agency with the Cleveland Jewish Community Federation, it decided to open Jewish group homes for mentally retarded adults. The criteria for licensing and funding required that they admit Christian residents, and the home consisted of both Jewish and non-Jewish residents and staff alike, who differed in the level of knowledge and interest about Judaism. There was also a recognition of the need to respect and provide expression for the Christian residents and staff.

The resolution of the debate regarding the observance of kosher food laws symbolized the agency's commitment to Jewish values and content and the feeling that it needed to justify the use of such content in its practice to enhance the quality of life programmatically and clinically.

> Kashrut had become a metaphor for their ambivalent feelings about how and to what extent to observe their Jewishness. With that recognition, ultimately, it was resolved that a kosher home does not discriminate against nonkosher or Christian residents, but a nonkosher home does discriminate against certain Jews. Therefore, if the homes were to provide a residence for any Jewish mentally retarded individual, they must be strictly kosher. (p. 56)

Coun (1983) reports on the experience of Jewish vocational service agencies and purchase-of-service contracts. These programs originated as sectarian employment and career counseling organizations whose image in Jewish communal circles had become tarnished as the result of extensive use of public funds. He argues that these funds have brought substantial benefits to Jewish clients in need and enabled vocational agencies to expand their service to the Jewish community and the community at large. The need to accept government funds was due to three main factors. First, the increasing and prohibitive costs of service delivery to special Jewish need groups (i.e., the elderly and disabled) were outstripping the resources of the Jewish community. A second reason was the sudden financial burden of serving thousands of arriving Soviet Jewish immigrants. Finally, substantial program income for indirect costs reverted to agency budgets for administering government contracts.

His own agency, the Jewish Vocational Service in East Orange, New Jersey, had a long history of receiving funds from the Office of Economic Opportunity (OEO), CETA, and other government sources. Various programs funded through public dollars served significant numbers of Jewish clients and were conducted alongside the agency's sectarian Jewish services of placement and career counseling, which were funded through the local federation allocation.

Over time, the agency gained a strong reputation in the field as a quality service provider which cared for its own constituency while sharing its expertise for the general welfare. It was often called upon to consult with government agencies as well as other nonprofit groups. In addition, agency staff were invited to serve on a host of area planning councils, advisory boards, and interagency coalitions. As a result, the agency was able to advocate for the interests of the Jewish community while also serving broader needs. Coun (1983) claims that vocational service agencies are able to maintain their basic sectarian mission while accepting public funds. In addition, much-needed dollars are generated to serve Jewish clients and the community relations benefits which accrued from giving service to the general populace were significant.

This author was employed during the late 1970s by a Jewish organization in New York that received federation funds as well as various contracts, primarily from different city government departments. He served as the agency's Assistant Director and the Director of its Youth Employment Training Program (YETP), funded through federal CETA funds and administered by the New York City Department of Employment. The agency and its program were based in a poverty-stricken neighborhood that had at one time been home to a very large Jewish population. By the 1960s, the Jewish community had, for the most part, relocated, with many older adults remaining behind. Most of the agency's programs provided services to the elderly Jewish population.

The YETP was a means-tested, job training program geared to prepare young high school dropouts or unemployed teens for secretarial, bookkeeping, clerical, and similar office positions, as well as assisting them to obtain their high-school-equivalency diplomas. The agency knew at the outset that the overwhelming number of trainees (80 per year) would not be Jewish.

In practice, ethical conflicts did arise because the agency had a commitment to serve sectarian needs. Each year a small number of Jewish youth applied to enter the YETP, often including recent immigrants from Eastern Europe. Some of these youth were not admitted based on eligibility criteria (financial status, educational attainment, scores on entrance exams, interview ratings, and affirmative action guidelines) despite the inclination to admit them. Still, the organization chose each year to apply for and accept funding for pragmatic and philosophical reasons. On the practical level, the grant provided income. It allowed the agency to hire staff who were able to fill roles for the agency beyond the tasks related to the YETP. For example, this writer worked with various board committees, handled other agency-wide tasks, and was the main liaison officer for community relations, working on interagency coalitions with other ethnic and religious groups. Philosophically, the agency had a commitment to the greater communal good. It felt that by providing this service, it was contributing to the improvement of the community as a whole and to needy individuals.

CASE STUDY: UJA–FEDERATION OF NEW YORK

The ensuing case discussion highlights as the unit of analysis the New York UJA–Federation, arguably the predominant agency and leading service provider in the New York, if not the national, Jewish community. Reference has earlier been made to the Jewish federation as an organizational entity. A few additional words of definition would be useful.

According to its mission statement (1989), the United Jewish Appeal–Federation of Jewish Philanthropies of New York (or UJA–Federation), is the primary philanthropic arm of the Greater New York Jewish community. As the result of the merger of two separate organizations—the United Jewish Appeal of New York, established in 1938, and the Federation of Jewish Philanthropies of New York, established in 1917—UJA–Federation is an umbrella network that raises and distributes funds to 130 social welfare agencies in New York, to agencies in over 50 countries worldwide, and to a network of human service programs in Israel. UJA–Federation is responsible for communal planning and serves as the central address of the New York Jewish community. UJA–Federation represents the notion of united, federated giving, macro-level social planning, central distribution of funds, and coordination of service delivery (UJA–Federation, 1994a, 1994b).

The New York organization is one of the nearly 200 local Jewish federations affiliated with the national Council of Jewish Federations. On an annual basis, UJA–Federation raises over $200 million dollars from individual contributions, foundations, bequests, and other sources. Although it does not receive government grants directly, its government relations and public policy activities include grants writing and liaison work to government to leverage public funds for its agencies.

It is UJA-Federation's mission to ensure the continuity of the Jewish people, to enhance the quality of Jewish life and to build a strong and unified Jewish community—in New York, in Israel and throughout the world; to help, through a series of affiliated agencies, individuals and families in need—the old and young, the unemployed, the homeless, the sick and the poor—and to resettle those who are persecuted and oppressed; to help meet human needs in the State of Israel and to strengthen the relationship between the people of Israel and the Diaspora. (UJA–Federation, 1989a, p. 2)

Although its primary concern is with the needs of its own community, UJA–Federation has historically served non-Jewish individuals through its beneficiary agencies and maintains an activist role in expanding its assistance to the general community (UJA–Federation, 1989b, 1993).

In recent years, however, a series of challenges have confronted the American Jewish community, the national federation system, and the New York UJA–Federation. Distressed by the high and rapidly increasing levels of intermarriage, assimilation, lack of affiliation with basic Jewish institutions, and troubling demographic patterns (such as a low birth rate, aging of the population, occupational shifts, and high residential mobility), the entire federation system has mobilized around the theme of promoting Jewish continuity. UJA–Federation of New York has defined Jewish continuity to mean "assuring in New York both the continued presence of a large and diverse Jewish community, and the continued quality, vitality, and magnetism of those Jewish institutions and experiences on which the self-identification of Jews as Jews will depend" (UJA–Federation, 1993, p. 18). In its Strategic Plan (1993, p. 18), UJA–Federation further pronounced that "assuring Jewish continuity is the most fundamental and most pressing challenge the New York Jewish community faces; and UJA-Federation must be centrally involved in meeting that challenge." Furthermore, UJA–Federation should provide the model for the community to follow:

It should exemplify the standards needed throughout Jewish organizational life. And because our campaign makes contact with many more Jews than does any other activity of any New York Jewish institution, UJA–Federation should conduct its campaigns so as not merely to maximize immediate revenues, but to build greater understanding of the needs, values and institutions of the Jewish community, and to enlarge the number of persons participating actively in them. . . . In the largest sense our task is to help create a Jewish community more learned in our classics and in current Jewish thought; more committed to observe the mitzvot (religious commandments) and to advance Jewish concerns; more familiar with Israel; and enriched by the capacity to refract all aspects of life through the prism of Jewish values and tradition. We can do that only by enhancing the capacity of the most effective Jewish institutions of many kinds. (UJA–Federation, 1993, pp. 24-25)

These statements represent a radical departure for UJA–Federation. Whereas its history has been that of a social service delivery system, leaving such education, program, and service content issues to its beneficiary agencies which include religious institutions, schools, and community centers, now it has set as a major institutional and system priority the cultivation of Jewish sectarian needs, beyond the provision of basic human services. As a result, these new priorities raise questions and conflicts for the agency that receives public funds and heretofore has been providing what amounts to nonsectarian services to all, regardless of religious affiliation. This is a particularly pertinent subject, since most of the UJA–Federation beneficiary agencies today are nonsectarian in character; that is, they provide service to a diverse clientele composed of religious, ethnic, and racial groups beyond just the Jewish community.

This policy thrust is very recent and it would appear that many more questions than answers have been raised by virtue of the continuity agenda. Although a distinct continuity fund-raising drive and special grant allocation process have been instituted, many policy issues for the network remain undecided, and professional practice knowledge on the issue is only now evolving. Still, the organization is pressing ahead and pushing its entire system to respond and upgrade the level of Jewish content in services.

This new agenda will ultimately cause UJA–Federation to rethink its own funding priorities in the coming years as well as reevaluate its position on the advisability in some cases of its agencies seeking contract dollars from government. It has been illustrated that acceptance of government money tends to allow a nonprofit agency to expand and increase its responsiveness to the community by offering new services and resources. However, a related tendency is the shift away from an agency's traditional sectarian mission with the infusion of public dollars. Ironically, the Jewish continuity thrust is articulated at a time when agencies are heavily dependent on contract money and government is implementing deep funding cuts. At the same time, continuity is pitted against powerful assimilatory forces and increasing Jewish intermarriage, as well as full Jewish participation in society at large.

As a funding umbrella agency for 130 agencies throughout the New

York area, the leadership of UJA–Federation perceives the organization's role as including planning for an entire community, advising its agencies on a whole host of matters, setting the pace policy-wise for the entire system, raising and juggling funds, reducing allocations when government grants increase, and targeting Jewish dollars to Jewish clients and services. Given this role, given the tensions and conflicts that confront sectarian agencies as well as all nonprofits, the unique circumstances related to being located in New York, and the evolving Jewish continuity agenda, UJA–Federation continuously reflects on what guidance and parameters it should provide for its network.

One of UJA–Federation's main concerns is its need to understand the proper mix, albeit forever shifting, of private philanthropy and government revenue. Philosophical and pragmatic issues emerge connected to the relationship of the federation and its agencies when the latter receive government contracts. Agencies naturally want to maintain the same level of federation grant even as their government dollars increase. But, from the federation's standpoint, the community needs to be able to reallocate funds in order to stretch its limited resources in line with overall communal needs. Selig (1973, p. 134) went as far as to suggest that

> it is necessary that programs funded by public funds should be discussed with the Federations prior to initiation and subject to the approval by the Federations. . . . This may be regarded as an intrusion on "autonomy"; but without such an orderly review the programs financed by government funds may not be related to the priorities of the Jewish community. They may be so general as to distort the function of the agency and its role in the Jewish community.

The use of public dollars has yet another effect on the relationship of the Jewish federation and it agencies. As the proportion of government contract dollars to agencies increase, the percentage of income from the federations decreases.

> "Dual alliance" then becomes "triple entente." We must not close our eyes to the real fact that the relationship of the agencies to Federations has become more attenuated, particularly, but not exclusively, with respect to the programs for which the Federations no longer have financial responsibility. (Selig, 1973, p. 128)

The potential once existed for federations to become the junior partners in the relationship (see, for example, Selig, 1973). Such a role reversal could undermine commitment to the federated system, disrupt central communal planning and coordination of services, destroy unified fund-raising campaigns, and transform the federation allocations process into a veritable war zone. A similar analysis pertains to the United Way system and its beneficiaries. Smith and Lipsky (1993, p. 69) found that "Overall, United Way funding is a relatively small source of total revenues for nonprofit service agencies." Their survey of 350 organizations revealed that United Way funding constituted just 4% of agency income, while state contracts amounted to 52% and 17% came from nonstate (mostly federal) contract government funding, such as SSI and Medicaid.

As of this writing, however, this concern about junior partnership with government should fade or diminish as a result of impending deep reductions in government funding for human services. As the availability of government dollars shrinks, federation allocations to agencies as a proportion of their total budgets will inevitably rise. Agencies will, in all likelihood, become more dependent on federation fund-raising and allocation, especially if federations continue to restrict the fund-raising activities conducted by beneficiary organizations. Ironically, while public funding cuts will send massive reverberations throughout the Jewish federation system, they will also have the effect of reinforcing the federation as the senior partner in its relationship with its agencies.

A serious concern on the part of UJA–Federation is whether its grants to agencies, which represent unrestricted funds, in effect pay for the administrative inefficiencies of the agencies that receive government contracts. According to a senior executive at UJA–Federation, various agencies habitually operate government programs at a deficit, due to either low reimbursement rates and/or inefficient management of contracts. In addition, these contracts almost always require some oversight by executive staff. Time spent by these staff members on troubleshooting or contracts management has cost implications: time lost from other worthwhile activities for which UJA–Federation has funded the organization. In other words, UJA–Federation must question whether Jewish philanthropy should be forced, by default, to subsidize administrative inefficiency.

Another crisis faced by the UJA–Federation network occurs when public dollars decline or are lost but a needy clientele has been established over time. From a planning perspective, is it necessary for Jewish communal dollars to absorb the cost, especially when the contracted service clientele may not be Jewish? In recent years, UJA–Federation has defunded agencies, reduced grants, or disaffiliated agencies that were no longer serving a predominantly Jewish clientele or neighborhood. In other cases,

UJA–Federation has sought to target its grants to agencies for specific Jewish needs, that is, Jewish chaplaincy services or research on Jewish diseases at a Jewish hospital that is now nonsectarian in its clientele, or Jewish family life programming at a social service agency. The choices are often difficult, given UJA–Federation's joint commitment to universal concerns as well as sectarian interests (Slomon & Sherins, 1992; Solender, 1992).

Various criteria have been suggested for use in making the decision to apply for public funding. Agencies should judge the essentiality of conducting the program under sectarian auspices. The identified human need may be real, but it may be possible for the service to be conducted under different auspices, such as the government, or in a cosponsorship arrangement with other nonsectarian agencies. The community would have the right to ask what the net loss to the (Jewish) community would be if an agency abandons a service which is not picked up by other organizations (Zibbell, 1978).

In an era of scarce resources, government cutbacks and difficult times for private philanthropy, and the compelling need to focus on a sectarian agenda (i.e., Jewish continuity), organizations may be obliged to conduct hard cost-benefit analyses and refuse public funds that they had once accepted in order to avoid being diverted from core purposes.

Similar to the case materials from the literature, kosher dietary practice has provided UJA–Federation with a paradigm for exploring the tension between sectarian needs and government funding. Not only does kosher food provision bear significant financial ramifications, but it also cuts across many service areas, including nursing homes, senior centers, hospitals, Jewish community centers, child care agencies, residential and outpatient treatment facilities, and even prisons (when Jewish organizations are asked to deliver food to prisoners). For example, due to government cutbacks, a network nursing home approached UJA–Federation for an increased grant to fund its kosher food service. For a 500-bed facility, this food service costs some $400,000 a year, much more than non-kosher service. A grant of $400,000 is far more than any of UJA–Federation's total grants to any single nursing home. The policy and practice issues are further accentuated by the fact that very few patients require or request kosher food, and a large number of residents of this and other network homes are not Jewish.

In an ironic twist, one outpatient rehabilitation agency (no longer in existence) that received government contracts and UJA–Federation funds, and served mentally retarded and handicapped individuals, offered nonkosher food service training to enable its clients to obtain jobs in the private sector. The agency received complaints from religiously observant staff and communal representatives asking why this Jewish organization did not maintain a kosher food policy. Ultimately, the service remained intact. It was explained that many of the trainees were not Jewish. But, more to the point, it was noted that the overwhelming number of job opportunities were not in the kosher food sector. To train clients otherwise was an exercise in folly.

The same agency experienced another serious value conflict between sectarian needs, religious practice, and government expectations. Certain Jewish religious holidays are 2 days in length, and when traditionally observed prohibit various forms of work. Many Jewish organizations, including UJA–Federation, have adopted the practice of closing for both days when they fall on a work day. The rehabilitation agency wanted to open on the second day of holidays (up to 6 additional days of operation) due to the special needs of its population and the heavy non-Jewish representation among its clientele. It was argued that these clients had difficulty coping with two consecutive unstructured and unsupervised days. Even more, the agency maintained that it generated more income in government reimbursements by opening up the additional days.

A final example that affected the UJA–Federation network came to be known as the Wilder Case, an affair which wound its way through the courts between 1973 and 1988 (*Wilder v. Bernstein*, 848F. 2d 1338, 2nd Cir., 1988). In this case, a foster care client sued various city and state officials and 33 private child care agencies, including UJA–Federation and its child care agencies, with another 19 child care agencies that entered the case as intervenors. The plaintiffs were represented in the case by the Children's Rights Project of the American Civil Liberties Union. The defendants and intervenors were represented by the corporation counsel of New York City, the attorney general of New York State, and 36 private law firms. Several more litigants entered the case as *amici curiae* (Kelley, 1990).

The issue revolved around the role of religion in the placement of children in foster care. New York City had long relied on sectarian agencies to provide this service. These agencies were largely under Roman Catholic and Jewish auspices, and gave preference to accepting children of their own faiths. Protestant, non-Catholic, and non-Jewish children were often unable to be placed at the remaining accredited private agencies. As a result, the number of Black children needing placement was too numerous for the less abundant agencies under Protestant auspices, and these children were often shuttled to whatever places could be found, often to allegedly marginal or inferior facilities or foster homes. The plaintiffs argued that this system discriminated against Black Protestant children

due to their religion. The inadequate placements available to Black children resulted from publicly financed and sanctioned religious preferences. This arrangement was attacked as a violation of the separation of
church and state, or the Establishment Clause, the First Amendment provision that government not make any laws respecting the establishment
of religion (Kelley, 1990). In addition, the plaintiffs argued that all children in the foster care system should have meaningful access to family
planning information, services, and counseling, a provision that was especially troubling to the Catholic agencies named in the suit.

Ultimately, a three-judge court found the system to be constitutional,
and a district court presided over a long and complicated negotiation to
settle the case. The settlement was not found to be satisfactory by the sectarian agencies, but they acceded when their appeals were rejected. The
symbiotic relationship between the sectarian agencies and government
was too deeply entrenched, and although these agencies could have opted
to leave the purchase-of-service arena to avoid public regulation, the agencies could not have found other ways to replace lost dollars for services.
The private agencies were required to accept foster care applicants on a
first-come, first-served basis independent of religious affinities (Kelley,
1990). The only exceptions allowed under the court's settlement pertained
to cases in which foster care candidates came from "pervasively sectarian"
traditions and could be served by agencies specifically designated to care
exclusively for these children.

For UJA–Federation, the outcome of the case raises concerns in a number of ways. For all intents and purposes, its network child care agencies
do not serve many Jewish children at risk, are now fully nonsectarian, and
provide a nominally recognizable sectarian service, prompting many of
the questions about mission and funding priorities discussed earlier.
Although the service agency must resolve its own dilemmas regarding purpose and program, UJA–Federation must grapple with the question of
whether it should continue to fund such an organization, especially in
light of the continuity agenda.

The value and pragmatic conflicts are palpable. UJA–Federation has a
commitment to the general welfare of the New York community, including, of course, foster care clients and their families. Within that univer-
salistic value stance, Jewish children would still be served by a UJA–
Federation agency regulated by the outcome of *Wilder*, although not on
a priority basis. Concomitantly, the level of Jewish programming would
be lowered as the Jewish element of the service population declines.
Alternatively, UJA–Federation could encourage its agencies to reject

government funding, although this is not a very realistic option. UJA–Federation could reduce its allocations to or defund its current agencies, and/or choose to create a new entity that would only operate with Jewish communal resources. These alternative paths might focus UJA–Federation efforts on a Jewish clientele and support its continuity goals, but with the forfeiture of its universal commitments, at least in the foster care domain. Neither decision is an easy or comfortable one, and at least for the present, UJA–Federation dissonantly continues to fund agencies that accept public funds and adhere to the *Wilder* settlement.

Another potential conflict relates to the possible extension of the *Wilder* decision to other institutions in its network, potentially spelling the end of many sectarian services, such as Jewish nursing homes expressing preference for admitting Jewish residents. (For the most part, Jewish nursing home facilities under New York UJA–Federation auspices have operated on a virtually unchanged basis. In the cases where the Jewish population of homes has declined, market forces have been more of a factor than government regulations.)

Steinberg's (1989) prescient analysis introduced earlier now comes back to haunt the social policy planner. In the interest of preventing discrimination and ensuring equal access to all, sectarian services are potentially undermined, let alone a commitment to the perpetuation of the ethnic or religious group. Such agencies would be ineligible for government funds and therefore placed at a great financial disadvantage. Furthermore, if organizations under sectarian auspices are enjoined to provide care or admission to facilities on a first-come, first-served basis, without allowance for ethnic/religious preference, the population in the agencies will change. The service content and agency environment would lose their sectarian character and consequently, many clients would be prevented from receiving treatment or service in a familiar, comfortable, and desired setting. Once again, the issue of government contracting accentuates the tension points between universal and particular commitments. Even more, the *Wilder* case conceivably places the whole notion of sectarian service in jeopardy and undermines the very foundation, if not the very existence, of systems like UJA–Federation.

CONCLUSION

Purchase-of-service contracting will remain an important source of revenue for the sectarian agency. Private philanthropy has never been in the position to provide enough resources to cover all human service needs and will never be able to produce sufficient income to offset government cutbacks. The ongoing challenge for the agency under contract will be to sustain the integrity of its sectarian purpose without being narrowly parochial and to continue to serve others outside its preferred population. Contracting with government will never be a comfortable or perfect process or relationship. The question will be how well the agency is able to manage the inherent tensions and conflicts (Fabricant & Burghardt, 1992; Wedel, 1991).

As of this writing, it would appear that managed care represents the wave of the future for human service delivery systems. The market forces implicit in the managed care revolution may pose a far greater threat today (i.e., directing clients to particular services and agencies without regard for the client's preference) than the availability of public funding in regard to whether an agency can maintain a Jewish quality and clientele. However, the extent and manner in which nonprofit organizations link up with managed care systems may in fact help to guarantee their survival. For example, because reimbursement is based on what insurance will cover, the number of people of various sectarian groups receiving services could actually increase, if their members heavily utilize commercial insurance (Solomon-Levine, personal communication, October 31, 1995).

Ultimately, sectarian agencies will need to answer the question of what they stand for. Regarding the Jewish sponsored organization, is it the pursuit of specific Jewish communal purposes and the servicing of narrow Jewish needs? Or is it the provision of a range of care to the general populace, characterized by a Jewish style of service delivery with a distinctive Jewish value base? For the foreseeable future, the Jewish continuity agenda may very well be the dominant force that will shape the direction of the Jewish federation system in the United States. One answer may lie in the notion of the prior action obligation introduced above. Serving one group first does not mean serving it exclusively, but can mean serving all groups needing assistance with a certain purpose and value base at the core of its philosophy and service style. The sectarian purpose can be primary, but the agency can still serve all who seek care.

Of course, from the public policy or government point of view—assuming government will continue to provide support for the delivery of social services either through its own systems or through nonprofit groups—the issue will continue to be how to fund religious or ethnic organizations without giving advantage to religion and without subverting the public interest. The agency that pursues a sectarian purpose as its primary objective while serving the general population cannot impose its own practices and values on unsuspecting or vulnerable clients. It is one thing to fund a sectarian entity as a means of fulfilling government's interest to extend service to needy populations. It is quite another matter to enable religious groups to influence public policy or service delivery in line with their narrow religious interests, i.e., debates regarding family planning, abortion, school prayer, tax credits, or vouchers for parochial education, standards of morality in entertainment, etc. Government, too, has a thin line to walk between funding and favoring religion.

This chapter began by briefly tracing the history of the sectarian and nonprofit social welfare sectors in the United States. It concludes now with a reference to the deeply religious foundations of American social welfare and sectarian service. Indeed, it might be timely for contemporary policymakers and public officials to reflect back on these important sources. Within Christian thought, the powerful notion of charity, derived from the Latin *caritas*, connotes benevolence, love, and good will toward all others, especially the poor. In Judaism, the term for pursuing charitable action is derived from the Hebrew word for justice, or *tzedakah*. Taken together, the message of the Judeo–Christian tradition compels us to work unceasingly to repair a terribly shattered world, to create universal justice and righteousness, and to act at all times in a spirit of love, caring and concern. Thus, in addition to important instrumental purposes achieved by entering into purchase-of-service contracts with government, the sectarian agency should serve as a moral compass by reminding all of us what our core responsibilities are to our fellow human beings and how to carry out these commitments.

REFERENCES

Bernstein, S. (1991). *Managing contracted services in the nonprofit agency: Administrative, ethical, and political issues.* Philadelphia: Temple University Press.

Blum, A., & Naparstek, A. J. (1987). The changing environment and Jewish communal services. *Journal of Jewish Communal Service, 63,* 204–211.

Boeko, J. L. (1992). A time for downsizing, a time for kehillah leadership. *Journal of Jewish Communal Service, 69,* 28–34.

Catholics report they lack tools to raise money. (1995, October 11). *Chronicle of Philanthropy,* p. 32.

Chernin, A. D. (1991). The liberal agenda: Is it good or bad for the Jews?

Journal of Jewish Communal Service, 67, 166–173.

Coun, R. I. (1983). Amplifying Jewish vocational services through publicly funded programs. *Journal of Jewish Communal Service, 60,* 53–55.

Council of Jewish Federations. (1995, October). *Government funding for human services in the Jewish community* (revised working draft). New York: Council of Jewish Federations.

Dawidowicz, L. S. (1966). *Church and state.* In M. Fine & M. Himmelfarb (Eds.), *American Jewish year book 1966* (pp. 128–150). New York: American Jewish Committee and Jewish Publication Society of America.

Dorf, M. (1995, September 19). Study shows Jewish agencies highly dependent on government. *JTA Daily News Bulletin,* pp. 1–2.

Elazar, D. J., & Goldstein, S. R. (1972). *The legal status of the American Jewish community.* In M. Fine & M. Himmelfarb (Eds.), *American Jewish year book 1972* (pp. 3–94). New York: American Jewish Committee and Jewish Publication Society of America.

Eskenazi, D. (1973). The Jewish community center and the United Way: The case for the sectarian agency. *Journal of Jewish Communal Service, 50,* 58–65.

Fabricant, M. B., & Burghardt, S. (1992). *The welfare state crisis and the transformation of social service work.* Armonk, NY: M. E. Sharpe.

Gibelman, M. (1995). Purchasing social services. In R. L. Edwards (Ed.), *Encyclopedia of social work* (19th ed., Vol. 3, pp. 1998–2007). Washington, DC: NASW Press.

Gilbert, N. (1983). *Capitalism and the welfare state.* New Haven: Yale University Press.

Hart, A. F. (1988). Contracting for child welfare services in Massachusetts: Emerging issues for policy and practice. *Social Work, 33,* 511–515.

Hartogs, N., & Weber, J. (1978). *Impact of government funding on the management of voluntary agencies.* New York: Greater New York Fund/United Way.

Horowitz, S. (1977). Issues in public funding of Jewish communal services. *Journal of Jewish Communal Service, 54,* 13–17.

Jolkovsky, B. (1995, July 7). Sages of Yeshiva issue: Dissent on Lamm's law. *Forward,* pp. 1, 4.

Kelley, D. M. (1990). *Public funding of social services related to religious bodies.* New York: The American Jewish Committee.

Levin, M. (1978). Another look at the open membership policy of Jewish community centers. *Journal of Jewish Communal Service, 55,* 98–104.

Levine, E. (1985). Jewish professional-professional Jew: Commitments and competencies for a Jewish mission. *Journal of Jewish Communal Service, 62,* 40–48.

Levine, E. (1990). The ethical-ritual in Judaism: A review of sources on Torah study and social action. *Jewish Social Work Forum, 26,* 44–50.

Miller, A. P. (1992). Jewish communal service and the new economy. *Journal of Jewish Communal Service, 69,* 6–12.

Nackman, B. C. (1984). Developing services to the mentally retarded/developmentally disabled. *Journal of Jewish Communal Service, 61,* 188–192.

Netting, F. E., McMurtry, S. L., Kettner, P. M. & Martin, L. M. (1994). Will privatization destroy the traditional nonprofit human services sector? In M. J. Austin & J. I. Lowe (Eds.), *Controversial issues in communities and organizations* (pp. 158–173). Needham Heights, MA: Allyn and Bacon.

Oates, M. J. (1995). *The Catholic philanthropic tradition in America.* Bloomington: Indiana University Press.

Ortiz, L. P. (1995). Sectarian agencies. In R. L. Edwards (Ed.), *Encyclopedia of social work* (19th ed., Vol. 3, pp. 2109–2116). Washington, DC: NASW Press.

Reid, W. J., & Stimpson, P. K. (1987). Sectarian agencies. In A. Minahan (Ed.), *Encyclopedia of social work* (18th ed., Vol. 2, pp. 545–556). Silver Spring, MD: National Association of Social Workers.

Roof, W. C., & McKinney, W. (1987). *American mainline religion.* New Brunswick, NJ: Rutgers University Press.

Rosenblatt, G. (1995, July 7). For YU, tough choices about gays. *The Jewish Week,* pp. 5–6.

Saltzman, A. R. (1987). The new season: Reruns and new episodes. *Journal of Jewish Communal Service, 64,* 77–80.

Selig, M. K. (1973). New dimensions in government funding of voluntary agencies: Potentials and risks. *Journal of Jewish Communal Service, 50,* 125–135.

Shadowed by budget cuts, HUD gives $900-million to help the homeless. (1995, July 27). *The Chronicle of Philanthropy,* pp. 30–32.

Sherriff, B., & Hulewat, P. (1990). Enhancing the Jewish dimension in Jewish family agency services. *Journal of Jewish Communal Service, 67,* 52–58.

Smith, R., & Lipsky, M. (1993). *Nonprofits for hire: The welfare state in the age of contracting.* Cambridge, MA: Harvard University Press.

Solender, S. (1978). The changing situation in the Jewish community and implications for Federations. *Journal of Jewish Communal Service, 55,* 148–154.

Solender, S. D. (1992). Pursuing excellence in Jewish communal policy, program and professional practice in times of change. *Journal of Jewish Communal Service, 69,* 35–42.

Solomon, J. R. (1995). Beyond Jewish communal service: The not-for-profit field at risk. *Journal of Jewish Communal Service, 71,* 303–308.

Solomon, J. R., & Shevins, B. (1992). Managing Jewish communal agencies in difficult times: Cutting and coping. *Journal of Jewish Communal Service 69,* 13–19.

Steinberg, S. (1989). *The ethnic myth.* Boston: Beacon.

Terrell, P. (1987). Purchasing social services. In A. Minahan (Ed.), *Encyclopedia of social work* (18th ed., Vol. 2, pp. 434–442). Silver Spring, MD: National Association of Social Workers.

UJA–Federation of New York. (1989a, November). *Mission statement.* New York: Author.

UJA–Federation of New York. (1989b, July 24). *UJA–Federation credo.* New York: Author.

UJA–Federation of New York. (1993). *One vision: The strategic plan for UJA–Federation of New York.* New York: Author.

UJA–Federation of New York. (1994a). *Report to the community 1993–1994.* New York: Author.

UJA–Federation of New York. (1994b). *UJA–Federation organizational objectives, 1994–1995.* New York: Author.

UJA–Federation of New York. (1995a, June 14). *Summary of the 1995–96 state budget adopted June 7, 1995.* New York: Author.

UJA–Federation of New York. (1995b, July 14). *Summary of the New York City budget for fiscal year 1996.* New York: Author.

Wedel, K. R. (1991). Designing and implementing performance contracting. In R. L. Edwards & J. A. Yankey (Eds.), *Skills for effective human services management* (pp. 335–351). Washington, DC: NASW Press.

Weinberger, P. E., & Weinberger, D. Z. (1974). The Jewish religious tradition and social services. In P. E. Weinberger (Ed.), *Perspectives on social welfare* (2nd ed., pp. 402–411). New York: Macmillan.

Wernet, S. P. (1994). A case study of adaptation in a nonprofit human service organization. *Journal of Community Practice, 1,* 93–112.

Wickenden, E. (1976). Purchase of care and services: Effect on voluntary agencies. In N. Gilbert & H. Specht (Eds.), *The emergence of social welfare and social work* (pp. 149–162). Itasca, IL: F.E. Peacock.

Zibbell, C. (1978). The Jewish component in Jewish communal service. *Journal of Jewish Communal Service, 55,* 141–147.

6

Fears Betrayed: Initial Impressions of Contracting for United Kingdom Social Services

James Richardson and Richard Gutch

INTRODUCTION

Purchase-of-service contracting is both new and relatively underdeveloped in the United Kingdom (UK) personal social services system. It already appears likely, however, that POS contracting will become the principal, and possibly sole, form of state funding for voluntary organizations in the social services field within the next few years. Unlike the United States, where contracting has developed on an ad hoc basis, in the UK it is a deliberate aim of government policy (Deakin, 1993).

This chapter first examines the background to the implementation of contracting in the UK personal social services system. It then compares current perceptions of the policy implications with the fears and hopes expressed by UK nonprofits when it first became apparent that state funding would shift to a contractual basis. Many of the initial fears of nonprofits arose out of assumptions about the market structure of the "mixed economy of care" that have not been borne out. Hence, the vision of a "contract nightmare" that many commentators warned of has failed to materialize (see Billis & Harris 1986; Chanan, 1991; Gutch, 1991, 1992; Leat, 1995; Qaiyoom, 1992a for an overview of the "contract nightmare" perspective). Instead, contracting has led only to incremental change.

However, a brief examination of the earlier implementation of POS contracting in the UK market for vocational training is used to suggest that UK nonprofits are uniquely vulnerable to for-profit competition. In the UK, unlike the United States, levels of charitable subsidy are unlikely to be sufficient to exclude for-profits. At the same time, unlike much of continental Europe, there is no institutional bias toward the use of non-profits. We, therefore, tentatively suggest that large-scale contracting by UK nonprofits, with its associated costs or benefits, may prove to be purely ephemeral, and not the seismic shift in the role of the sector that many commentators have predicted.

Case studies have been the principal methodology applied in studies of implementation and we draw on a range of these that together provide a wide range of insights (Common & Flynn, 1992; Flynn & Hurley, 1993; Goulding, 1993; Harris, 1993; Hedley & Rochester, 1991; Lewis, 1993, 1994; Meadows, 1992; Wistow, Knapp, Hardy, & Allen, 1992). By contrast, little sample survey evidence exists. However, we conducted a small-scale survey for this study (Richardson, 1995) to complement and complete the picture provided by the case studies.

We surveyed 135 UK nonprofits in October 1994. The sample frame chosen was expected to contain a higher than average proportion of agencies involved in significant contracting, and included only agencies with at least some access to external advice to minimize effects arising purely from ignorance. The intention of the survey was to assess whether the hopes and fears of the nonprofit sector about POS contracting had been borne out. Questions were asked to elicit current views on the issues identified as key hopes and fears by the National Council for Voluntary Organizations (NCVO) (1989).

Finally, both authors have been directly involved in developing policy and advice for UK nonprofits, primarily through the National Council for Voluntary Organizations, an umbrella body for nonprofits in England. We have drawn on this experience to provide anecdotal support for the claims of more rigorous studies to be universally applicable. Taken together, these sources provide a rich body of evidence on the development of POS in the UK personal social services system, although there is clearly still a need for more widespread empirical evidence in this area.

THE DEVELOPMENT OF POS IN THE UNITED KINGDOM

For most of the postwar period, the development of the UK welfare state assumed a state hegemony of provision. Although long forgotten by the time of the arguments about POS contracting in the late 1980s, UK non-profits had received substantial contractual income during the 1920s and 1930s as the state gradually took over responsibility for social welfare (Davis Smith, 1995). Despite the wishes of its progenitor, Beveridge, however, the postwar welfare state had direct state provision at its heart, with non-profits playing very much a junior role (Deakin, 1995). Although voluntary nonprofit organizations always maintained certain niche roles, the bulk of services was directly provided by the state. Indeed, many nonprofits saw their role as setting up new services which would ultimately be subsumed within state provision.

Throughout this period, the overwhelming majority of statutory funding for nonprofits was on the basis of grants: monies given in support of the general objectives of the organization, without legally binding obligations and often with little accountability (Hawley, 1992). Although some contractual arrangements did exist, these were very much an exception.

By the 1970s, this model of the welfare state was coming under pressure from both ends of the ideological spectrum. Liberals had become disillusioned with the paternalism of uniform state provision, and pressure for greater individual choice and involvement in service provision was accompanied by the growth of self-help organizations. The New Right criticized the welfare state as creating a "dependency culture" and expressed concern at the apparently inexorable rise in government expenditure, accompanied by levels of unemployment hitherto unseen in the postwar period.

The key determinant of the shift toward POS contracting, however, came following the election of the Thatcher government in 1979. The confluence of two factors led to a massive expansion of the service provision role of UK nonprofits. In the postwar period, the relation of nonprofits to the welfare state had been as an "extension ladder" (Sydney & Beatrice Webb, cited in Davis Smith, 1995), complementing and enhancing mainstream state provision. Now, nonprofits were again to be offered, and bribed or cajoled into accepting a major role in provision of social services.

The new government was taking the first steps in an attempt to bring about a complete transformation of the nature of governance. At the same time, it faced an immediate need to provide services for a rapidly growing body of unemployed people. The government sought to substitute market values for those of public bureaucracies, accompanied by a reorientation of attitudes toward public services. In this view, users see themselves as customers, rather than citizens, and act accordingly (Deakin, 1993).

Through the years of continuous Conservative government since 1979, this philosophy and accompanying programs has manifested itself in a series of fundamental changes in the nature of the British state, including: privatization of nationalized industries; the effective transfer of social housing from local government to nonprofit housing associations; spinning off of service providing sections of the central government bureaucracy into semi-autonomous ("Next Steps") agencies, with a stronger managerial emphasis and business ethic; compulsory competitive tendering of many local government services; and the introduction of an internal market into the National Health Service. Although a full-fledged assault on traditional health and social services provision did not occur until some time after the Conservatives' third election victory in 1987, earlier, more subtle policy shifts paved the way for the widespread introduction of POS contracting by the third Thatcher government.

At the same time as this initiative was being launched in 1979, the new government was faced with rapidly increasing unemployment following the second oil shock and the highly deflationary economic policies pursued by Chancellor of the Exchequer Geoffrey Howe. With the new ideological shift away from state service provision, the government looked to nonprofits to provide a means to keep the newly unemployed occupied and reduce the burgeoning unemployment figures. Funding was offered to nonprofits under the government's Community Programme: an employment creation scheme under which the government paid the wages of formerly unemployed workers engaged in "socially useful" activities—in practice largely personal social services or environmental projects—provided that the work undertaken would not otherwise have been done for 2 years. The Community Programme was ineffective at reducing unemployment (Layard, 1994) but rejuvenated the service provision role of nonprofits (Hawley, 1992). Although the sums of money involved were small for government, they were significant for the sector.

Thus a major impetus to the regrowth of nonprofit direct service provision was provided, which had largely been in abeyance since the Second World War. When the Community Programme was phased out, many providers successfully lobbied local government to take over responsibility for funding activities set up under it (Hawley, 1992). Unbeknown to those concerned at the time, the scene had been set for the introduction of POS contracting into the UK personal social services system. Although the principal driving force arose from developments in central government policy, the legacy of the Community Programme led some, though by no means all, in both local government and the nonprofit sector to have their own reasons to support POS.

Hence, within all three organizational constituencies involved in the development of contracting, there were those with reasons to support it, albeit with their own interpretation of what it would imply. Not surprisingly, despite a new rhetoric to the contrary, neither service users nor carers played any significant role in the decisions that led to POS contracting. Indeed, there is no data about the views of users or carers on the principle or implementation of POS contracting.

Reasons for Introducing POS

The key factor behind the introduction of POS was undoubtedly central government's policy of Community Care, arising out of the white paper *Caring for People* (Secretaries of State for Health, Social Security, Wales and Scotland, 1989) and resulting in the passage of the National Health Service and Community Care Act of 1990. Rapidly increasing costs of residential care for elderly people, together with a long-standing paper commitment to reduce residential services in favor of care within the community, had led the government to re-examine the whole system of provision in 1988.

Unusual for the UK welfare state, before the introduction of the new policy, residential care for elderly people was available on what was essentially a voucher basis. Care costs, up to a maximum of £160 ($240) per week (£183/$275 in London), were paid directly to residential care homes for those assessed as eligible. The choice of provider lay with the individual, provided that the chosen home did not charge more than the state would bear. Most homes were in the private, for-profit sector. Together with other aspects of the UK benefit system, this entitlement created an incentive for elderly people to go into residential care (Glennerster & Le Grand, 1994), regardless of whether they might better be cared for at home. Of more direct concern to the government was the impact that this open-ended commitment was having on the social security budget. The cost of support for people in independent residential and nursing homes rose from £10 million ($15 million) in 1979 to £1,000 million ($1,500 million) in May 1989 (Secretaries of State for Health, Social Security, Wales and Scotland, 1989).

These rising costs led the government to commission a leading businessman, Sir Roy Griffiths, to examine the provision of services not only to the elderly but also to people with learning difficulties (mental handicap), mental illness, or physical disability. His recommendations formed the basis of the subsequent Community Care policy, implementation of which began in April 1992. In direct contrast to most of the government's reforms of public service, the new proposals allocated a large role to local authorities. Authorities would have the principal role in managing services and assessing needs.

In line with the government's intention to introduce a market ethos into statutory services, actual provision would largely be the role of the "independent" sector—nonprofit agencies and for-profits. Local authorities were to become "enablers" rather than providers. Although the legislation did not specifically require the use of contracts, the development of POS contracting as the primary mechanism for ensuring service provision was a central element of the policy. Central government expected a formalization of relations between local authorities and nonprofit service providers through the use of binding legal contracts. Indeed, grants were redefined as a form of contract appropriate in limited circumstances (Department of Health, 1991), thus extending the notion of contracting as the norm to previously existing arrangements.

If central government's reasons for promoting POS contracting were primarily ideological, those of local government and elements of the nonprofit sector were far more practical. A shift by some local authorities, away from paternalism and toward greater choice and involvement for users of services, led to a new emphasis on quality and evaluation. Local authorities sought to ensure that services provided by nonprofits were subsumed within this new ethos by imposing tighter conditions on grant aid.

At the same time, and of wider significance, local authorities became increasingly concerned about how nonprofits were spending public money and sought greater accountability for the use of public funds. This was probably an inevitable corollary of the expansion of funding in the 1980s (Hawley, 1992), but was promoted by three further factors. First, cuts in local government funding in the late 1980s, together with capping limits on local government expenditure imposed by central government, led authorities to scrutinize their expenditure more carefully than they had in the easier financial climate of earlier years. Second, funding by some authorities of often highly politicized and easily stereotyped groups representing marginalized sections of society, especially black or lesbian and gay groups, attracted considerable adverse publicity. This led to both greater public concern about the use of statutory funds to finance nonprofit agencies and greater caution by elected representatives and local government officers in the distribution of grants. Finally, the expansion of funding exposed problems of under-management in nonprofit agencies, compounded in some cases by a culture of amateurism.

Pressure was also concurrently building within the nonprofit sector for more long-term funding. The annual grants cycle left nonprofits exposed to higher risk and higher costs, particularly where long-term financial commitments, such as leases, were required to set up service provision on the scale now expected. The more professionalized end of the nonprofit sector sought escape from the risk of arbitrary decisions inherent in the old grants culture and saw attractions in legally binding, long-term funding commitments. In addition, there was an increased recognition in parts of the sector of the need to become more professional and efficient in operations; what has been termed the "new managerialism" (Deakin, 1995) was beginning to emerge. For many in the nonprofit sector, however, the very language of contracting, and its implications of commercialization, were anathema.

Moreover, while there were those within all three constituencies who had reasons to support POS contracting, they each had their own interpretation of how the policy should be implemented. Central government saw the "enabling" role of local government as one of market creation and the "mixed economy of care" as a market in which statutory provision would play a purely residual role. Central government argued that a multitude of competing providers would encourage innovation, increase user choice, and lead to higher quality services and better value for money (Secretaries of State for Health, Social Security, Wales & Scotland, 1989).

In contrast, those local authorities that saw any advantages in an "enabling" role interpreted it as a complement rather than a substitute to direct provision, a means of mobilizing community-based resources and reaching out to traditionally excluded sections of the community (Wistow et al., 1992). Although there was a recognition that direct service provision would be reduced in the future, most local authorities sought to ensure that statutory services maintained a significant presence in the "mixed economy".

Finally, where nonprofit organizations could see attractions in the new proposals, it was as a means for leveraging larger amounts of state funding, on a more secure basis, for mission-centered activities. The appropriateness of those missions as a basis for state-funded provision was never questioned, nor was the basis of accountability that would be implied when service provision is determined by nonprofit missions rather than democratically elected authorities. A large part of the nonprofit sector, however, responded to the proposed change with caution or outright hostility.

CONCERNS VERSUS EXPERIENCE
WITH PURCHASE OF SERVICE

Fears, Hopes and Reality

The arrival of POS contracting on the nonprofit policy agenda brought forward a torrent of publications and opinions that has yet to abate. Most of the views shared a common analysis and raised similar issues. In large part, the debate was conducted on theoretical grounds, with few attempts to examine cross-national empirical evidence. It was not until 1992 that US experience was brought into the debate in the UK (Gutch, 1992) and examination of continental European models still remains rare today. Even the earlier experience of UK nonprofit providers of vocational training were largely ignored (although see NCVO, 1991a, for an exception).

In 1989, in an early response to the developing policy, the National Council for Voluntary Organizations convened the Voluntary Sector Working Group on Contracting Out. The Group's second guidance notes for voluntary groups (NCVO, 1989) listed 10 problems and ten opportunities presented by contracting. Although some ingenuity was required by the authors to present the views of the sector in this neatly balanced form, the notes provide a comprehensive picture of the hopes and fears of many UK nonprofit social services agencies at the time. As such, they make a useful benchmark against which to assess the subsequent implementation of POS contracting. Although it is still too early to assess the final impact of the policy on the shape of the UK nonprofit sector, evidence to date suggests that many of the fears were exaggerated or misplaced, while modest progress toward the hoped-for gains has been achieved.

Fears

Fears about contracting clearly outweighed expected advantages, even in those analyses, such as NCVOs, that sought to portray a balanced view. The key problems were seen as:

Distortion and Loss of Independence. Agencies feared that funders would use contract specifications to increase their control over the nature of services, the client group, or both, to the detriment of voluntary sector independence and mission-led activity. Nonprofit independence needs to be seen along a number of dimensions (Perri 6, 1994a) and concerns about aspects of independence clearly underlie a number of the fears expressed. Equally, greater statutory funding was often seen as a benefit of contracting, even though this would undermine financial independence.

Mission distortion was clearly seen as the principal threat to independence. However, there is little evidence that this has taken place. For example, Hedley and Rochester (1991, p. 7) found, in a study of respite care providers, that in all but one case examined, the providers had been able to maintain their "bottom line" principles: "Most schemes felt that they had gained financial security without compromising any of their principles." Goulding (1993) supports the contention that nonprofit agencies have been able to contract for service provision without substantial mission distortion, as does our own survey.

In particular, nonprofits seem to have been able to resist attempts to impose control over the nature of services they offer through the specification within the contract of services to be provided. Our survey found that service specifications written exclusively by funders were rarer even than those written exclusively by providers, whereas the overwhelming majority were jointly determined. In only 10 of the 12 contracts studied by Common and Flynn (1992) was the service specification imposed on the provider. The text of some contracts contains an explicit statement of the nonprofits' mission and independence.

Lewis (1994), Hedley and Rochester (1991), and our survey all point to attempts by funders to increase their control over referrals to the service. This can be seen as an attempt to target service provision to clients who are a high priority for the authority, or simply as an attempt to prevent "creaming" by nonprofits serving low-dependency clients. In addition, this behavior would conform to the analysis of Leat (1988) that authorities might not find it time-efficient to make nonprofits accountable. If it is not viable for authorities to control the nature of service provision, it may be more rational for them simply to determine the clients to be served. However, even here nonprofits have generally been able to maintain a power of veto over referrals (Common & Flynn, 1992; Hedley & Rochester, 1991).

Loss of Advocacy and Campaigning. Traditional advocacy and campaigning roles were thought to be at risk, because agencies would fear "biting the hand that feeds them;" because the pressures of contract management would squeeze out other activities; or because agencies would not be able to advocate or campaign about services they themselves would be running. These fears, another aspect of independence, have only partially been borne out.

Hedley and Rochester (1991) found some evidence that contracting had led to a reduction in advocacy, principally because resources were being diverted into contract management. However, our survey found no evidence of reduced campaigning or advocacy among nonprofits which had seen a significant increase in their contractual income over the last 2 years.

The issue cannot, however, be addressed solely through micro-level studies. Although some organizations, offered large contracts, will inevitably shift away from campaigning and toward service provision, this is only part of the picture. It is easy to find examples in the precontract era of UK nonprofits, established as advocates, which became primarily service providers. It would be surprising if this did not occur in the future. However, a casual glance at the makeup of the UK nonprofit sector would suggest that these advocates-turned-providers are replaced by a new generation of campaigning and advocacy organizations, so that the loss of campaigning at the micro level is compensated within the sector as a whole. A comprehensive macro-level study would therefore be needed to address the claim that advocacy and campaigning is being undermined by contracting. In the absence of such a study, and with the micro data lending only qualified support to concerns about loss of campaigning, the most that can be said with any confidence is that at the organizational level, there have been some cases of shifts away from campaigning and advocacy.

Inflexibility and Loss of Innovation. Contracts were seen as locking agencies into fixed ways of working, stifling innovation and development. This again does not seem to have been borne out.

The claim to innovation by nonprofits needs to be treated with some scepticism. Empirical studies are thin on this ground and agencies may label incremental change as innovation (Osborne, 1994). Even allowing for a wider range of activities than those that should properly be termed "innovative," however, our survey found no evidence of restrictions arising from contracting. Osborne (1994) attributes the tendency of nonprofits to interpret developmental activities as innovative as a response to actual or perceived funder expectations. This may undermine attempts to identify the impact of contracting on innovation, with agencies underreporting the impact of contracting on innovation as a market response to actual or perceived funder demands. It also requires that the initial claim to be innovative be treated with caution, however.

Impact on Volunteers. It was thought that volunteers might react against the "commercial" ethos of contracting and that use of volunteers would decline, or that their roles would be downgraded. Our survey could find no evidence to support this, with no greater tendency for volunteer use to fall among agencies that had seen a significant increase in their contractual income over the last 2 years. However, Lewis (1994) cites a day-care provider whose volunteer manager resigned over increased "professionalization" and a shift away from direct involvement in providing services toward greater management responsibility. Meadows (1992) also express concern about the impact of increasing management demands on volunteers.

In particular, contracting has placed a heavy burden on board members (Harris, 1993) that could potentially lead to difficulties in recruitment and retention. In extreme cases, if board members no longer feel a commitment to the agency's purpose, they may simply fail to turn up at meetings, thus resigning by default (Collins, 1988). This may be acting as a check on pressures toward mission distortion (Rochester, 1992).

The position is complicated by increasing demands on the pool of citizens from which board members are drawn. Harris (1990) indicates that board members come from a fairly restricted group of "socially conscious" citizens. The demand for the services of such people is rising as a consequence of other elements of the government's project of redefining governance, such as local management of schools or the transference of hospitals to semi-independent NHS Trusts. There are indications that demand for board members may begin to outstrip the available supply (Harris, 1989), a situation that can only be compounded by the greater demands that contracting makes.

Squeezing Out. Small agencies and those tackling "unpopular causes" feared that they would lose out to larger more mainstream agencies, both because small agencies would lack the resources needed for contract management, and because cautious purchasers might prefer "household name" providers.

There is little evidence that contracting has had an adverse impact on small agencies per se. In many cases, contracting has involved a change in the nature of existing relationships (Common & Flynn, 1992; Hedley & Rochester, 1991; Meadows, 1992) rather than the development of new government/nonprofit relations, so that the existing pattern of service providers has been maintained. Contracting has often been the responsibility of local authority officers formerly responsible for relations with the local nonprofit sector. Furthermore, many nonprofits are essentially local monopoly providers so that the possibilities of squeezing out do not arise.

The position of agencies tackling "unpopular causes" or representing marginalized communities is, however, less clear. Although there is no evidence that such agencies are losing funding as a result of contracting, our survey suggests that agencies tackling "unpopular causes" may be more prone to interference by funders in the nature of service provision, which would lend some qualified support to the squeezing-out hypothesis. However, this result could arise because such agencies are more sensitive to the actions of their funders and hence more likely to interpret actions as interference. Qaiyoom (1992b) argues that the Black nonprofit organizations may lose out because of the discretion inherent in the negotiated, as opposed to openly competitive, processes of contracting advocated by much of the rest of the nonprofit sector (e.g., NCVO, 1991b).

Charitable Subsidy. Agencies were concerned that they would have to use charitable resources to underwrite contracts for services that previously had been seen as the responsibility of the state.

Some degree of charitable subsidy of contracts seems common. Meadows (1992), Lewis (1993), and our survey all identify cases of financial "topping up" of contracts. In some cases, the additional funds clearly come from other statutory sources, but charitable foundations were the most widely cited source of "top up" in our survey. Subsidy is not universal, however, all but one of the respite care schemes examined by Hedley and Rochester (1991) had avoided using their own funds to support contracts. Similarly, the learning difficulties charity studied by Goulding (1993, p. 18) "negotiated care costs up to the level they required to fully operate the scheme."

Equally, the extent to which subsidy is a result of contracting is difficult to determine. It is likely, in many cases, that subsidies have continued where contracts have replaced former grant agreements. Impressionistic evidence suggests that subsidies are more likely where grants have been converted into contracts than where wholly new services have been established on a contractual basis. In part, this may reflect the view that, whereas in the past nonprofit service provision was "the icing on the cake" of the welfare state, services now being contracted are the cake itself, and hence should be paid for entirely by the state. Certainly there is widespread resistance to using charitable funds to subsidize services that are clearly seen as statutory responsibilities.

Increased Costs and Liabilities. Agencies were concerned about the costs of preparing for, negotiating, and managing contracts. In addition, charity trustees were concerned above the high levels of personal liability incurred by taking on large-scale contracted provision.

High transaction costs have been an overriding feature of the development of POS contracting in the UK, just as they also dominate UK literature on the US contracting experience (e.g., Gutch, 1992; Richardson, 1993). All the studies emphasize the length of time taken to negotiate agreements and the diversion of resources into developing contracts. Common and Flynn (1992) cite one organization that incurred £30,000 ($45,000) of staff time costs negotiating a single contract. Contract negotiations generally took between 6 months and 2 years to complete. Lewis (1993) cites the case of a nonprofit director who now spends 75% of her time working on the contract. These are not isolated cases: the weight of evidence in case studies suggests that high transaction costs are virtually universal.

These problems have been exacerbated by years of under-management within many nonprofits and a "cascade of change" (Audit Commission, 1992) imposed on local authorities. The rapid growth of nonprofit service provision during the 1980s, in an environment where nonprofits "came to see themselves as having a priority call on public money and grant aid as a natural right" (Hawley, 1992, p. 18), led perhaps inevitably to chronic undermanagement in many organizations. Services, and in some cases whole new organizations, sprung up overnight on the back of job creation schemes. Management development inevitably lagged behind, in some cases hindered by a culture that saw the language and practices of professionalism as alien and unwelcome.

By the early 1990s, the "new managerialism" had begun to arrive, and contracting probably only acted as a spur to many processes, such as the implementation of proper financial controls, monitoring, and evaluation procedures, that would have been needed in any case. Our survey found that in the last 2 years alone, 45% of respondents had undergone internal restructuring, 25% had launched a new corporate image, and 24% had used management consultants. These developments were attributed only in a minority of cases to the impact of contracting, and organizations that had not seen a significant increase in their contractual income were as likely to have undertaken change as those that had.

Furthermore, local authorities were subjected to a series of changes that impacted heavily on social services departments, which were responsible for the majority of contract negotiations. The NHS and Community Care Act of 1990 required authorities to separate their purchasing units from direct provision, leading most authorities to implement sweeping internal restructuring. Many of those with responsibility for contract negotiation were new in the role.

In addition to this internal restructuring, the government announced a review of the structure of local government in general across most of the UK in 1990. The review was initially expected to recommend widespread replacement of existing two-tier local government by unitary authorities. County councils, which have responsibility for social services, were expected to be the main casualties of the process, and most embarked on a fight for survival. At the same time, social services departments had to implement wide-ranging reforms arising from the Children Act of 1989, while local government in general was facing the extension of compulsory competitive tendering into many white-collar services (though not social services) and the introduction of a new local tax to replace the politically disastrous poll tax.

Meadows (1992) and Hedley and Rochester (1991) both emphasize the problems this turmoil caused in some contract negotiations. Hedley and Rochester cite one nonprofit agency that had to liaise with 13 different Health and Social Services officers in the course of negotiating a single contract. Some well-briefed nonprofits were able to exploit the lack of preparation of many local authority negotiators (Age Concern, 1990). However, many others were baffled by continual changes of personnel, departmental structures and objectives.

Overall, it is clear that POS contracting has involved some deadweight costs, although the extreme level of costs involved in some early contracting negotiations almost certainly include a large element of necessary management development and one-off adaptation costs.

The effect of greater liability is harder to determine. Interest in trustee liability insurance has risen over the last few years (Gill & Kirkland, 1993). This does not generally cover contract risks, however, and is more likely to be a result of greater interest in the role of trustees (NCVO, 1992) and a consequent greater awareness of existing liabilities. While POS contracting has been a factor behind this new interest in the role of trustees, it needs to be seen within the context of greater interest in issues of accountability and governance of nonprofits generally.

Our survey does find a slightly greater propensity to incorporate among agencies with significantly increased contract income. Contracting was rarely cited as the reason for incorporation, however. There is little evidence to suggest that contracting has led to a substantial exodus of board members. We are aware of only one publicized example of liabilities being incurred by trustees through the collapse of contracts (Edwards, 1992). Local authorities may, in any event, prove reluctant to pursue claims against voluntary board members.

Impact on Partnership. Nonprofits were concerned about a shift away from cooperative relations both among agencies and between agencies and funders. Although, in fact, nonprofits had always competed for grants, they feared that a more openly competitive environment would undermine cooperative working practices. Furthermore, the rhetoric of partnership between local government and nonprofits had become a major theme in the 1980s. Organizations that had adopted insider lobbying strategies were also concerned that their influence would be reduced in a world of competitive tendering.

These fears have not been borne out. Partnership between funders and nonprofits was frequently little more than rhetoric in the first place. Lewis (1994) argues that partnership often meant little more than determining grant allocations and that it was not until the enactment of the same legislation that paved the way for contracting that voluntary agencies were given a role in joint planning:

> Thus renewed emphasis on the importance of partnership in the sense of collaboration has to be put alongside the parallel shift in the way in which the role of voluntary organizations as service providers is being seen. (p. 209)

Moreover, contracting has rarely involved arms-length relations with funders. Common and Flynn (1992) found that formal selection procedures were rare, with purchasers generally looking to known providers. They also emphasize the role of trust and individual relations in managing the contracting relationship. More formal contract relations were generally only found in residential care, where the existence of a large number of providers previously operating in a voucherized market has led to more traditional market-type relations.

More open competition among nonprofits has not emerged. In part this reflects the near-monopoly position that many nonprofits enjoy in their locality (Hedley & Rochester, 1991). In part, it arises from a deeply entrenched culture of cooperation. When one English County Council proposed to put contracts out to open competitive tender, local nonprofits responded by forming a cartel. In time, such responses may attract the attention of the regulatory authorities (Perri 6, 1994b). Anecdotal evidence suggests, however, that such responses are common where purchasers have attempted to promote greater competition.

Inadequate Infrastructure. Many nonprofits, especially at the local level, looked to external agencies for the provision of free technical assistance. Although the UK had a better developed infrastructure than many parts of the US, it was far from universal. It was widely feared that agencies which depended on this source of advice and technical assistance would not be able to obtain adequate support. At the same time, there was concern that the existing infrastructure would be run down, as purchasers concentrated on frontline service provision.

To date, there is little evidence of a collapse of infrastructure. The sheer volume of publications, seminars and training programs that have been produced on contracting over the last few years means that nonprofits are now more likely to face too many sources of advice rather than too few. Although, as stated above, previous undermanagement meant that the demand for advice within many agencies was very high, it would be hard to sustain an argument that an equal supply of advice has not been made available, often subsidized by central or local government.

Opportunities

Security. Principal among the perceived advantages of POS was greater security of funding—in particular, longer-term agreements and an escape from the annual grants cycle. There was a widespread expectation that contracts would be for longer durations than grants.

Although experiences have been mixed, many contracts are for longer durations than the traditional 1-year grant cycle. Seven of the twelve contracts studied by Common and Flynn (1992) were for more than 1 year, and one was of indefinite duration. This is fairly typical, certainly among contracts negotiated early in the shift toward POS. Greater financial security was widely seen as an advantage among the respite care organizations examined by Hedley and Rochester (1991). One scheme coordinator described how "For the first time I really feel the scheme is here to stay (p. 7)," after over 10 years of annual grant applications. Furthermore, there are examples of nonprofits using their new legal rights to prevent proposed funding cuts (NCVO, 1991c).

However, some local authorities have refused to offer contracts for more than 1 year, arguing that because their own funding is uncertain year-to-year, they are not in a position to make long-term commitments. Our survey found that, where contracts replaced existing grants, 37% were for longer durations, but the majority were for the same period. This may reflect a greater caution among purchasers as the scale of contracting increases. The risk to purchasers of entering a few long-term agreements is very low, especially where contracts are for mainstream services that are almost certain to be protected against any cuts. However, as the scale of contracting has grown (Mocroft, 1995), the risks to authorities of long-term agreements have risen accordingly. Although authorities could almost certainly manage the risks involved far more easily than often undercapitalized nonprofits, there appears to be an increasing tendency to transfer the whole of the risk onto providers. Richardson (1993) has argued that, in the long run, this is likely to increase total costs and could lead to a withdrawal of providers.

Moreover, we found that many contracts have no-fault termination clauses. These effectively reduce the length of the contract to the length of the termination period. Although there is no evidence of the widespread use of such clauses, they must bring into question how real the apparent increase in security is.

Overall, it appears that a significant minority of nonprofits has gained greater security, both through the greater duration of funding agreements and from the binding nature of contracts. However, risk aversion by local authorities has limited the extent of these gains, and may become a more significant factor as contracting comes to encompass a higher proportion of total expenditure.

Clarity. It was hoped that the process of negotiating and agreeing on contracts would help voluntary agencies to become more mission-focused and raise standards.

This is probably the most widely accepted gain from POS contracting. Meadows (1992), Hedley and Rochester (1991), and Lewis (1993) all point to increased clarity arising out of the contracting process. Contracting appears to have acted as a welcome spur to improve management and information systems that had lagged behind the growth of service provision in the 1980s.

Income Generation. There was an expectation that contracting out of existing services might give the sector an opportunity to expand its role and increase income. There was also a hope that the end of the assumption of direct provision by local government would open a debate about provision in which nonprofits would be better able to promote mission-based service provision techniques.

Wistow et al. (1992) showed that few local authorities, regardless of political persuasion, were convinced of the case for contracting out existing direct service provision. Instead, most saw contracting as concerned with formalizing existing grant aid agreements and as a means to develop new services outside of the statutory sector. Unlike the case in the US, few authorities have engaged in widespread transfers of existing statutory services to nonprofit or for-profit providers. In addition, most of the funding transferred to local authorities for Community Care will go to residential care for elderly people, where the bulk of provision is already in the for-profit sector.

Thus, expectations of substantial increases in funding available to nonprofits have not been met. Survey evidence of total local authority funding (Mocroft, 1995) confirms this view. Growth of the market is also limited in many cases by supply-side constraints (Wistow et al., 1992). In many cases, potential providers simply do not exist, and capital shortages arising from the nonprofit distribution constraint may limit the ability of nonprofits to exploit rapid increases in the market if they do occur. However, there does appear to be a greater openness to the provision of new services in the nonprofit sector. Together with central government requirements that 85% of funds transferred under the policy be spent on purchasing contracted services rather than direct provision, the result will be a gradual increase in the size of the market for care.

Equality. The grant culture was often perceived as putting nonprofits into the role of supplicant. The shift toward an explicit service provision role and the replacement of grant applications with contract negotiations was seen as an opportunity to develop a more equal relationship with local authorities.

At least for some contracting nonprofits, this hope has been realized. Hedley and Rochester (1991, p. 7) describe a new recognition of nonprofits as bona fide service providers, "more than icing on the cake." This was seen as reinforcing security gains, as nonprofits felt, sometimes for the first time, that purchasers understood and valued their services and saw them as an integral part of overall service provision, rather than an easily cut optional extra.

User Involvement. A more open process of determining services to be provided was seen as providing an opening for greater involvement by service users (and nonprofits as their advocates) in planning and managing service provision.

Flynn and Hurley (1993) found no evidence that contracting had led to greater user involvement or user choice. Services were designed by purchasers or providers with little user input. Even monitoring and evaluation showed no significant element of user involvement. Moreover, contracting had not led to increased choice for users, which had been one of the claims made for it by central government (Secretaries of State for Health, Social Security, Wales and Scotland, 1989). In many cases, monopoly provision precluded choice. Even if there were multiple providers, there was rarely enough slack in the system, at least in the short term, to offer a choice.

Other Gains. Two further possible advantages were listed in the Working Group guidance: improved cost-effectiveness, and a more open process. Although heavily hedged, there was a recognition that competitive tendering might lead to cost savings. It was also argued that better costing of services might lead to increased resources by removing hidden subsidies (a point somewhat in contradiction to the concern about abuse of charitable subsidies). Traditionally marginalized agencies hoped that a more open process of determining funding might make it easier for them to obtain statutory funds (this is clearly contrary to the argument about squeezing out). Since both of these claims were based on an assumption of openly competitive tendering that has not been borne out, it is unlikely that these advantages have been realized. However, no direct evidence exists either way.

IMPLEMENTATION

Many of the concerns expressed by nonprofits about the proposed shift toward POS contracting arose from assumptions about the shape of the proposed market for care that have not been borne out. Virtually all the fears expressed are best understood as arising from a vision of a market dominated by a single, powerful purchaser (the local authority for most service providers) determining the services to be provided, writing the contracts, and contracting with the lowest bidder prepared to meet the purchaser's needs. In such a market, nonprofit mission or independence would count for little. The details of the services to be provided would be determined exclusively by the local authority, down to the number of potatoes on the menu (Wistow et al., 1992).

Such a vision was not without foundation. Nonprofits looked to the experience of Compulsory Competitive Tendering (CCT) following the Local Government Act of 1988. This required local authorities to put services such as rubbish collection and building cleaning out to competitive tender. The procedures to be followed were complex and tightly defined. Their stated purpose was to ensure that councils could not unfairly favor in-house bids. Opponents of the policy argued that the rules were intended simply to prevent in-house bids from winning, thus forcing provision out into the for-profit sector. In practice, the majority of contracts remained with in-house providers, although in some cases only after cuts in the pay, conditions, or numbers of staff. Contracts, however, were invariably non-negotiable, written in immense, often excessive, detail and subject to open competitive tender. Transaction costs were substantial (Walsh, n. d.).

Although examples of social care contracts let on this basis can be found in the UK, this model has not made substantial headway. The closest examples are to be found in residential care for elderly people, where there was already a highly developed voucherized market in operation. Instead, most contracts with nonprofits have been let on a negotiated basis, often to providers with long-standing relations with purchasing authorities that have simply been adapted to the new funding regime. Several reasons can be identified as to why the market for care did not develop along the lines that were clearly feared by nonprofits. This analysis will give some indication as to how the market might develop in the future.

First, the legislative framework was very different. CCT has not been applied to social care, giving local authorities considerable discretion in their purchasing policies. Although nonprofits in the late 1980s could not be sure that the introduction of POS contracting would not be accompanied by the extension of CCT to social services, it was never likely to be a viable option for government. Even the extension to white-collar services, such as legal or finance, where there were existing markets, involved a substantial alteration of the procedures to account for the greater complexity of these tasks.

Moreover, because few local authorities were enthusiastic about CCT, it was unlikely that they would use its procedures when they were not forced to. Even those authorities which were ideological supporters of contracting out generally preferred to do so on their own terms, rather than applying centrally determined rules which many saw as a bureaucrat's vision of how a market ought to work, owing more to textbook economics than real life.

In practice, most authorities, regardless of political persuasion, saw social care as different (Wistow et al., 1992). There was little support for tightly drawn or excessively detailed service specifications, the expectation of which fuelled many nonprofit fears. Instead, most understood that drawing up such specifications invited providers to exploit loopholes or led to impossibly high administrative costs. The expressed desire instead was for flexibility and trust.

This attitude reflects the fact that implementation of the policy was in the hands of social work professionals whose traditional values and culture were far removed from notions of market development. Indeed, their attitudes were frequently closer to those of the nonprofit providers with whom they were negotiating than to the intention of the policy. This was often brought into stark relief by the involvement of purchaser staff from outside of social services, especially lawyers, who often failed to understand the prevailing ethos and sought to work more in the CCT tradition (Goulding, 1993).

Moreover, the vision of the market as determined by monopoly purchasing power (monopsony) in the hands of local authorities ignored two critical aspects of the market for care as it existed when POS was being introduced. First, many nonprofits failed to recognize that they, too, had considerable monopoly power; and second, there was a general failure to realize the restrictions imposed on purchasers by the impact that their decisions would have on the shape of the future market. These factors would almost certainly have prevented the "nightmare vision" of contracting from arising even in the absence of other restraints.

Unused to thinking in market terms and viewing themselves as supplicants for grant aid, many nonprofits failed to recognize their true market position. Many nonprofits saw themselves as powerless against the monolith of the statutory welfare state. Once expanded, however, direct provision ceased to be a politically acceptable option. Many providers enjoyed substantial or even absolute local monopoly power, particularly in niche markets for specialist services. Because a major purpose of the new policy was to support people within the community, using providers from outside the locality was rarely an option.

For some services, particularly in sparsely populated rural areas, the number of clients is always likely to be too small to sustain more than one provider, and once established, a provider agency will enjoy considerable power. Moreover, where continual service to a client group is a factor, there will be substantial welfare costs involved in any attempt to award the contract to a competitor. Hence, first mover advantages will act to further limit competition.

Furthermore, because of their monopsony power, purchasers cannot ignore the consequences of their purchasing decisions. Providers which lose contracts cannot pick up business elsewhere and may simply go out of business, reducing the extent of competition in subsequent contracting rounds. Thus the opportunities for purchasers to use competition to bid down prices may prove self-defeating in the long run. Furthermore, if local authorities wish to increase competition, they will have to subsidize or otherwise encourage new market entrants (Knapp, 1995). Development of a market for care is likely to be slow for as long as funding remains tight.

The State of the Market

The market for care that was to be the centerpiece of the UK government's Community Care policy remains underdeveloped and patchy. Alternative visions of contracting, monopoly power, and limitations in the nature of the market itself combined with conflicting priorities and natural caution among local authority staff dealing with vulnerable people to ensure that change has been incremental rather than radical.

This is not to say that implementation has been painless, either for nonprofits or local government. Years of under-management have had to be rectified within nonprofits, some of which faced a continual struggle simply to survive in the face of rising demand and falling funding. At the same time, negotiations have often been complicated by continual changes imposed upon local government, itself sometimes facing a struggle to survive in the face of the Local Government Review. Moreover, although some of the hoped-for benefits have undoubtedly been fulfilled, purchasers have frequently transferred both risks and administrative costs onto nonprofit providers. But the balance has been in the fulfilment of hopes, rather the realization of fears.

The fears with which nonprofits approached implementation substantially arose from a vision of the market based more on ministerial rhetoric than practical reality. Misled by the experiences of Compulsory Competitive Tendering, nonprofits failed either to recognize their own market power or to understand the limitations on purchasers' intentions or freedom of action. Three years into implementation, it is apparent that policy has been reinterpreted in such a way as to be compatible with the values and interests of those responsible for implementation (Wistow et al., 1992), rather than the policymakers. The current state of the market better reflects local government's desire for greater accountability over the use of public money, and nonprofits' desire for a larger stake in a pluralist welfare state, than the victory of market values over the traditions of social care.

Developments

If the "contract nightmare" has failed to appear, nonprofits may yet have reason to be concerned about the developing market for care. Part of the reason that contracting has not had the scope of impact predicted is that market development is a slow process, especially when funds are restricted. There are further changes to come, and they may yet threaten the position of many nonprofit service providers.

Although POS contracting is a relatively new development in the UK, it is hardly so elsewhere. Both in the US and in Continental Europe, mature contracted markets for personal social services exist, and nonprofits are often dominant providers. In both cases, however, competition is restricted by features of the market that have not been reproduced in the UK.

United States social services provision depends to a great extent on charitable subsidy. Most nonprofits subsidize their contracts by 10 to 20% from private sources, and such subsidies are often seen as evidence of value for money by purchasers (Richardson, 1993). This acts as a substantial barrier to for-profit competition; there is little incentive for for-profits to bid for contracts that need to be subsidized.

The attitudes toward welfare provision that underlie this funding structure are not replicated in the UK, however. Despite Ministerial attempts to dismiss its significance, the public still holds to collectivist values in welfare and expects the state to fund provision (Deakin, 1993). Although the boundaries of statutory responsibility have become increasingly blurred, there remains a deeply felt hostility within the nonprofit sector to the use of charitable funds to subsidize statutory services. Indeed, some charitable foundations have used contracting as an opportunity to review existing policies with the intention of phasing out current subsidies.

Moreover, levels of giving are simply not high enough to sustain such an approach. Because both individual and corporate donors pay higher taxes in part to fund the welfare state, they are understandable unwilling to donate again on the scale that would be needed. Wholesale undercutting of for-profit competition through the use of charitable subsidy is not an option in the UK.

Where there is a substantial element of nonprofit service provision in Continental Europe, such as in Germany, the Netherlands, or Italy, nonprofits are protected from competition by institutional biases toward the use of nonprofits. Such biases are unlikely to operate within the UK. Central government sees both nonprofits and for-profits as part of an "independent sector" and has, if anything, been more concerned about promoting the role of for-profit providers (Department of Health, 1992).

Some local government officers and elected representatives favor nonprofits. One metropolitan authority in the north of England has apparently refused to contract with any for-profit providers, with one councillor reportedly saying he would rather burn the council's care homes than see them taken over by the private sector. Such attitudes, however, are now unusual as local authorities, regardless of political persuasion, increasingly look to work in partnership with local businesses.

For-profit providers also rarely fit the negative stereotypes of "profit before people" that underlie such attitudes. Many are run by people of the same social care background as purchasers; increasingly, for-profit providers are being established by former local government staff, who no longer see a future for direct statutory provision.

Without either financial or institutional barriers to for-profit competition, it is questionable whether nonprofits will be able to survive outside of particular market niches. The development of a contracted market for vocational training for unemployed people is an instructive example here. When government first sought to contract out provision to external providers in the late 1970s and early 1980s, the only available contractors were nonprofits, which consequently dominated the market. As the policy matured, however, and against a background of continual changes in programs and funding, for-profit providers gradually took over. Nonprofits now survive only in niche markets, such as training for ex-offenders or people with disabilities.

Nonprofits face a number of disadvantages in competing with for-profits. Because they cannot distribute profits, nonprofits have difficulty in accessing capital, and many are chronically undercapitalized. At the local level, this has often been exacerbated by the insistence of local government on drawing back any unspent monies at the end of each year, undermining the ability of nonprofits to build up a hedge against temporary setbacks (Smith & Lipsky, 1993). A tradition of consensual management and often conflicting aims and opinions among board members can also lead to nonprofits being unable to react quickly to changing developments.

Furthermore, nonprofits' mission focus can serve to make them a poor choice for purchasers. Where government is prepared to hand over control of day-to-day service provision to contractors, nonprofit missions may be seen as providing a distinct advantage in trustworthiness over for-profits (Wistow et al., 1992). The extent of the democratic mandate over the nature of service provision remains high within the UK, however. Where purchasers continue to see it as their role to determine how services are to be provided, with contracting serving purely to promote efficiency and not pluralism, there is likely to be a tension between the priorities of democratically elected councillors and those of mission centered nonprofits (Richardson, 1993). Unless mission and democratic decision happen to coincide, purchasers will rightly be concerned that nonprofits will put their missions before the priorities of government. Under such circumstances, it may prove more attractive to contract with for-profits.

CONCLUSION

It is too early to judge the ultimate implications of purchase-of-service contracting for the UK nonprofit sector. Although some contracts go back further, and a number were introduced in anticipation of the policy shift, the main impact of POS with UK personal social services arose out of the implementation of Community Care beginning April 1992.

To date, the impact of the policy has been largely incremental. Transaction costs have been high, and resources have been diverted into contract management that could perhaps have been better used in delivering services. In many cases, however, contracting has served as a spur to rectify undermanagement, and has fed into the wider processes driving a new managerialism in the sector. Contracting has been a difficult change for many agencies, although many of the changes it has brought may have been inevitable anyway.

The fears with which the sector faced the initial prospect of contracting have largely failed to materialize, however. In particular, we have argued that many of these fears arose from a vision of the shape of the market for care that has not been borne out. Contracting has been guided more by the desire of local government for greater accountability over the use of public money and by nonprofits for a larger role, than by the demands of market-making.

In the long run, the greatest threat to the sector may come not from the all-powerful purchasers, as originally feared, but from for-profit competition. UK nonprofits are uniquely vulnerable to for-profit competition, lacking either the buffer of charitable subsidy present in the US, or the institutional protections of Continental Europe. Ultimately, it may prove that large-scale mainstream service provision by UK nonprofits will be a temporary stage between a welfare state dominated by state provision, and one dominated by for-profits.

REFERENCES

Age Concern. (1990). In practice. *Contract Unit News, 1*(1), 3.
Audit Commission. (1992). *Community care: Managing the cascade of change.* London: HMSO.
Billis, D., & Harris, M. (1986). *An extended role for the voluntary sector: The challenge of implementation.* (PORTVAC Working Paper No. 3).
Chanan, G. (1991). *Taken for granted* (Community Development Foundation Research and Policy Paper No. 13). London: Community Development Foundation.
Collins, C. (1988). *Struggling to survive: An analysis of four voluntary organizations' experience of losing GLC funding.* (Case Study 6). London: Centre for Voluntary Organization.
Common, R., & Flynn, N. (1992). *Contracting for community care.* York: Joseph Rowntree Foundation.
Davis Smith, J. (1995). The voluntary tradition: Philanthropy and self-help in Britain, 1500–1945. In J. Davis Smith, C. Rochester, & R. Gedley, (Eds.), *An introduction to the voluntary sector.* London: Routledge.
Deakin, N. (1993, July 20–22). *Contracting in the UK: The policy context.* Paper presented at the Contracting Selling or Shrinking? conference, London, England.
Deakin, N. (1995). The perils of partnership: The voluntary sector and the state, 1945–1992. In J. D. Smith, C. Rochester, & R. Hedley, (Eds.), *An introduction to the voluntary sector* (pp. 40–65). London: Routledge.
Department of Health. (1991). *Purchase of service.* London: HMSO.
Department of Health.(1992). *Implementing community care.* London: Author.
Edwards, K. (1992). *Contracts in practice.* London: NCVO/Directory of Social Change.
Flynn, N., & Hurley, D. (1993). *The market for care.* London: Public Sector Management, London School of Economics.
Gill, T., & Kirkland, K. (1993) *Trustee liability insurance: Is it for you?* London: NCVO.

Glennester, H., & Le Grand, J. (1994). *The development of quasi-markets in welfare provision.* London: Welfare State Programme, London School of Economics.

Goulding, J. (1993). *A contract state?* (Case Study 5). London: Centre for Voluntary Organization, London School of Economics.

Gutch, R. (1991, December 16). Speech to the Contracts for Care - Building Site or Battlefield?

Gutch, R. (1992). *Contracting lessons from the U.S.* London: NCVO.

Harris, M. (1990). Voluntary leaders in voluntary welfare agencies. *Social Policy and Administration, 24,* 156–167.

Harris, M. (1993, July 20–22). Voluntary management committees: The impact of contracting. Paper presented at the Contracting Selling or Shrinking? conference, London, England.

Hawley, K. (1992). *From grants to contracts.* London: NCVO/Directory of Social Change.

Hedley, R., & Rochester, C. (1991). *Contracts at the crossroads.* Rugby: Association of Crossroads Care Attendant Schemes.

Layard, R. (1994). *Preventing long-term unemployment: An economic analysis.* London: Centre for Economic Performance, London School of Economics.

Leat, D. (1988). *Voluntary organizations and accountability.* London: NCVO.

Leat, D. (1995). Funding matters. In J. D. Smith, C. Rochester, & R. Hedley. (Eds.). *An introduction to the voluntary sector.* London: Routledge.

Lewis, J. (1993). Developing the mixed economy of care: Emerging issues for voluntary organizations, *Journal of Social Policy, 22,* 173–192.

Lewis, J. (1994). Voluntary organizations in new partnership with local authorities: The anatomy of a contract. *Social Policy and Administration, 28,* 206–220.

Meadows, A. (1992). *Reaching agreement.* London: NCVO.

Mocroft, I. (1995). A survey of local authority payments to voluntary and charitable organizations, 1992/93. In S. Saxon-Harrold & J. Kendall (Eds.), *Dimensions of the voluntary sector.* London: Charities Aid Foundation.

National Council of Voluntary Organizations. (1989). *The contract culture: The challenge for voluntary organizations: Guidance notes on contracting for voluntary groups* (No. 2). London: Author.

National Council of Voluntary Organizations. (1991a). Lessons from the training world. Supplement to Contracting In or Out? London: Author.

National Council of Voluntary Organizations. (1991b). *Working in partnership: NCVO Codes of Guidance. No. 2—Contracting.* London: Author.

National Council of Voluntary Organizations. (1991c). Contract used to reverse funding cuts. Contracting in or out? London: Author.

National Council of Voluntary Organizations. (1992). *On trust.* London: NCVO.

Osborne, S. (1994). *The once and future pioneers?* Birmingham: Aston Business School.

Qaiyoom, R. (1992a, Summer). Contracting: A Black perspective. Contracting In or Out? London: Sia.

Qaiyoom, R. (1992b). From crisis to consensus: A strategic approach for local government and the Black voluntary sector. London: Sia.

Richardson, J. (1993). *Reinventing contracts: Transatlantic perspectives on the future of contracting.* London: NCVO.

Richardson, J. (1995). *Purchase of service contracting: Some evidence on UK implementation.* London: NCVO.

Rochester, C. (1992, May). Pressure Points. *NCVO News.*

Secretaries of State for Health, Social Security, Wales and Scotland. (1989). *Caring for people.* London: HMSO.

6, Perri. (1994a). *The question of independence: The future of charities and the voluntary sector* (Working Paper 3). London: Demos.

6, Perri. (1994b). Should the monopolies and mergers commission investigate charities? In *The Henderson top 2000 charities 1994.* London: Hemmington Scott.

Smith, S. R., & Lipsky, M. (1993). *Nonprofits for hire.* Cambridge: Harvard University Press.

Walsh, K. *Service specification.* Birmingham: Institute of Local Government Studies.

Wistow, G., Knapp, M., Hardy, B., & Allen, C. (1992, Spring). From providing to enabling: Local authorities and the mixed economy of social care. *Public Administration, 70,* 25–45.

7

Accountability in Purchase-of-Service Contracting

Peter Kettner and Lawrence Martin

Any discussion of accountability in purchase-of-service contracting (POSC) must begin with an understanding that it is an evolving, not a static, concept. The focus of accountability in POSC has undergone significant change over the last 20 years and will undoubtedly undergo even more change in the future. In order to fully appreciate what POSC accountability means today, it is useful—perhaps even necessary—to place the issue in historical context. In the case of POSC accountability, the past really does provide a framework for considering the present and speculating about the future.

Although POSC as a concept can be traced back as far as colonial times (Gibelman & Demone, 1989), the roots of POSC accountability can be found in the social services titles of the Social Security Act (49 Stat. 620). Of particular importance is Title XX (Public Law 63-647) and its complementary program, the Social Services Block Grant (SSBG) (Public Law 97-35). The reasons for characterizing the origins of POSC accountability in this manner are threefold. First, the social services titles of the Social Security Act have for some time represented the major human services funding sources in this country. Second, the reliance of Title XX and the SSBG on POSC as the means to carry out programs influenced state contracting in other human service areas, including mental health, developmental disabilities, job training, aging, and others. Finally, Title XX and the SSBG have been the subject of numerous studies dealing with POSC and related accountability issues.

THE NATURE OF POSC ACCOUNTABILITY

Accountability means being answerable for one's performance and implies a set of expectations on the part of one party and a set of responsibilities on the part of the other. To understand the accountability relationship, one must be able to answer the following questions: Which party is answerable and to whom? For what performance expectations is the party answerable?

From the earliest days of POSC, the answers to these questions have been framed from two different perspectives: (1) the level of accountability, and (2) the focus of accountability.

The *levels* of accountability can be described as micro and macro. The micro perspective views POSC accountability in terms of contractors' answerability to government funding sources for the contracted services they provide. The macro perspective views POSC accountability in terms of the answerability of government agencies to their citizens for how contracted services contribute to the overall development, maintenance, and performance of the human services system.

The *focus* of POSC accountability refers to two different types: fiscal and program. Fiscal accountability deals with stewardship issues in relation to resources made available for POSC. Program accountability deals with issues of service design, service outputs, and client outcomes.

Both of these perspectives on POSC accountability were recognized in an early procedures manual (Franklin & White, 1975). Developed under the auspices of the then Department of Health, Education and Welfare (HEW) and designed to guide POSC efforts in the states of California, Hawaii, and Nevada, the manual noted that:

> Contracting . . . is just one part of the total service delivery system. It is a method available to the public agencies to provide services according to their state plans. Public agency responsibilities lie both in the provision of services and in accounting for the funds expended in providing services. In a sense the provider agencies become an extension of the public agency when they provide services to eligible clients. This includes accountability responsibilities on all levels. (p. 2)

This passage from an important and one of the earliest POSC procedures documents accomplished the following:

- acknowledged both the micro and macro perspectives on POSC accountability;
- acknowledged the importance of both fiscal and program accountability;

- identified two compliance measures for micro-level POSC accountability;
  1. state agency control and supervision of the services provided by
     contractors, and
  2. state agency accounting for the funds expended by contractors;
- identified two compliance measures for macro-level POSC accountability,
  1. provision of services according to state plans, and
  2. accounting for total program funds expended.

The state plan measure for macro POSC accountability was in keeping
with one of the major goals of Title XX: to make states accountable to
their citizens, rather than to the federal government (Benton, & Millar,
1978; Muller, 1980). To accomplish this goal, Title XX mandated that
states establish statewide systems to plan, monitor, and evaluate service
provision, but did not mandate what types of human services states were
to provide (Slack, 1979).

At the first national conference on POSC, Kahn (1978) commented
on the subject of POSC accountability:

> In beginning a discussion of purchase of services, there is a temptation to
> focus first on issues surrounding purchase rather than on issues surround-
> ing services. The legitimate concerns and practical concerns of contract
> management tend to overshadow the fundamental issue: the role of the
> baseline public system in the provision of social services. (p. 11)

Kahn again identified both the micro and macro perspectives on POSC
accountability and speculated that micro accountability concerns might
become the major focus of attention to the detriment of macro accountability concerns.

DEVELOPMENTAL STAGES OF POSC ACCOUNTABILITY

If accountability in POSC is an evolving concept, cross-sectional snap-
shots taken over time should provide a sense of the nature and direction of that evolution. To this end, it is possible to look at POSC
accountability during three time periods: (1) the late 1960s to the late
1970s; (2) the 1980s; and (3) the early to mid-1990s. These three time
periods are somewhat arbitrary, as are most attempts to impose a
chronology on social phenomena. Nevertheless, they do help in track-

ing and understanding the history of POSC accountability.

The first time period provides insight into the nature of POSC account-ability during its formative years, when state human service agencies began to widely use POSC. The second time period provides insights into the nature of POSC accountability during its maturing years, a period when POSC became institutionalized as a major, if not the predominant, approach to human services delivery. Finally, the third time period provides insights into refinements in POSC accountability during what might be called the performance years, while also providing a basis for specu-lation about its future directions.

For each of these three time periods, the national human services con-text in which POSC occurred is a vital backdrop, as context largely deter-mined the form that POSC accountability took.

The Formative Years (1968–1979)

The National POSC Context. Prior to 1968, POSC was used in a limited way in fields such as health and vocational rehabilitation. In the 1962 amendments to the Social Security Act, states were, for the first time, authorized to enter into agreements with other public agencies (Slack, 1979). In social services, however, widespread state adoption of POSC began in 1968, due to three major developments:

1. changes in social services titles of the Social Security Act authorized states, for the first time, to contract with private nonprofit organizations (heretofore, states could only contract with other public entities);

2. the federal government authorized states to use donated funds to satisfy state matching (25%) requirements; and

3. the federal appropriation for the social services titles of the Social Security Act was open ended, meaning Congress had imposed no upper limit or ceiling (Pacific Consultants, 1979, p. 16; Slack, 1979, p. 8).

Entrepreneurial state and private nonprofit human services adminis-trators exploited to their mutual advantage what was essentially a loop-hole in the federal law. A nonprofit agency could donate funds to a state human services agency and, in return, receive a contract for services that represented a return not only of their donated funds, but of three addi-tional federal dollars for every one dollar donated. States and private non-profit agencies working together in a type of partnership arrangement were able to expand services, create new services, and extend services to previously unserved and underserved client populations, all on federal money. No new state or private dollars were required to make this system work.

It was later observed that this practice initiated a "gold rush on the federal treasury" (Kettner & Martin, 1987, p. 24). The years between 1968 and 1975 were referred to by many human services administrators as the era of "hatch it and match it." In most states, virtually any human service agency (existing or newly created) addressing any human service need was considered worthy of a state POSC contract, provided that the necessary donated funds were made available. Federal reimbursement to states under the social service titles of the Social Security Act quickly skyrocketed to $1.7 billion in fiscal year 1972. When estimates climbed to $4.7 billion for fiscal year 1973, Congress moved to cap total reimbursement at $2.5 billion and made specific allocations to the various states (Martin, 1986, p. 13). The $2.5 billion cap was continued when the various social services titles of the Social Security Act were rolled into Title XX in 1975.

A second "gold rush" of sorts ensued when federal reimbursement was capped. States that were not spending up to their newly established federal limits engaged in even more POSC in order to keep their share of federal funds from lapsing or being reallocated to states such as California that had already reached their federal ceilings.

The Nature of POSC Accountability. During this formative period, POSC accountability was primarily fiscal in nature, with program accountability receiving scant attention. This general observation is equally true for micro as well as macro POSC accountability. An American Public Welfare Association study (Slack, 1979) laid the blame for this financial orientation to POSC accountability squarely at the feet of the federal government in observing that "concentration at the highest federal levels on financial management and efficiency (have resulted in) . . . a relatively weaker focus on quality, adequacy and effects of services" (p. 30).

POSC accountability at both macro and micro levels during this period was concerned primarily with service design issues: inputs (funding) and to a significantly lesser extent, process (service delivery issues). Little attention was paid to performance issues, either outputs (service volume) or outcomes (client results).

Based on their actions during this period, one might conclude that state human service agencies considered fiscal accountability to mean:

(1) insuring that their federal allocations were properly expended and accounted for, and (2) also insuring that most, if not all, of their federal allocations were obligated and spent. To a great extent, being answerable to state electorates at this time was viewed by state human service agencies as being able to assure elected officials, advocacy groups, private non-profit agencies, clients, and other stakeholders that federal social services funding was being exploited to its fullest potential.

The authors of this chapter had some firsthand experience with POSC accountability during this time period. The director of Title XX contracting for the state of Arizona was given the task in fiscal year 1976 of using POSC to insure that at least 85% of the state's federal social services allocation was expended. It was made clear that the type of service purchased was not important. Neither was the need for the service, the fit of the service into the larger human services system, nor the merits of POSC versus direct government delivery. What was important was spending the federal funds allocated to the state so that they wouldn't be reallocated to other states.

Subsequent analysis of state performances during this era shows that Arizona's actions were not atypical. Most state human service agencies had similar goals and similar fiscal accountability orientations to POSC during this era (Benton et al., 1979; Slack, 1979). Studies of POSC undertaken during the 1970s made several observations about both macro and micro POSC accountability:

- Half of all state human services agencies had made little or no attempt to evaluate Title XX services, either those involving POSC or those delivered by public agencies (Benton et al., 1978);
- Most state Comprehensive Annual Service Plans, the key planning documents that were supposed to implement Title XX in a rational fashion, were not plans at all in the opinion of the American Public Welfare Association (Slack, 1979);
- Consistent state agency policies governing when POSC was to be used instead of direct state agency delivery simply did not exist (Benton et al., 1978);
- The primary reasons for using POSC in many states were: (1) to increase the amount of human services through the mechanism of donated funds, and (2) to shift state-funded human services to federal funding (Booz-Allen & Hamilton, 1971);
- Little or no concern was expressed by state human services agencies as to what POSC might be doing to the larger services system, nor

was the cost of POSC services viewed as a particularly important concern (Benton, 1978).

Some program accountability in POSC was evident at the micro level, if one considers filling out forms as a type of accountability. One particularly vocal contractor in Massachusetts made the comment during this time that "We could be running a zoo here and they wouldn't care as long as I filled in the little blocks on the forms" (Massachusetts Taxpayers Foundation, 1980, p. 16).

Because they frequently provided the state 25% matching funds, many contractors felt that they should not be answerable to state agencies. Contractors used their political muscle with elected and appointed state officials to avoid issues of POSC accountability altogether (Massachusetts Taxpayers Foundation, 1980). In many instances, contractors believed that their contracts were really grants with few or no strings attached.

To counter the view that POSC was a grant rather than a contract, and to begin making contractors cost-conscious, state agencies began to move from a primary focus on inputs (funding) to more of a concern with process (service delivery issues). Short-form contracts that contained very little specificity and were essentially funding documents were abandoned in favor of long-form contracts that spelled out in greater detail the services to be provided as well as other expectations for which contractors were to be held accountable (Pacific Consultants, 1979). State agencies also began making their first tentative moves toward establishing performance expectations by defining units of service for various human services programs and by requiring contractors to collect and report on data on the types and number of units of service they provided (American Public Welfare Association [APWA], 1981; Pacific Consultants, 1979).

Despite the shift to long-form contracts and accounting for units of service, the principal payment mechanism in POSC remained cost reimbursement. Because of the nature of cost-reimbursement contracts (i.e., the separation of performance from payment) micro POSC accountability still demonstrated little real concern with either output or outcome performance issues (Kettner & Martin, 1993a).

By the end of the formative period (about 1979), POSC had become in many states little more than a funding mechanism for private agencies. State human services agencies had lost control not only over POSC, but over their human services systems as well. As one author pointed out, in Michigan, POSC was viewed by state officials as a way of funding favorite private nonprofit human services agencies, rather than as a method of purchasing human services (DeHoog, 1985). In another state, Massachusetts, POSC became so contractor-dominated that a citizen's group published a report entitled, *Purchase of Service: Can the State Gain Control?* (Massachusetts Taxpayers Foundation, 1980).

Somewhere between the years 1975 and 1976, a significant threshhold was passed. More Title XX funds for human services were expended via POSC than were expended by direct state agency delivery. What Karger (1994) has called one of the most significant developments in the human services since the advent of the welfare state went largely unnoticed at the time.

In summary, POSC accountability during the formative years can be said to have had the following characteristics:

- It was primarily fiscal in nature;
- Few criteria had been established for use in program accountability;
- At the micro level, state agencies were only beginning to establish program control over contractors by switching to long-form contracts and incorporating unit of service measures; and
- The principal contract type was cost reimbursement and few state agencies evidenced any real concern with performance issues in general or with client outcomes in particular.

The Maturing Years (1980–1990)

The National POSC Context. By the beginning of the 1980s most states had reached their ceilings on federal Title XX funds. The 1980s also saw the advent of Reaganomics and block grants which resulted in generalized cutbacks in federal funding for human services. The Title XX program became the Social Services Block Grant (SSBG) and its funding was likewise reduced.

During the decade of the 1980s, human services funding was no longer increasing; it was decreasing. The win-win strategy that had worked for both state and private nonprofit human service agencies created by POSC in the formative years gradually became a zero-sum game. State human service agencies could no longer fund new or more critical services without reducing the funding levels of other services. Because of the prominent role now played by POSC, cutting funds to a particular service or services also meant cutting funds to specific contractors. Services, target groups, and contractors began to find themselves in competition with each other for diminished resources.

The Nature of POSC Accountability. The harsh new reality of finite funding for human services created demands for new approaches to state POSC accountability at both the macro and micro levels.

At the macro level, states attempted to regain control over their human service systems. A study of 10 selected states conducted at the end of the decade found that the use of POSC to aid in planning and controlling the human services system had become a major concern of most state human service agencies (Kettner & Martin, 1993b).

At the micro level, states also sought to gain control over their contractors. By the mid-1980s the need for aggressive monitoring of POSC contractors had become generally recognized (DeHoog, 1985; Kettner & Martin, 1985). POSC monitoring was still heavily fiscal in nature, but by this time had also been expanded to routinely include client eligibility determination, service provision considerations, case record-keeping systems, facilities review, staffing ratios, administrative practices, and compliance with licensing and certification standards (Tatara & Pettiford, 1989). State human services agencies were also becoming more concerned with issues of contractor performance.

Performance, as measured by the amount of service provided by contractors and/or by contractors' achievement of client outcomes, was becoming increasingly important. While no clear definition of what constituted performance contracting existed at the time, evidence suggests that by the end of the decade of the 1980s, state human service agencies were routinely engaging in contracting for units of service. Performance contracting involving client outcomes, however, had not yet caught on as a working concept (Kettner & Martin, 1995).

In summary, POSC accountability in the 1980s could be characterized as having the following features:

- Fiscal concerns continued to dominate;
- States were making progress at regaining control over their contractors and over their human service systems;
- Planning and controlling the human services system was becoming an increasingly important aspect of macro POSC accountability; and
- Performance related issues were beginning to emerge as a part of contract expectations at the micro level.

The Performance Years (Early to Mid–1990s)

The National POSC Context. Beginning in the early part of the 1990s, the national POSC context took a decidedly different turn. Rather than being dominated by a single major piece of federal legislation, such as Title XX or SSBG, the national POSC context can be characterized as moving into a performance environment. Policy and administrative actions emanating from all levels of government (federal, state, and local) began to include expectations for performance and results. These policy and administrative actions are directed toward government programs in general and not just human services programs. The influential best seller *Reinventing Government* (Osborn & Gaebler, 1992) sums up succinctly this new performance thinking: "What gets measured gets done" (p. 146).

The new emphasis on performance is being expressed in many ways, as illustrated by the following examples:

- Congress has passed The Government Performance & Review Act of 1993 (Public Law 103-62) requiring the establishment of outcome performance measures for all federal programs;
- The National Performance Review (Gore, 1993) has established the requirement that performance standards be developed for federal agencies and departments;
- The Department of Labor now requires that POSC involving JTPA (Joint Training Partnership Act) funds be performance based (Osborn & Gaebler, 1992); and
- Many state and local governments across the nation are busily engaged in developing performance measures for their programs (Epstein, 1992; Fountain & Robb, 1994).

Some of these performance initiatives, like JTPA performance-based contracting, have already had a direct impact on POSC in the human services; other initiatives are only now beginning to be felt.

Another factor that may have had some influence on POSC accountability is that POSC was the focus of a good deal of criticism in professional literature during the 1980s. Privatization in the form of POSC was seen as undermining a long-standing commitment of public social services to provide services based on need (Abramovitz, 1986).

Smith (1989) found that government agencies were exerting increasing control over the functions of the provider agency, reducing discretion in decision making, and even imposing certain methodologies. He also raised questions about the ability of government agencies to calculate costs that accurately reflected the cost to the provider. Kramer and Grossman (1987) characterized private agencies that contract with government as quasi-public agencies that had become dependent on government contracting dollars for survival. Gibelman and Demone (1989) warned about bureaucratizing the private sector through the contracting process. Criticism of a strictly fiscal approach to POSC accountability was increasing (Hill, 1983; Salamon, 1989).

The Nature of POSC Accountability. Addressing the issues of programmatic and fiscal POSC accountability at the macro level in an era when the focus is increasingly on performance requires that states take steps to insure that:

- Statewide and community needs are being met to the greatest extent possible; and
- Collectively, the contracts awarded are providing the highest volume of services affordable, the best quality services available, and are achieving the best possible client outcomes.

Addressing the issues of programmatic and fiscal POSC accountability at the micro level also requires states to insure that:

- Contract expectations for quality and quantity of services and client outcomes are established and monitored; and
- Methods of determining the cost and price of services insures that contract awards go to potential contractors that demonstrate the capability to provide the best quality services at the lowest possible cost.

Translating these principles into practice, in turn, requires that POSC systems include the following components:

1. A systematic approach to needs assessment designed to insure that funding is directed toward areas of greatest need;
2. A system of fair and open competition for contracts to insure that awards are made on the basis of ability to address community needs and not on the basis of political connections;
3. A system that establishes contract expectations which insure that contractors meet client need, are fiscally responsible, and are paid a fair rate for services provided; and

4. A database that permits monitoring of individual contractor compliance and performance and evaluates community-wide impact on problems and needs identified at the beginning of the planning cycle.

Current Management and Accountability Practices

In the early 1990s the authors undertook two national studies of state POSC practices. The first study examined five programs (residential treatment, alcohol, drug and mental health, employment and training, child day care, and specialized transportation) in 10 states. The focus was to determine the relative importance of factors affecting contract awards. The factors explored included

1. Funding and fiscal considerations;
2. Planning and controlling the POSC system;
3. Client outcomes;
4. Continuation of business-as-usual;
5. Service volume, and
6. Politics and external pressures.

(For a full report of the study, see Kettner and Martin, 1993b. This will be referred to as the 1993 study.)

The second project was a 50 state study of management practices in four program areas (children, youth and family services, mental health services, adult and aging services, and employment and training services). This study was an attempt to better understand state management practices in the areas of

1. Planning for community-wide services;
2. Calculating costs;
3. Establishing contract expectations;
4. Monitoring, and
5. Payment.

(For a full discussion of this study, see Kettner and Martin, 1994. This will be referred to as the 1994 study.)

Findings from both studies have relevance to the issues of micro and macro POSC accountability, as well as to both fiscal and program accountability. In making observations about management and accountability practices in POSC in the 1990s, we will draw on the aforementioned studies of contracting practices as well as other literature where relevant in an attempt to reflect the state of the art of accountability in POSC.

Comprehensive Planning and Determination of Need. Accurate determination of community-wide need for services can be an important issue in evaluating macro-level program accountability. In the absence of some orderly, systematic method for assessing need, assumptions tend to be made that needs of the past continue in the same order of priority, that existing services continue to be needed in the same order of priority, and that newly emerging needs can be addressed only when funding surpluses exist. In the absence of community-wide planning and needs assessment, POSC tends to be used simply as a funding mechanism, and fails to deal with macro-level accountability issues.

In the 1994 study, respondents were asked to indicate if they used any of five possible formats for determining need or whether they, in fact, did not assess need at all. Only 14% responded that they did not assess need for services. The remaining 86% used one or more of the following methods, in this order of importance: (1) community advisory groups; (2) direct contact with clients; (3) contractors; (4) formal needs assessments; or (5) public hearings.

Although the finding that 86% of state programs attempt to assess community need might be considered mildly encouraging, the findings do not represent a strong statement about macro-level program accountability in POSC. It could be argued that using community advisory groups, clients, and contractors as the major source of information about service needs essentially serves to reinforce the need for existing services. In short, POSC accountability practices in the early 1990s do not reflect a strong commitment to the identification of newly emerging problems and needs and inclusion of these needs in the planning process.

Competition for Contracts. A second issue related to macro-level accountability is the issue of competition. Evaluated in the context of accountability, competition becomes a complex variable. On the one hand, sound macro-level management of POSC systems would tend to promote a partnership relationship between government funding sources and contractors in selected areas of service (Kettner & Martin, 1990). These would be services that, in the best interest of clients, promoted stability and continuity over time. Child residential treatment and foster care would be examples of services best provided in a partnership type of environment.

On the other hand, certain types of services lend themselves to competition in the interest of purchasing better-quality services at a lower cost, thereby expanding the resources available. POSC systems that fail to encourage competition in areas where it can be effectively used may be running a quasi-government system that deemphasizes contractor performance and may not necessarily be in the best interest of the human services community or its clients or consumers (Kramer, 1994).

Competition is also important because of its impact on cost and price. When adequate competition is present in a procurement, the objective of the financial review is to establish a fair price. When adequate competition is not present, the objective of the financial review is to establish a reasonable price (Kettner & Martin, 1987). The Office of Federal Procurement Policy (1980) has established criteria for use in determining whether or not adequate competition is present.

Findings from the research on the issue of competition are mixed. In the 1993 study, state agencies indicated that driving down costs (and by implication, competition) was the most important decision factor in awarding contracts. In the 1994 study, whereas almost 64% of administrators of state agency programs studied stated that they actively solicited bids and proposals as a part of their POSC procurement process, almost 40% stated that they also followed the practice of simply renewing existing contracts.

In summary, on the issue of generating competition for contracts, the following concerns about POSC practices in the 1990s need to be raised:

- Perhaps the most powerful factor influencing decision making in POSC in the 1990s is the need to lower costs (which would tend to support competition and accountability);
- This factor runs counter to a strong tendency to continue business-as-usual with established contractors (which would tend to reduce competition); and
- Competition, alone, of course, does not meet the expectations of good POSC accountability practices.

Regardless of competition, rigorous monitoring of contractor performance is essential.

Establishing Contract Expectations. Both fiscal and program accountability at the micro level require that each contract specify precise expectations and that contractor performance be regularly monitored to insure that the expectations are met.

Contract expectations tend to cluster around two types of factors: (1) technical, clerical, and bookkeeping considerations such as ensuring client eligibility, record-keeping, and staying within the budget, and (2) client service considerations, such as quantity of service, quality of service, and client outcomes. The former indicators tend to be used in fiscal accountability and the latter in program accountability.

In some of the earliest literature on POSC, concerns were expressed about the ability of government contracting agencies to specify expectations. Wedemeyer (1970) raised questions about whether specifically definable end-products could be produced, requisitioned, and delivered in quantifiable units or whether measures of performance and quality could be identified, defined, and enforced. Lourie (1979) also advocated clear definitions of the services to be provided by contractors. In many ways, clear expectations of contractors are the sine qua non of program accountability.

In the 1993 study, fiscal and cost considerations ranked as the #1 or #2 decision criterion in all five programs studied, emphasizing, once again, that fiscal accountability dominates POSC practices at both micro and macro levels. Client outcomes emerged in two statewide programs (employment and training and special transportation) as the number one consideration in making decisions about contract awards, but ranked lowest as a decision criterion in residential treatment and midrange for the remaining programs.

In the 1994 study, state contract administrators were asked to specify the types of expectations that were imposed on their contractors (e.g., keeping within budget, insuring client eligibility, specific client outcomes, etc.). Although "staying within budget" and "client eligibility considerations" proved to be basic to most state-level program expectations, a significant majority of respondents also established minimum expectations for quantity and quality of services provided, and almost 45% expected specific results with clients. The same pattern of findings emerged in relation to contract monitoring.

It is worth noting that, from the limited literature available on the subject, it appears that accountability standards for contractors tend to exceed accountability expectations for programs delivered by public social service agencies. A recent study of CEOs in state departments of social service, mental health, and corrections revealed that monitoring and evaluating departmental programs was mentioned as an important administrative activity in only 8.1% of the total responses (Meinert, Ginsberg, & Keys, 1993). Hoefer (1993) discovered that management skills (including program planning, evaluation/research, MIS, statistics, database, and spreadsheets) ranked last in importance for all levels of administration. Gustafson and Allen (1994) chronicle the many management shortcomings in child welfare and propose a new model of management that includes establishment of performance standards for all programs. As the need for program accountability for services delivered by public agencies is increasingly recognized, improved practices internally could have a positive influence on the quality of program accountability in POSC as well.

From these findings and related literature, the following observations can be made about establishing contract expectations and monitoring:

• Fiscal accountability in terms of cost control continues to dominate POSC practices;

• POSC systems seem to be responding to the trend to establish performance expectations and to monitor contractors in terms of quantity and quality of service and client outcomes;

• As public social service agencies establish accountability standards for the services and programs they provide, their experiences could, in the future, have a positive effect on the quality of program accountability in POSC as well; and

• The more precisely contract expectations can be defined, the more likely the contract will focus on programmatic accountability, while the greater the difficulty in defining contract expectations, the greater the likelihood that the contract will focus on fiscal accountability.

Determining Cost and Price of Services. Fiscal accountability at both the macro and micro levels may, on the surface, appear to support a "low bidder" mentality. However, on closer examination, quality of service and client outcomes also need to be considered. This is based on the premise that accountability requires attention to purchasing the best available service for the lowest price—not simply purchasing the lowest-priced service.

Fiscal accountability is addressed from a variety of perspectives. First, to what extent does cost or price drive decisions? Second, how are costs and prices of services determined? Third, how are contractors paid?

In both the 1993 and 1994 studies, it became clear that the cost of a contract dominates the decisionmaking process. In the 1993 study, fiscal considerations were considered the number one or number two factor in all five programs studied. In the 1994 study, cost was described as "a major factor" by 47% and "the major factor" by another 5% of the respondents.

The way that costs and prices of services are determined can be based on projected total program costs, on estimated unit costs, or on a fixed price. Unit costs (e.g., cost per hour of service) would probably be considered the most competitive and accountable formula because they lend themselves best to comparison across providers. Projected total program costs and fixed-price contracts often leave questions about comparability of what is included in the budget.

In the 1994 study the majority of state contract administrators determined cost by using the potential contractor's line-item budget as the basis. Unit cost also appeared to be widely used, although programs were almost evenly split between unit cost being determined by potential contractors and unit price being determined by the government agency. Fixed price was the least used mechanism.

The most used method of contract payment was cost reimbursement—repayment of expenses actually incurred and billed. Over half of the respondents paid contractors only for the number of units actually provided. Only 4% paid based on outcomes of service.

In light of these findings, the following observations can be made relative to determining cost and price of services:

- POSC systems appear to be strengthening and improving their skills in determining cost or price of services in ways that increasingly permit comparisons across potential contractors; and
- In most programs, while cost and price are important, they do not stand alone, but rather appear to be coupled with another factor, which changes from program to program (e.g., in residential treatment, cost plus system stability; in employment and training, cost plus client outcomes).

The Future

As POSC moves into the latter part of its third decade, several trends are worth noting. Practices in the first two decades produced increasing attention to fiscal accountability. They also produced concerns about meeting client need, the relevance of certain services, and the need for clearly defining performance expectations. These concerns were echoed in two efforts undertaken by the Clinton Administration, both of which, if enforced, will have profound effects on POSC accountability: (1) the

Government Performance & Results Act of 1993 (Public Law 503-625) and (2) the National Performance Review.

The Government Performance and Results Act specifies that beginning with fiscal year 1994, at least ten federal agencies must begin experimenting with performance measurement. In addition, by 1998, all federal agencies must develop 5 year strategic plans linked to measurable outcomes (Gore, 1993). This will inevitably have a ripple effect from federal agencies to state agencies to contractors, since it will be impossible for government agencies to measure performance without requiring provider agencies to generate and compile data on performance (such as quantity and quality of services provided and client outcomes).

The National Performance Review extends and expands upon the initiatives of the Government Performance & Results Act. The National Performance Review requires that the federal Office of Management & Budget alter the fiscal year 1996 budget process to require federal agencies to track and report performance measures with specific emphasis on outcomes (Gore, 1993). This change will affect all federal agencies and, in turn, all states and those organizations that contract with federal and state governments. As provider agencies are increasingly required to define and collect data about performance, the focus of POSC accountability will inevitably shift to indicators that reflect not only cost, but quality of services and client outcomes as well.

SUMMARY AND CONCLUSIONS

POSC accountability has come a long way in 20 years. The early years were characterized by state-level contracting systems being hurriedly created and pressured to maximize use of newly available federal funding. The federal agenda seemed to be to encourage development and expansion of human service programs. States responded by directing the maximum resources available to private, nonprofit agencies. Accountability did not become a dominant factor until federal funding was capped and ceilings imposed on the states.

The next decade brought greater sophistication in measurement. Fiscal measurement tools such as units of service introduced greater precision and comparability into fiscal accountability during this era. Program accountability emerged as a concern, and gradually increased in importance. Measurement tools relating to quality of services, to program outputs, and to client outcomes moved POSC accountability ahead significantly in evaluating program performance at the micro level. Advances in measuring both fiscal and program performance led to much greater control being exercised over the POSC system in the 1980s.

In the 1990s POSC systems have become increasingly stable. Some even describe them as quasi-governmental service delivery systems. From an accountability perspective, this raises new problems. Macro-level, community-wide accountability depends, to a certain extent, on information about the full range of community problems and participation by a wide range of contractors. These elements do not appear to be as much a part of POSC systems as they might be.

In establishing contract expectations and monitoring contracts, POSC systems appear to be making their greatest strides. The full range of fiscal and program indicators is widely used, although use of performance indicators tends to be limited to programs where measurement is fairly straightforward (e.g., job placement), and avoided in areas where less tangible client improvement must be demonstrated. Great strides have also been made in accurately calculating the cost and price of services, but cost reimbursement is still favored as a payment mechanism over payment for units of service provided.

In closing, there is one factor that the authors have learned from first-hand experience with a number of states that has a profound impact on POSC accountability. Although state legislatures and high-level state administrators consider accountability an extremely important part of a POSC system, few states have developed the data processing and information management capacity (either in hardware or software) needed to move POSC accountability to the next level.

Macro-level POSC accountability requires aggregation of data from all contractors to aid in understanding the extent to which community-wide services match up to community-wide needs. Micro-level accountability requires comparisons across similar contractors. Without adequate data and information management capacity and appropriate staffing, these functions cannot be accomplished.

POSC is now in an era where fiscal and program accountability are ready for refinement to fairly high levels of precision if adequate infrastructure is provided. If attention and resources are devoted to this component of the system in the latter half of the 1990s, the entire human services system could become capable of making some important contributions, not only on the accountability front, but also in refining services and improving results.

REFERENCES

Abramovitz, M. (1986). The privatization of the welfare state: A review. *Social Work*, 31, 257–265.

American Public Welfare Association. (1981). *Study of purchase of service in selected states.* Washington, DC: Author.

Benton, B., Field, T., & Millar, R. (1978). *Social services: Federal legislation vs. state implementation.* Washington, DC: The Urban Institute.

Booz-Allen & Hamilton. (1971). *Purchase of service: A study of the experiences of three states in purchase of service under the provisions of the 1967 amendments to the Social Security Act.* Washington, DC: U. S. Department of Health, Education & Welfare.

DeHoog, R. (1985). Human services contracting: Environmental, behavioral, and organizational conditions. *Administration & Society, 16,* 427–454.

Epstein, P. (1992). Get ready: The time for performance measurement is finally coming! *Public Administration Review, 52,* 513–519.

Fountain, J., & Robb, N. (1994). Service efforts and accomplishment measures. *Public Management, 76,* 6–12.

Franklin, D., & White, M. (1975). *Contracting for purchase of services: A procedural manual.* Los Angeles, CA: Regional Research Institute in Social Welfare, University of Southern California.

Gibelman, M., & Demone, H., Jr. (1989). The evolving contract state. In H. Demone, Jr. & M. Gibelman, (Eds.), *Services for sale: Purchasing health and human services* (pp. 17–57). New Brunswick, NJ: Rutgers University Press.

Gore, A. (1993). *Creating a government that works better and costs less: Report of the national performance review.* Washington, DC: U. S. Government Printing Office.

Gustafson, L., & Allen, D. (1994). A new management model for child welfare. *Public Welfare, 52,* 31–40.

Hill, R. (1983). Thoughts on the history and future of purchase-of-care in Massachusetts. *New England Journal of Human Services, 3,* 36–49.

Hoefer, R. (1993). A matter of degree: Job skills for human service administrators. *Administration in Social Work, 17,* 1–20.

Kahn, A. (1978). The impact of purchase of service contracting on social service delivery. In K. Wedel, A. Katz, & A. Weick, (Eds.), *Proceedings of the National Institute on Purchase of Service Contracting* (pp. 11–16). Lawrence, KS: University of Kansas, School of Social Work.

Karger, H. (1994). Is privatization a positive trend in social services: No.

In H. Karger, & J. Midgley, (Eds.), *Controversial issues in social policy* (pp. 110–116). Boston: Allyn & Bacon.

Kettner, P., & Martin, L. (1985). Issues in the development of monitoring systems for purchase of service contracting. *Administration in Social Work, 9,* 69–82.

Kettner, P., & Martin, L. (1987). *Purchase of service contracting.* Beverly Hills: Sage.

Kettner, P., & Martin, L. (1990). Purchase of service contracting: Two models. *Administration in Social Work, 14,* 15–30.

Kettner, P., & Martin, L. (1993a). Performance, accountability and purchase of service contracting. *Administration in Social Work, 17,* 61–79.

Kettner, P., & Martin, L. (1993b). Purchase of service contracting in the 1990s: Have expectations been met? *Journal of Sociology and Social Welfare, 20,* 89–103.

Kettner, P., & Martin, L. (1994). Purchase of service at 20: Are we using it well? *Public Welfare, 52,* 14–20.

Kettner, P., & Martin, L. (1996). Performance contracting in the human services: An initial assessment. *Administration in Social Work, 19,* 47–61.

Kramer, R. (1994). Voluntary agencies and the contract culture: Dream or nightmare? *Social Service Review, 68,* 33–60.

Kramer, R., & Grossman, B. (1987). Contracting for social services: Process management and resource dependencies. *Social Service Review, 6,* 32–55.

Lourie, N. (1979). Purchase of service contracting: Issues confronting the government sponsored agency. In K. Wedel, A. Katz, & A. Weick (Eds.), *Procdings of the First National Institute on Purchase of Service Contracting* (pp. 17–28). Lawrence, KS: University of Kansas, School of Social Work.

Martin, L. (1986). *Purchase of service contracting: An analysis of state decision making.* Doctoral dissertation, Arizona State University.

Massachusetts Taxpayers Foundation. (1980). *Purchase of service: Can state government gain control?* Boston: Author.

Meinert, R., Ginsberg, L., & Keys, P. (1993). Performance characteristics of CEOs in state departments of social service, mental health and corrections. *Administration in Social Work, 17,* 103–114.

Muller, C. (1980). Five years later: A look at Title xx: The billion dollar social services fund. *The Grantsmanship Center News, 8,* 26–37, 56–68.

Office of Federal Procurement Policy. (1980). *Desk guide to price and cost analysis.* Washington, DC: U.S. Government Printing Office.

Osborn, D., & Gaebler, T. (1992). *Reinventing government.* Reading, MA: Addison-Wesley.

Pacific Consultants. (1979). *Title XX purchase of service: A description of states'
service delivery and management practices.* Berkeley, CA: Author.

Salamon, L. (1989). *Beyond privatization: The tools of government action.*
Washington, DC: The Urban Institute Press.

Slack, I. (1979). *Title XX at the crossroads.* Washington, DC: American Public
Welfare Association.

Smith, S. (1989). The changing politics of child welfare services: New roles
for the government and the nonprofit sectors. *Child Welfare, 68,*
289–299.

Tatara, T., & Pettiford, E. (1989). Purchase of service monitoring and eval-
uation policies and practices. In H. Demone, & M. Gibelman (Eds.)
Services for sale: Purchasing health and human services (pp. 331–342). New
Brunswick, NJ: Rutgers University Press.

Wedemeyer, J. (1970). Government agencies and the purchase of social
services. In I. Winograd (Ed.) *Proceedings of the First Milwaukee Institute
on a social welfare issue of the day: Purchase of care and services in the health
and welfare fields* (pp. 3–20). Milwaukee, WI: School of Social Work,
The University of Wisconsin at Milwaukee.

8

The Political Future of Privatization

Harold W. Demone, Jr.

The forecasting of events in our existential world is fraught with unanticipated events and actors. Privatization and its important subset, the purchase of services (POS), is no less subject to the vagaries of our times. Yet there are some identifiable activities, even some trends, that may help to provide some insight into the next decade or so. In this final chapter, some of those factors that may influence the use or nonuse of purchase of services as a means to realize privatization goals are discussed. This chapter begins with a brief overview of the broad trends and issues in privatization.

WHITHER PRIVATIZATION?

By definition, privatization has the government transferring one or more of its functions to the private sector as a gift, for a nominal sum or for the full value of the operation. In classical terms, the former governmental responsibility would now be that of the private sector. There are modifications of this scenario. The federal government may establish federally charted entities, such as the U.S. Post Office, the Federal Deposit Insurance Corporation, and the Export-Import Bank. In its December 1995 report to Congress, the GAO surveyed 58 entities that it believed were governmental corporations (GCS), which it defines as "federally chartered entities created to serve a public function of a predominately business nature" (General Accounting Office [GAO], 1995b, p.1).

In many states there are state-established authorities that manage toll roads, bridges, tunnels, steamship authorities, and conference centers, among others. At both the federal and state levels, they generally provide business-type services. They may also be known as quasi-governmental or "quangos." Basically, they are responsible for their own financing, budget, and operations, and at the state level they sometimes become patronage havens for the political party in power. In a deficit situation, they are often able to turn to government for financial assistance.

THE FUNCTIONS OF GOVERNMENT

The future of privatization is inseparably linked to the determination of what is inherently public and what is and should be inherently private. (A similar close linkage is to be found in the current close association between privatization and the purchase of services, with privatization as much the senior partner. As such, much of the forecasting to follow is targeted on privatization.) There are several essential components in this long-standing debate about what should be public and what should be private.

In the second volume of this series, former Massachusetts Governor and the 1988 presidential nominee Michael Dukakis (1998) contended with the limits of contracting for state government by reflecting on his own experiences as governor. What are the appropriate functions of state government? Dukakis' global view is that government must be willing and able to manage a first-rate service system. Specifically, he would never contract adult maximum and medium correctional institutions. Transitional facilities are excepted. He feels similarly about the care and treatment of the severely and chronically mentally ill. As with adult corrections, he is comfortable about purchasing other mental health services. His review is humanistic, pragmatic and experiential. He does not theorize. He does not ask who has the authority to establish the limits and from where they emanate.

There are experiences in other states where both of the populations excluded by Dukakis have been served by purchased programs. The Corrections Corporation of America (C C A) receives contracts from 11 states to manage 45 prisons or detention centers, housing more than 20,000 inmates. Nationally, about 50,000 inmates are in such privately operated settings (Purdy, 1996, citing C C A literature). In many, perhaps most states, services for the severely mentally ill are now being purchased. Thus, neither alternative is beyond the choice of some governor at some time in some state.

The Libertarian-Republican Mayor of Indianapolis, Stephen Goldsmith, and Party's nominee for Governor was prepared for that city to sell or commit to competitive bidding everything except police and fire services. Thus, he established parameters for the essential local governmental functions (Will, 1994). Yet even within this narrow definition of public boundaries, these crucial services have been provided privately in some municipalities. Private volunteer, not-for-profit fire departments are widespread across the nation. There are about 12 for-profit fire protection firms operating in 25 communities in three states (Arizona, Oregon, and Tennessee) with a New York village testing the waters (Williams, 1996). For most of the nation's history the majority of the police/security forces have been employed in the private sector, both for-profit and not-for-profit. And for about the last 30 years or so, both in the United States and Canada, members of the public police forces have once again been in the minority, as they were in the last century.

Thus efforts to distinguish between that which is fundamentally public or private by two national leaders, one a Democratic Governor and the other a Republican Mayor, suggests that the choices for local and state government are mixed and not at all clear. They are driven by both pragmatism and ideology. Local circumstance also affects decisions. To some, there are no ambiguities. Michael Huffington, the wealthy businessman nominated in 1994 by the Republicans in California for the U.S. Senate, campaigned (and lost) with the slogan "I want a government that does nothing" (Berke, 1996, p. E1). Morry Taylor, successful businessman and one of several Republican candidates for the presidency in 1996, recommended that the State Department be dynamited and its essential functions moved to the states. For most of the other federal agencies, dismantling or diminishing is proposed (Pertman, 1996b).

The mid-1990s found a proposal by the Clinton–Gore administration testing the acceptable limits. In "reinventing government" they closed a federal unit responsible for some governmental security clearances and established it as a private for-profit company that received a sole-source 3-year contract to provide those same security clearances. The debate took many forms, but ultimately focused on whether this work is "inherently governmental" (Gillers, 1996, p. A23). To the critics the answer is affirmative. Other functions uniquely governmental offered by Gillers are enforcing the law and approving new drugs.

To the Public Citizen's Research Group located in Washington, D.C., only the federal and state governments should be responsible for the regulation of hospitals. They find the current accreditation body—the prestigious national not-for-profit Joint Commission on Accreditation of

Healthcare Organizations—to be lax and accepting of lower standards than appropriate (Bass, 1996).

SHARPENING THE DEBATE

Clearly, an unanticipated advantage of the several experiments in privatization is that they help to sharpen the debate about that which government does and the degree to which it is unique. The U.S. General Accounting Office (GAO) came down on the equivocal side:

> None of these documents the GAO reviewed clearly defined inherently governmental functions. The basic principle to adhere to is that the government should not contract out its responsibilities to serve the public interest or to exercise its sovereign powers. A key criterion in determining whether service contracts are appropriate is whether the government maintains sufficient in-house capability to be fully in control of the policy and management functions of the agency. In this context, governmental decisionmaking power means more than simply being a final authority or signatory to a document. Government officials should be active throughout the decision-making process. (GAO, 1991, p. 3)

The GAO report was written in response to a request by then Democratic Senator David Pryor of Oklahoma, Chairman of a subcommittee of the Committee on Governmental Affairs. Senator Pryor had expressed concern about the government's growing reliance on consultants to administer its core activities that may include "inherently governmental functions" (GAO, 1991, p.1). The 136-page report expanded its review to include contracts along with the use of consultants as requested by Senator Pryor.

To prepare this report the GAO examined the *Federalist Papers*, for the framers of the *Constitution* were concerned even then, and perhaps especially then, about the appropriate functions of the federal government. Among more current documents, the Office of Management and Budget (OMB) Circulars A–76 and A–120 addressed governmental functions in a context in which the executive branch has generally been concerned about its appropriate functions. The circulars establish the principle that contractors are not to be hired to perform the work of a policy, decision-making, or management nature, for these are the responsibilities of the officials of the agency. Some of the federal agencies have also issued their own guidelines on governmental functions.

In preparation, the GAO reviewed more than 100 contracts from four federal agencies. They critiqued and analyzed relevant literature, court cases, and government policy and practices. Two symposiums were held on the subject, and the draft final report was disseminated widely in and out of government for reaction and comments. The task was taken very seriously.

Results of the GAO Study

The GAO was unable to find any document which clearly defined those functions which are inherently those of the federal government, and it thus concluded that the basic principles are those enumerated above. The concluding principle was that the government should not contract out its responsibilities to serve the public interest or to exercise its sovereign powers.

The GAO recommended that the Office of Management and Budget (OMB) develop a short generic list of inherently governmental functions, to be supplemented with similar agency-based lists. OMB did not agree that the individual agencies should supplement their work or that Congress could play a clarifying role, as also advised by the GAO. Some of the outside consultants were equally unhappy with the major responsibility being assigned to OMB. They preferred a public–private panel of experts which would establish a forum to develop the needed guidance.

The GAO is very pragmatic. It finds service contracts to be essential, but does not want the federal bureaucrats to relinquish total governmental control to contractors, which, they assert, has happened on occasion. Government needs to retain an ability to manage effectively. It would allow substantial experimentation as long as government retains some in-house competence.

THE DEBATE CONTINUES

Given more than 200 years of uncertainty and ambiguity and with no clear consensus about the inherent governmental functions, there is no reason to believe that truly definitive definitions will soon be forthcoming. The marketplace of ideas and experiments is still in flux. More harm than good may evolve from a premature conclusion, especially in an era in which privatization has become a political cachet.

We see experimentation continuing with the boundaries under constant testing. Despite forces gathered on both sides of the issue, most of the public is flexible and uncommitted. They await results, and do not see the debate as reflecting fundamental choices.

Heilbroner and Milberg (1996) view the contemporary marketplace as needing a dynamic public sector to bring balance into the forces of modern capitalism. This government will need to be resourceful and adaptive.

Of the potential roles to be played in the delivery of human services, several are highly significant. Needs identification comes first, priority-setting next, followed by resource assessment and development, financing, allocating, planning, coordinating, service delivery, and monitoring. Can any of these roles be classified as exclusively public or private and on what grounds? The rhetoric of political debates aside, there is no real disagreement on the point that only the public sector has the financial wherewithal to confront major financial demands, thus, de facto, the financial purpose is a function the government must play in varying degrees in varying situations. The question becomes only to what extent government will fulfill this function.

Only the government has a taxing authority under which no one can be determined to be exempt. Similarly, any financial responsibility includes some planning and monitoring concerns. Given a current consensus about the negative features of monopolies, if government plays a major role in financing, planning, and monitoring the other functions would logically be assigned elsewhere. The private for-profit and/or not-for-profit sectors are the legitimate alternatives.

There are examples of role-reversal in which the sectors have played roles directly contradictory to those outlined above, thus requiring some flexibility in making ultimate judgments. Government has long used the private sector to advise in allocation decisions, planning, and monitoring, but only as consultants, grantees, or vendors under contract. They were agents of the government in these roles.

Private armies, sometimes known as mercenaries, have a long-standing international history. Papua New Guinea hired a London-based mercenary company to crush armed rivals (Lynch, 1997). In recent years, Somalia, Haiti and Bosnia all saw the Pentagon making use of an army of civilians playing a range of noncombatant roles ("America's private army in Bosnia," 1996). Private sector foreign policy-making is similarly endowed. A recent example was found in the administration of President Ronald Reagan, when Colonel Oliver North was a major catalyst in such an enterprise.

Finally, there is one uniquely exclusive franchise of government: concern with equity and fairness for all residents within its borders.

A WORLD VIEW OF PRIVATIZATION

Trends toward privatization of government functions in the United States are best understood in the context of a worldwide movement. Indeed, the United States has been among the more reluctant nations to privatize. Purchase of service has been the "middle-of-the-road" position.

Those nations owning and operating most activities are to found in the former communist and socialist states. Eastern nations thus have more with which to experiment and to devolve. Even China, Cuba, and North Korea, countries which are still proclaiming their socialist purity, are engaging in behaviors allowing for major private responsibility. Savas (cited in Tierney, 1995) listed the not-privatizing countries in the world as Burma, North Korea, and Cuba.

Eastern Europe and the Soviet Union

According to *The Economist* ("Privatization in eastern Europe," 1990) about 90% of the industries of Poland and Hungary in 1990 were in state hands, and these Eastern Europe nations were viewed by the Soviet Union as experimental laboratories, for they (the Soviets) had much further to go.

Compared to the denationalization of Great Britain or France in the 1980s and into the mid-1990s, the changes in these former communist nations were daring multiples of 100 times the risk ("Privatization in Eastern Europe," 1990). Each alternative had been tried in some form or another. They all presented risks, likely political corruption, limited fairness, and lack of information to make responsible judgements. There are no clear solutions. Russia, Poland, and the Czech Republic all tried governmentally distributed vouchers, which allowed every person, adult or child to buy shares in some newly developed private businesses, shops, and factories (Shapiro, 1992). By 1995, American entrepreneurs were making major investments in Czech industry, including the installation of American managers following a sweeping nationwide privatization. The Czech managers, in turn, were balking at brash American replacements (Perlez, 1995).

By mid-1996, the Czech Privatization Ministry was abolished because 70 percent of the gross domestic product was produced by the private sector through the transfer of 4,700 large governmental agencies to the private enterprise. The banks were still largely controlled by the State (Rocks, 1996).

These were notable events. The head of the East German agency charged with privatizing its companies was shot to death in his home for his actions. The Red Army faction claimed responsibility for the killing (Associated Press, 1991).

Each of the Eastern countries has been faced with constant, seemingly never-ending problems, although anecdotal stories of great success are also reported regularly, and matters seem to be better, not worse (Dobbs, 1993). One important result is that the inflation rate seems to have declined in some of the countries.

Assassination aside, after roughly 4 $^1/_2$ years the agency established by Germany in 1990 to lead its privatization efforts was closed. It had privatized thousands of East German state-owned-and-operated companies, despite great political opposition and many problems (Protzman, 1994).

Blasi (1994), an American advisor to the Russian government, studied 200 large state-owned organizations that had been privatized, and was heartened by the results. Employees are majority stockholders in most of the companies. Managers still retain firm control of the operation and outside investors are increasingly active. The public, too, has a stake, and many of the companies are much more efficient than in the past.

In late 1995, Hungary and Poland were still struggling with their commitment. The people in Hungary were opposed to selling state-owned property, according to the polls, yet to survive and compete they seemed without options. Hungary, Poland, and the Czech Republics seem on the verge of significant commitments to privatization (Nash, 1995). The interconnections of the world economies seemed to narrow the options.

The Ukraine has been even more complicated. A year-long effort to sell 8,000 state-owned companies found only 300 actually transferring ownerships despite massive United States financial and expert assistance. The Ukraine followed only Israel, Egypt and Russia in the receipt of American financial aid. The public employee's directors and the general public demonstrated either or both resistance and disinterest. For most Ukrainians, privatization was found to be incomprehensible or doubtful (Perlez, 1995).

Western Europe

Although most of the Western European countries had nationalized many more industries than the United States or Canada, there was still a very strong and internationally competitive private sector, even a not-for-profit sector of sorts. Thus their efforts to privatize or even to deregulate was often more similar to what was happening in North America than those in Eastern Europe.

A more typical example is the problem faced in the European Commission's effort to deregulate the telecommunications industry. The national postal monopolies that were opposed to many of the reforms have succeeded in blocking the denationalization ("Neither snow, nor rain, nor fax" 1990).

Richardson and Gutch, in Chapter 5, describe many of the problems occurring in Great Britain as the government attempts to contract for human services that it once provided directly, in a model more typical of the United States. It differs now in one important respect. In the United Kingdom (UK) POS is a product of formal governmental policy, whereas in the United States it has a more ad hoc character.

Within the UK, the purchase of services is also part of a larger privatization movement with a well-established history. By 1994 the British Conservative government had dropped its plan to sell the Post Office. Public enthusiasm for privatization after 15 years of effort appeared to be slowing down. Dozens of state-run organizations had been sold in the previous 15 years, including British Airways, Jaguar, British Petroleum, and British Steel, generating more than $80 billion and strengthening some of the units (Reuters, 1994a). In 1995, the headlines read "Britain is streamlining its bureaucracy, partly by privatizing some work" (Stevenson, 1995, p. 10). Now in the UK, as in the United States, discussions about privatization more often refer to POS.

PRIVATIZATION IN THE UNITED STATES

The United States has fewer pure options for privatization. The post office could be spun off, but as a quasi-governmental authority it does not now receive federal subsidies. Conrail was sold in 1987 (Glassman, 1994). The next major privatization was the sale of the government's uranium enrichment operations. Following the decision to divest this operation by the Congress and the Administration, Morgan Stanley and Company was hired to identify the option which would best meet several objectives:

1. provide the most value to the government, estimated to be in the neighborhood of nearly $2 billion;
2. insure the domestic supply of enriched uranium; and
3. protect national security (Strom, 1995).

According to the General Accounting Office (GAO, 1995c), the major divestiture proposals currently under consideration (in addition to the Helium Program, which will be discussed later) were the Naval Petroleum Reserves, the United States Enrichment Corporation, and the four Power Marketing Administrations. The sale of Amtrak in the northeast US is also a possibility.

A very different set of recommendations came from the National Research Council. This prestigious group was established by Congress, as a private group, to advise the government. In 1995 Congress requested that the council examine how the federal government allocates federal funds for science and technology. In this case, unlike the generally negative view of the accomplishments of the government by the general population, the 18-member panel of distinguished scientists was very laudatory of the federal government's post-World War II research accomplishments. How to maintain these successes in the future, given budget deficits and worldwide changes, was the charge. As a beginning, the Council wants the government to clarify its expenditures. Nearly half of the federal research expenditures are used in the development of new aircraft and weapons and establishing new production lines, not in the creation of new knowledge or technologies. In regard to privatization, it recommended that grants should finance projects and people, not institutions, and that academic research should take precedence over that done by industry and that which takes place in federal laboratories. This could include the closing of the federal laboratories, generally considered models of successful governmental operations (Broad, 1995).

There are also airports, utilities, bridges, tunnels, and turnpikes, NASA, fire and police departments, correctional institutions, mental health, public health, and public welfare departments, among others. Jack Kemp, when Secretary of Housing and Urban Development and most recently, Republican Vice Presidential candidate, was an advocate of the sale of low-income public housing to its tenants. The new governor of New York, George Pataki, in his first address on privatization, referenced Kemp, and proposed the sale of some of the state's 21,000 housing units to individual tenants or entire projects to the private sector (Hernandez, 1995). The sale of Social Security to the private sector has long been advocated. Interest in the private collection of taxes is resurfacing.

There are truly logical candidates for privatization. The state-operated lotteries and off-track betting (OTB) are examples. Despite the face validity of such an option, these have remained solidly public operations, sometimes under state authorities (quasi-government), and more frequently as state agencies. Nor should we forget the occasional municipal program. In New York City the off-track betting agency generated more than $17.4 billion in income from 1970 to 1991 (Marriott, 1992). The reasons for the failure to privatize are likely two; they are hot beds of political patronage and there are no special interest or professional groups vying for their control (Marriott, 1992).

Tongue in cheek, the *New York Times* in one editorial asked "Why not privatize New York's streets?" (1983, p. A30): "The streets are worse than ever, nothing else is working, why not sell them?" But the *Times* then reminds the reader that some streets and bridges were privately owned at one time, and the need for equity and the common good soon replaced such ownership. The *Times* suggests that just as the construction of streets is contracted, daily maintenance might also be contracted.

To Congress, as noted earlier, a near-classic example of a federal program ripe for privatization, and one cited by politicians of all major political persuasions, is the governmental operation in Texas of a plant to produce helium. It was established in 1925 to insure that the Army Air Corps would have an adequate supply of helium. It was enlarged by Congress in 1960 when there were no private producers in the United States (by 1960, helium was also being used in the new rockets). There are now 14 private helium producers in the country producing 91% of the helium sold in the United States. The balloons and blimps now use less than 1% of the federally produced helium at a price 10% above the price of the market. (The federal agencies are required to make their helium purchases solely from the Federal Bureau of Mines' plant). The U.S. produces more than eight times the helium produced in the rest of the world and is the world's largest exporter. The federal reserve is sufficient to supply the government for 100 years at its present consumption rate (Brooke, 1995). The sale of the reserve is likely, but at a price that will not undermine the private sector. Given these limits, the future of the 50-year-old plant is uncertain.

But privatization is seldom easy to do well or completely. As the legislation making the necessary devolution of the manufacture of helium was wending its way through the legislative chambers, the American Physical Association, a professional association of American physicists, warned of serious problems. Given the growth in utilization and the practice of discarding about half the supply of helium recovered each year, the physicists estimate that this nonrenewable substance will be depleted in 21 years. They do not advocate a continued governmental role in storage, but instead argue that government should play a major role in stimulating conservation (Browne, 1996).

How equity and the common good, when required, can be guaranteed is largely ignored by most of the advocates of the above transfers, for most of the programs discussed were at one time the responsibility of the private sector and were converted to public sector control because of gaps or flaws in their operation. Lekachman (1987), in a post-mortem of the Reagan years, sees the United States serving as a playground for the rich, and not an accommodating place for the poor and vulnerable. Privatization he views as a development to be equated with unemployment, militarization, and a victory for plutocracy.

Private toll roads are now once again hot properties. Both California and Virginia were scheduled for such openings in 1995 (Glassman, 1994). Both the internationalization and the irony of privatization (US corporations are all over Eastern Europe and Asia) is evidenced by the funding sources of Virginia's toll road, the Dulles Greenway—Banks from Germany, Britain, and Switzerland were in the lead (Glassman, 1994). Even more ironically, the private toll road in California was constructed in Orange County (Ayres, 1996), the nation's wealthiest county, as measured by the income of its residents; but this is consistent with the country's recent behavior. Rather than increase its taxes to pay the debts that it owed, it chose to go into bankruptcy. Six months after its opening, the 10-mile road is described as a success in a front-page story in the *Boston Globe*. The developers are discussing whether to extend the express lanes by 15 miles in each direction, as permitted in the contract with the state (Pertman, 1996a).

INSIGHTS FROM THE PAST:
TRENDS FOR THE FUTURE

The trend is obvious: privatization will continue and likely expand in the United States and elsewhere. As privatization accelerates, the likelihood is that POS will grow selectively. Efficiency is the catchword across both government and corporations and since POS is seen by many to be consistent with this objective, its current popularity is enhanced. (The issues of ideology will be addressed in more detail below.)

In Britain, the Conservative government is trying to make governmental units develop specific performance and financial goals and to compete with the private sector (Stevenson, 1995). Large departments are decentralized. For routine tasks, the private sector is increasingly called upon.

The Clinton Administration continues to "reinvent government" under the aegis of Vice President Albert Gore. Under Ronald Reagan there was the President's *Private Sector Survey on Cost Control* (also known as the Grace Commission).

American corporations which are downsizing both employees and functions are themselves a major test of contracting functions. The traditional model of the vertical organization is being severely tested and found wanting. More and more, corporations are contracting for goods and services rather than manufacturing or delivering them themselves. The ultimate example can be found in the UltrAir Line in Houston, Texas, which leases the entire operation: planes, pilots, attendants, agents, gates, office space, and six Boeing 727 aircraft. The chairman says the objective is to own nothing; to be maximally flexible in a tenuous environment (Woodbury, 1993).

In Germany, according to *The Economist* ("DIY in Germany" 1996), outsourcing is being balanced by insourcing. The criteria for survival of internal manufacturing appears to be two: strong unions, which negotiate limits on outsourcing by offering greater flexibility in working conditions and wages, and those companies who occupy small niches and sell high-margin merchandise, and focus on quality rather than on price.

Whither Continuing Governmental Responsibility and Programming?

Depending on the level of desired change, the opposition can shift. Even the one quasi consistent major source of opposition, public employees' unions, is showing some willingness to compromise, as reported in the chapter by Demone (Gibelman & Demone, 1998, Vol. II). Nor at any time was there consistent comprehensive opposition by organized labor as a whole. Both privatization and purchases of service may be to the benefit of some unions which might gain new members by the changing developments.

In the Argentine, according to the World Bank (GAO, 1996), despite a reduction in the number of governmental employees employed in public enterprises from about 348,000 in 1990 to 67,000 in 1994, there was little opposition from organized labor. The combination of low public sector wages, generous severance benefits and the large proportion of employees holding more than one position appeared to blunt the resistance (GAO, 1996).

In France, members of the CGT communist-led trade union demonstrated to halt the sale of the government's 49% of the Renault corporation and other proposed privatization. The Renault workers invaded the French Wall Street. Curiously, the company had only been nationalized after World War II (Reuters, 1994b) and provides another example of the cyclical nature of many of these crossnational events. The framework also included a plan by the French government to convert 21 state companies to private ownership, which included, in addition to Renault, Air France, insurance companies, and banks. The only large state companies not on the privatization list were the telephone and power companies (Echikoson, 1993). And note that the latter two, although publicly regulated, are almost always in the private sector in the United States.

Sacred cows may be culture-bound. The social welfare contract in France has more strength than its American counterpart. Even modest recommended changes led in late 1995 to major strikes and demonstrations. The privatization recommendations had to be withdrawn and other proposals negotiated ("Political Warfare in France," 1995b).

Another cyclical example is to be found in the banks of Mexico which went from private to nationalized to private in about a decade from the mid-1980s to early in the 1990s ("Mexican bank privatization," 1991). Also in common with France, the Mexican public employees are engaged in concerted opposition to the proposed sale by the government of some of its petrochemical operations (Dillon, 1995).

In Haiti, the immediate past president (Aristide) and his close friend and successor have broken over the privatization of nine state-owned companies. Although both had pledged to implement such a program as a component of their American and other financial aid, President Aristide opposed such a commitment after leaving office. He said such action " has never improved the lot of citizens in any country" (Rohter, 1996, p. 6).

In England, the Liberal Party and the civil service unions have continued to attack both the proposals and the programs of the Conservatives (Stevenson, 1995). The planned sale of the post office failed when the

Conservative party lost some of its own members from rural constituencies who feared the closing of some of their local offices (Reuters, 1994a).

Shifting Values and Ideology

Attitudes Toward Government. Nearly 30 years ago, Peter Drucker (1968) was alerting his readers to a major shift in values in the Western world. We had cycled out of a belief in the capacity of government as the principal problem-solving institution. Politization was declining in acceptance; Privatization was on the assent. Drucker called it "reprivatization" then. To Senator Pat Moynihan (Purdom, 1994, p. 52), "The century began with vast expectations of what government could do and ended up with a huge amount of disappointment."

Robert Samuelson, in his book *The Good Life and its Discontents* (1996) talks about the transformation of the American dream into the American fantasy. We expected everything to be solved by government. Our ambitions were unattainable, and it is these that we measure rather than actual accomplishments.

There appear to be several corresponding simultaneous overlapping forces at work. The rise of capitalism, renewed interest in federalism, support for decentralization and/or devolution, anti-tax fever, states' rights, disenchantment and distrust of government, especially at the central level, hostility toward both elected and appointed officials (known invidiously as politicians and bureaucrats) and big governments, all spark the debate.

Support for the federal government, in the U.S. and elsewhere, is limited. The Volker Commission on the Public Service found that less than 10% of honors students in the colleges and universities would consider governmental employment, and that includes the still slightly more legitimate state and local government (Peters, 1995). In 1995, at one major school of public health, almost all of the Health Policy and Management graduates went to work for the private sector at salaries substantially in excess of the usual practice.

Most of the cited "values" are quite pragmatic. They reflect a disenchantment with big government, including those aspects which have or have not worked. Most of the attention has been directed to allegations of failures. If government could eliminate poverty, make progress in the "war" on cancer that it also committed itself to achieve, the public would be more sanguine, even though the superordinate goals of eradication were totally unrealistic. Unfortunately our adversarial political system, increasingly reflecting our judicial system's problem-solving methods, is committed to overpromising, and remains in the memories of most people as having failed to fulfill its promises.

There is one ideology, that of federalism, which is often cited by politicians to justify their positions. George Will (1992) periodically reminds the body politic of its existence. Politicians revel in its simplicity. They can cite its support of almost any position. Historians and political scientists see complexity and are intrigued by its potential role. (For a recent analysis see Elkins and McKitrick (1994) in *The Age of Federalism* and Banning (1995) in *The Sacred Fire of Liberty.*

Although now claimed by the Republican party, manifestations of the new federalism can be found in the administrations of every recent American president from Eisenhower to Clinton. Each administration has searched for ways to decentralize the federal government, which they referenced under the rubric of federalism. Eisenhower appointed committees to study and to propose ways to return programs to the states. For example, one plan had the federal government dedicating a substantial percentage of the federal telephone tax revenues to the states in return for the states giving up selected grants in aid.

During the Kennedy/Johnson years efforts were made to strengthen federal regional offices and to consolidate a variety of categorical programs into block grants to the states. Johnson spoke of this as creative federalism. The most unique features of those years were the series of grants bypassing the states and going directly to the counties and cities and towns. The states, vigorous supporters of grants to themselves, were consistently opposed to permitting the cities, towns, and counties the same privileges. Another innovative feature of these grants was that newly established not-for-profit agencies or quasipublic agencies were established to receive the funds in many jurisdictions.

The Nixon/Ford Administrations' "New Federalism" (Office of Management and Budget OMB), (1973) focused on

1. cooperation among all levels of government;
2. channeling resources to that level best able and willing to meet the needs of the people;
3. reversing the trend to centralization; and
4. instilling a new respect for personal freedom and individual responsibility.

Not cited under the statement of principles was the identification of six operating procedures, one which included the private sector in part as follows; "if a public service can best be provided by the private sector, what program changes are required to take advantage of that opportunity?" (OMB, 1973, pp. 6–7).

To Jimmy Carter it was the "new partnership." The implementation language was remarkably similar to that used by his several predecessors.

Ronald Reagan was fond of noting that the federal government had been created by the states, echoing the Nixon values. President Bush was similarly inclined, and President Clinton sought to both reinvent government and expand block grants to the states.

Historical inaccuracies by the presidential speechwriters aside, the Constitution states " We the people of the United States . . . do ordain and establish this constitution . . . ," not state or local government. The successful practicing politician (as measured by reelection) is a pragmatist. As noted earlier, the true believer would eliminate all federal activities except some defense and limited foreign affairs, and thus acts as an anchor at one end of the continuum. Attacks on the size of the federal bureaucracy are equally uninformed. Excluding military employees, the actual number of federal employees has remained roughly stable in size for more than 30 years. On a proportionate basis, as the population has grown, the ratio of employees has been declining steadily for about 40 years. The increase in expenditures is a function of growth in entitlements, voucher equivalents, income transfers, pensions (including Social Security), aid to the states, and contracts, not in the number of full-time federal employees. "Star Wars" is a classic example of major capital expenditures not requiring a significant real increase in the federal work force. It is accurate to say that there had been a substantial actual growth in the numbers of employees in state and local government, although even that has stabilized in recent years. The opposite end of the continuum is archered by those who believe government can solve our problems.

The popular ideology at the end of this century seems to be centered around several main and not always consistent themes:

1. government is too large and should be substantially decreased in size;
2. taxes should be reduced;
3. governmental functions should be transferred to governments closer to the people;
4. a safety net should be retained for the worthy poor, but not as an entitlement; and
5. the unworthy poor are to be on their own.

The goal is to undo the New Deal, the Great Society, and their several manifestations. More recently, more attention has been placed on the marketplace as the appropriate locus for most decision making. More on this later.

A battery of books (by James Carville, E.J. Dionne, Jr., and Jacob Weisberg) argue that government and the country have done well in recent years (Flint, 1996). Even conservative columnist Robert J. Samuelson, in his book *The Good Life and its Discontents* (1996), comparing the nation with its 1940 status, finds that Americans are living much better.

Curiously, in Canada, it is the Federalists who have been fighting to retain a single nation, opposing the separation of Quebec as a freestanding country, whereas contemporary American federalists are opting for a nominal national government.

Given this continuing long-standing debate about the role of federalism—really, the role of government—what are the implications for privatization and the purchase of services?

Federalism in most of its operating forms is conceptually supportive of privatization and contracting in general. Given our focus on the human services, the picture is more mixed. The devolution of functions to the states accompanied by a substantial reduction in resources and reduced federal regulations means substantial cuts somewhere. For the states to compensate for the budget cuts, they have to operate more efficiently, and under no circumstance are the federal regulations responsible for 20–25% of the operating budgets of these agencies. The bulk of the regulations serves one of three purposes: (1) to reduce the likelihood of malfeasance of misfeasance; (2) to make sure that a minimum standard of quality is in place; and (3) to elaborate the enabling statute. All three are there because of demands on the system, and often engender considerable negative publicity. All three also reflect a desire for a zero error rate. All three are often functions of failed or flawed state and local operations in the past. In any case, the devolution to the state means that the nation will once again operate with 50-plus full sets of state, district, and territorial regulations, with all sorts of untoward consequences. The *Federal Personnel Manual* alone runs for about 10,000 pages, supplemented by thousand of addenda pages (Putzel, 1993).

Another likely scenario, more pertinent to our topic, is that given declining resources, budget reductions are essential. Depending on the nature of the program, most direct service programs are heavily invested in human resources. Income transfer programs, of course, are much less invested in staff. Personnel downsizing is essential in one, reductions in income transfer in the other. Experience tells us that if personnel reductions are required, they will occur last, if at all, among governmental employees. The vendors are the first to feel the effect of budget reductions. An interesting exception may be in the making. In respect to the proposed substantial budget reduction in the federal Environmental Protection Agency, which uses contracting extensively, Congress has indicated that it wants the burden shared equally between the private sector and the Agency (Cushman, 1995).

The history of contracted services in the District of Columbia (Gibelman, 1998, Vol. 2) is a near classic example of how much damage can be done to the not-for-profit sectors when a government out of control abandons its obligations. For the most part new POS activities come from new money and programs, with the least negative effect on the existing bureaucracy, which will fight to maintain its existing positions. Despite these complications, growth in privatization and POS will likely continue with the few remaining city hospitals and mass transportation agencies with a for-profit potential being the next likely candidates.

The clients, too, face a world that had gradually been changed and will doubtless cycle back into considerations of "worthiness" as a criterion for assistance. It is likely that they will be the ones most at risk. As examples, young unmarried pregnant women and crack users have been found to be "unworthy" and subject to invidious discrimination.

Disenchantment About Government

Because well-designed survey research is an invention of this last half century, we cannot be fully certain that the negative attitudes toward government are uniquely a contemporary phenomena. There are historical anecdotes suggesting otherwise. The staff supplied to Washington on his inauguration was minimal. Jefferson's remark to the effect that the least government was the best government was well quoted.

We suggest, of course, that the large worldwide interest in privatization is substantially a product of this disenchantment. For some, the feelings are even more intense. The government is the enemy. As long as it continues, these efforts to reduce or modify government will continue at a steady pace.

How Deep Is the Disenchantment with Government? Maureen Dowd (1995) was "thunderstruck" to learn that the Montgomery, Maryland county government is eliminating the word "government" from letter-heads, business cards, and official cars, among other alternatives. The reason, according to the county executive of this wealthy county, a Democrat, is that the word is "arrogant" and "off-putting" (p. E13). This formulation is more drastic than some others that come to mind, but it is not entirely new. An example of rather long-standing antipathy to government was a personal experience with state-supported alcoholism clinics located in general hospitals in Massachusetts in the late 1950s. One of the clinics had persuaded one of the three national television networks to do a half-hour Sunday prime time story about their clinic. At no time during the program was there any reference to its status as a state clinic or the fact that the state was its principal financial supporter. A more current example is the executive of a not-for-profit social service agency who proclaims enthusiastically and loudly of the superiority of the private sector over the public sector. His entire budget is based on contracts with the public sector. At the very least, his self-proclaimed expertise does not suggest very enlightened self-interest. His public agency peers are not happy with his constant public criticisms, and since his contracts depend on their continuing support, he may be writing his own obituary.

But the trend is not only one-sided. The libertarian-Republican governor of Massachusetts, William Weld, who ran in 1990 as a strong advocate of privatization, toned down his enthusiasm in 1994 when he successfully ran for reelection. The polls and focus groups and strong political opposition made evident the negative as well as positive features to him as an elected official. Later, as a candidate for the U.S. Senate, he resurrected "privatization" as a compaign issue but integrated it along with downsizing government and lowered taxes as a total package.

Rutgers University, one of ten pre-Revolutionary universities in the United States, did not become New Jersey's state university until after World War II. It is periodically facing critics who want to change its name to the State University of New Jersey. The current solution is for all official documents to describe it as Rutgers, the State University of New Jersey.

A quick scanning demonstrates the depth of the lack of confidence in all three branches of the federal government. The year 1966 was special. The Harris people developed its confidence measure in the institutions of this nation and never again, to this writing, have they ever been so high as in 1966. Medicine, higher education, and the military were all then held in high esteem. A decade later the White House, under Lyndon Johnson, was respected by only 20% of the population, but it has been viewed with more favor subsequently, in a context in which all the other institutions declined in the subsequent measuring periods (Harris, 1987). In the golden years of 1966, half of the top 7 $\frac{1}{2}$ measured institutions, of a total of 15, were governmental; the military, the U.S. Supreme Court, Congress (# 7) and in the middle (# 8), was local government (Harris, 1987).

In 1973 Harris was reporting a mixed finding. Compared to an earlier 1970s study, there was a general increase in the confidence level of most Americans in their institutions, with some exceptions; falling below 33% were all three branches of the government, combined with similar negative attitudes toward the press, major companies, and organized labor. In fact, compared to the findings of the study in 1966, all the major key institutions except the press and television news were well below the former confidence levels. The major declines were found in the federal executive branch, the U.S. Supreme Court, and the major corporations. In context, the Vietnam conflict had ended and the press and Congress had successfully investigated the Watergate corruption. In the general population 53% felt there was "something deeply wrong in America" ("In trashmen we trust," 1973). Nor was any improvement found 3 years later. *The U.S. News and World Report* ("How Americans judge basic institutions," 1976), in another survey of the general population, ranked 26 "institutions" on two sets of criteria; (1) honesty, dependability, and integrity, and (2) competency, or ability to get things done. Seven of the bottom half, 13 in all, of those rated under "honesty" were governmental units, including state government. Local government escaped the bottom half by ranking 13th. The other six which were rated in the bottom half (not covered under government) were the two major political parties, the legal profession, large businesses, advertising agencies, and labor union leaders.

The rating of "competency" found some shifting views: governmental bodies assumed 10 of the bottom positions, while the legal profession and the two political parties constituted the remaining three slots.

By 1979, the last year of the Carter administration according to Yankelvich ("Trust in government," 1985) national confidence in government had sunk to about 20%. By late 1984, confidence in government had risen to between 40% and 45%.

Not to be intimidated by quantitative survey data, Ronald Reagan informed the nation in his first inaugural address that "Government is not the solution: government is the problem" (Reagan, 1982).

In 1986, Gallup was reporting that of seven major services delivered, those delivered by local government were evaluated the poorest. Supermarkets received a 58% "very high" rating, compared to 22% for local government services (Shriver, 1986).

In 1989, in a *Washington Post*–ABC News poll, about 75% of the respondents were saying that members of Congress would lie to them if the truth would hurt them politically. A similar proportion believed that Congress favors special interests more than they favor the average citizen. Curiously, but consistently, they offer a much more favorable opinion about their own congressional member (Morin & Balz, 1989).

In the same year, the UCLA Institute for Social Science Research reported on a study of 1,000 Southern California residents regarding confidence in government ("Study reveals Southern California attitudes," 1989). The most confidence in government was placed in the state government (59%), next in local government (54%) and last, the federal government (51%). When the question was reversed and focused on "not much confidence" the percentages are about the same (28 to 30%). Although these are not exciting figures for the governmental advocate, they suggest some confidence among slightly more than half of the respondents. Equally important, among those who see decentralization as the solution to lack of confidence, the data do not suggest that much difference among the three levels of government.

By 1990, the alienation from government had continued to grow. Compared to its 1987 study, those with annual incomes above $50,000 were less likely to have grown more concerned than those with lower incomes. According to the two surveys by the *Times-Mirror* Center for the People (Oreskes, 1990, p. A26) the "cynicism toward the political system in general is growing as the public in unprecedented numbers associates Republicans with wealth and greed, Democrats with fecklessness and incompetence."

The 1994 *Washington Post*–ABC News Poll reported similar findings. More than 60% of the public did not approve of the way Congress was doing its job (Morin & Broder, 1994). Nor was there a change for the better 2 months later. Kevin Philips (1994) reported that only 3% of the middle class felt things were becoming better for them, and that only 25%, compared to 10 or 20 years ago, felt there were more opportunities for the average American to get ahead today; 49% described fewer opportunities.

These negative attitudinal reports are mirrored at the extremes, in part, by the bitter antigovernment hate groups which are now sweeping part of the West. They see themselves as protecting the country from outside forces (Stern, 1996). Acts of civil disobedience are being reported more frequently. Federal employees are being threatened. Shots are fired at them (Larson, 1995). Their cars are bombed. Vigilante groups and militia are more popular. By late 1995, northern Nevada was completing a 2-year wave of violence targeting federal employees. Four separate incidents of bombings had been identified (Noble, 1995).

Roger Morris (cited in Turner, 1996), in his cynical analysis of the Clinton Administration, finds fault with all of Washington. Congress is corrupt, the political parties are venal, the bureaucracy and their Congressional staff peers are self-serving, overpaid, and arrogant. The press and corporations are equally blessed. Scorn underlies Morris' evaluations.

In this context, POS pales as an issue. If changing some roles and introducing the private sector into the equation has some positive potential, then it is worth a serious effort. It is to be noted again that when big business or state and local governments are compared with the federal government; they do not fare well either. A majority of the public is similarly disenchanted with all of them. The residents of Derry, New Hampshire, polled in October 1995 in anticipation of the presidential primaries, saw the Clinton Administration, the Congress, and the Derry town government in similar dreary terms. Only about 5 to 8% described any of them as "very effective." The state government reached a 18% approval rating, hardly a shining example, but certainly better than its peers (Rezendes, 1995). The differences between the various levels of government (elected and appointed), large business, organized labor and lawyers, and the media are modest. None do well. The assumption that the devolution of authority from the federal to state governments will help to deal with the inherent difficulty facing all governments is surely simplistic and flawed, and likely to create more problems than it solves.

The companion naïve notion has to do with the capacity of the American voluntary associations that politicians claim will replace the services and funding of government. As the federal government downsizes and state and local government stabilize, according to Robert D. Putnam, the participation in voluntary associations has declined between 25 and 50% in the last 30 years (Lewis, 1995; Roberts, 1995).

Monitoring

One of the few matters on which both opponents and supporters of privatization agree is that the quality of monitoring the programs, whether they are operated by the public or private sector, needs to be effective. (The conservative, however, may not be willing to pay for the function. The marketplace may be satisfactory.)

Opponents and proponents may even find common ground on some of the alternative means that are available. For a comprehensive view of human service monitoring developments in the last 15–20 years, see Chapter 7 by Kettner and Martin (this volume). In the second volume of this two-volume series Davidson (1998) and her colleagues describe their effort to evaluate a new Veterans Administration program in gerontology, and Fishbein and McCarty (1998) describe their effort to design a new procedure to monitor substance abuse programs.

An important overarching issue is to separate the idiosyncratic from the systemic. The superordinate objectives may either be so global and idealistic as to be generally unfeasible; or they may be so concrete that they dominate the program and prove to be counterproductive to the other objectives.

Public Provision v. Public Financing. One area of difference is the question of whether monitoring is better facilitated when the employees delivering the service are employed by the same governmental agency responsible for the funding and monitoring, or whether the governmental agencies' objectives are better achieved when the employees are employed by the organization under contract to the public agency. Having played all four alternative roles (a public manager, public employee, a private manager, and service deliverer) sometime in my career, the authors believe that the public manager is provided better short-term options only when the employees are members of the staff of a small public agency early in its history. For large agencies and for long-term and cost-effective results, the public administrators' role is generally enhanced when the employees are not direct members of the staff of the public agency executive.

The extent of the nomenclature encompassing monitoring—program evaluation, oversight, laws, regulations, auditing, policing, and comptrolling—is impressive. Demone (1998, Vol. II) identifies the substantial range of ascribed and achieved monitors. The public sector is replete with them. Some are in the formal criminal justice system, some in the public justice system and most are a standard component of the bureaucracy.

Effective monitoring must be helpful, supportive, and enhancing of the goals of the contract. To convert it to a police-type function is to abrogate the purpose for which the program was originally established. Pragmatically, we are convinced that every complex organization needs effective, helpful, cost-effective monitoring procedures. They are best constructed from a comprehensive management-planning information system. A useful system must be built component by component, with those responsible for the direct collection of the data set closely involved in the design and pretest.

In regard to program evaluation, we are equally convinced that to be maximally useful, the cost of the evaluation will often exceed the cost of the intervention being evaluated, and if the program is important, such an expenditure is well warranted.

The future issues are several; some are of possible vital importance. Among the several reasons that government is so ill-situated is that we, the public, have required that both elected and appointed officials compete with overpromises reflecting the worst of our product advertising. To Samuelson (1996) it is the politics of overload, the overuse of government. The public does not believe the manufacturers of the products; they know that they exaggerate and puff up their wares. But somehow, even though we distrust our elected officials with equal vigor and also those who aspire to such posts, we still assume that the new or modified programs are going to achieve something of that which was promised. We also require a zero error rate. Errors are not to be tolerated, and corruption is forbidden.

To achieve these impossible objectives, we layer the bureaucracy. Each scandal almost inevitably leads to the addition of more managers and rules to control abuses. More often than not, the cost of controlling potential corruption is greater than the unscrupulousness to be controlled. In reaction to alleged abuses, we may well drive the costs of developing and managing the additional control mechanisms so high as to effectively reduce or eliminate the savings from privatization. The goal of perfection may well be the enemy of good.

To limit the ravages of patronage, a civil service system is invented and then further encumbered with the organization of the same people into labor unions (Stevenson, 1995).

The press and the politicians, both of whom are highly vulnerable to criticism, are falling over each other looking for exposes to uncover.

This combination of a government ill-conceived and supported with self serving enemies constantly in the attack mode will likely enhance the move to both privatization and the purchase of more services. Neither will come easily, and each step will be increasingly opposed by those who see themselves losing by the changes and by those who are ideologically opposed to both options. They will seek private-sector calumny with equal ferror and press toward the same unachievable objectives, standards, and fiscal and personnel procedures that effectively made incompetent the public sector.

We may well find ourselves with two overmanaged, overregulated, bureaucratized sectors, public and private.

Cost Control and Savings

For many of the advocates of privatization, two companion assumptions are at work. The first is that government, by definition, is inefficient; and the second is that the private sector is efficient. These purists also define "private" as equivalent to for-profit. If asked, they will classify the not-for-profits as possibly more efficient than government, but not by any substantial margin. Thus in this and the following section, in an effort to be future-oriented, we will look first at the issue of cost savings and then follow with a fresh look at the similarities and differences of both the for-profit and not-for-profit sectors as players in privatization.

Dukakis (1998, Vol. II) talks about the importance to the state of having several vendors competing with each other for contracts. Bendick (1989) in his analysis of when not to contract, comes to the same conclusion. Other nonideological reasons not to contract include (1) too high administrative costs, (2) when corruption is found in the contracting process, and (3) if excess and unnecessary costs are placed in the contracts.

Another tactic is to determine where the alleged savings are to be found. In Massachusetts, Johnston (1998) notes that the state pays line staff substantially more than do the private vendors providing the same service. Other sources of savings may also be counterproductive. In some contracts, compared to direct public management, it has been noted that staff-client ratios are increased while staff qualifications are lowered. Similarly, supervisor–staff ratios may be higher, or less pre-service and in-service training may be required with fewer full-time equivalent specialists permitted. It may be that the governmental programs were overstaffed, overpaid, and overqualified, but there is little empirical evidence to that end. It is clear that efficiency is not a high priority in governmental employment. There are many other goals which rank higher.

Given the likely relevance of these issues, what are the implications for the future of privatization? Will the public permit government to be more efficient? Will our priorities change? Will technologies stimulate higher levels of efficiency even though our priorities do not change?

Many local and state governments are establishing procedures by which governmental agencies may bid competitively on contracts. Several jurisdictions, to protect the public agencies, require that those proposing that activities be contracted demonstrate that clear savings will occur to government. In none of these options, to the best of our knowledge, have clear, explicit requirements been established to accurately cost out the public expenditures. In our experience, the overhead items are constantly understated, because they fail to include the substantial infrastructure costs which permeate government. If this trend to protect public sector employees continues, expansion of POS is limited.

Brodkin and Young (1989) suggest that the size of the government unit may be a critical variable. Small government units may well be competitive with the private sector, whereby the large, more complex governmental organizations are structurally constrained.

An even more damning trend is to be found in the substantial human service budget cuts at all levels of government. If the goal is to contract, as we have noted elsewhere, employees already occupying positions protected by civil service and organized labor or because of political patronage are certainly less vulnerable than more recent and unorganized employees in small not-for-profit agencies. Large for-profit organizations with deep pockets may be in a better position to demonstrate their strength and largesse, but not many of them are in the human services, exclusive of the health industry.

Regarding technologies, there is still no clear evidence in the private for-profit sector of a current correlation between the major integration of modern technology and productivity. The Bureau of Labor Statistics for 1980 through 1994 found productivity increases averaging as low as 1.4% ("Overcoming the productivity paradox,"1995a). This flies in the face of the widely held belief of most executives that technology has made their organizations more productive. The data do not support that contention and is symptomatic of other corporate myths.

There are areas in which technology is a clear choice. Tax collection and airport traffic control are examples of units both desperately needing contemporary technology and seemingly unable to effectively manage internal changes (GAO, 1995a). In some examples, of which tax collection is one, the public may be very satisfied with the delays in improving their tax-collecting technology, but airport safety delay is different and totally unacceptable. Yet the integration of contemporary technology seems to be beyond the capacity of those making the decisions.

Corporate America has substantially modernized its technology. Government is several steps behind in its implementation. But independent of the stage of technology development, significant improvement in productivity has yet to be felt. Thus, the influence of technology on the future of POS/privatization seems to be unclear at this time.

Differences and Similarities in For-Profits and Not-for-Profits As They Participate in Privatization

Brodkin and Young (1989) lean to the use of the not-for-profits in the delivery of complex services, as in day care or nursing homes, for these providers can be better trusted. When services can be readily classified (and better monitored) the for-profits may be more efficient and thus be allowed to bid.

Bendick (1989) is similarly inclined. He would limit for-profit providers to specific conditions when goals and performance standards can be articulated, and are "amenable to explicit, arms-length monitoring and control" (p. 113).

Alternatively, if program simplification is feasible to facilitate better monitoring, some programs not contractible in general or specifically to the for-profit sectors, might be converted to purchase form (Bendick, 1989). This means that there would be clear constraints on individual decision making by the vendor staff.

In essence, there are essential complex services of sufficient importance to humankind that the profit motive must not be allowed to be superordinate. Lord Dahrendorf, the former head of The London School of Economics was quoted recently as warning against "an economism run amok" and attitudes that scorn "non-economic motives that lead people to do things because they are right, or because people have a sense of duty, a commitment" (Lewis, 1995, p. A17).

Of special concern is the future of those segments of the voluntary not-for-profit sectors, the bulk of whose budget is derived from government. There is a general agreement among the students of the nonprofit sector that POS (not privatization) has had a significant impact on that sector. One major concern has to do with the diminution of the nonprofits' capacity to act as advocates for their clients in an environment when the very public agency funding the vendor is the one that should be criticized. Curiously, as of this writing, conservative members of Congress are trying to remove the remaining declining advocacy capacity by statutory means. They say that organizations most able to offer constructive advice should not be criticizing the hand that feeds them. For-profit organizations with governmental contracts are not to be similarly constrained. In Colorado, via initiative and referendum, the 1996 ballot held a measure to eliminate property tax deductions from religious and most other nonprofit organizations ("Coloradans propose," 1996). These increasing constraints are all occurring as the voluntary sector is being asked to be the savior. Ann Kaplan (1996), the editor of *Giving USA*, notes that during the last decade the major growth in the financing of nonprofit organizations has been in fees and charges, not in contributions and support from government. She also derides the increasing regulations and taxes, as the not-for-profit sector is simultaneously being asked to be the protector of the poor and viewed as a swindler in need of bureaucratic controls. "Realistic appraisals of the possible must precede ambitious leaps into the future" (Kaplan, 1996, p. 12E).

Universities are comparably placed. Given the post-World War II growth of federal research and training support, the nation has departments and schools at many of our major research and teaching universities receiving more than half of their income from federal grant and contract support. Despite this apparent potential impediment, they have found it possible to be informed critics and advocates, even in their financially dependent situation. It may be that they are more cautious or more indirect, but they continue to find ways to have their voices heard. Thus, there are examples of like organizations with longer histories which have found ways to maintain their freedom of voice. The academic environment, however, may be an important enabling influence.

It should also be noted that most contracts are with organizations in the individual service delivery business. Organizations focusing almost exclusively on advocacy are less likely to offer a service of use to governmental agencies.

The other roles that have been traditionally played by the nonprofits are more at risk. Kramer (1994) notes that in the personal social services, prior to the major growth in POS, the agencies were seen as offering alternate, supplementary, or complimentary roles. Now, under contract, they more often are a substitute for government. Experimentation and innovation may be negatively influenced. Certainly, dependency on government is enhanced.

One certain new development is managed social services, paralleling managed health care. Some of the components, for example, flat fees for a particular function, have been a staple of some service contracting for years. The provision of bonuses to not-for-profits for controlling costs will be a new development, although it has precedence in the foster care-adoption field, where the federal government has used bonuses to encourage the states and local communities. The Defense Department has long used bonuses to encourage contractors. Massachusetts, on a formal basis, entered the managed care world in 1996 with a $45 million plan to serve 800 troubled youth, ages 12 to 18, then in residential care (Grunwald, 1996). This group represented some of the most difficult clients facing the Department of Social Services.

Changes are manifested in the voluntary agency's primary service focus, types of programs offered, mode of operation, and style of management. There may well be unintended consequences occurring over time on an incremental basis. In the quest to expand, supplement, or add to the services that they offer to their client group, they have often entered a financially dependent relation with government with little consideration to long-term consequences. Will the specific contract enhance, inhibit, or be neutral in respect to the long-term direction of the agency? Is this relation one that has a long-term viability associated with it? Should a contract be sought which is not consistent with its superordinate objectives, but will bring in needed income (Demone & Gibelman, 1989)?

One of the more interesting developments in the health industry, but equally relevant to the entire not-for-profit sector, is that occurring in the Blue Cross and Blue Shield (BC/BS) industry. Because of the major competitive developments and the need for capital to expand, not readily available to the-not-for profit sectors, some of the state-wide Blues are converting to for-profit status in their entirety or by establishing for-profit subsidiaries. Some of the health maintenance organizations originally established as not-for-profits, Harvard and Rutgers Health Plans, for example, have found themselves in similar situations. Because of the perceived benefits in their not-for-profit status, corporate laws in many states require that they turn over their assets to the public if they dissolve their status. In California, after 3 years of debate, the Blue Cross turned more than $3 billion in stocks and cash to two newly established foundations. In Georgia, the Blue Cross by legislative action was allowed to retain its assets when it converted to for-profit status. The basic debate is whether the service to patients will be enhanced by the need to meet the financial demands of investors (Freudenheim, 1996).

These and other like concerns are posed in several of the chapters in this volume. The not-for-profit sector needs to be continually testing itself on the decisions it is making. The boundary-blurring proposition is often offered as a reason why the not-for-profit sectors should not accept contracts from governments. Grants, with their less restricted focus, are sometimes exempted from this proscription. There is a vision of pure types which distinguish the two, but, as noted earlier, those functions exclusively public are not easily differentiated, and given that the public sector is one half of the body, distinguishing that which is exclusively private—other than organized religion—may also be tenuous. There are several subsets of questions which need identification. Are there any generally accepted theories about the private sector, profit and/or not for profit, which clearly differentiate them from the public? Next, are there clear-cut empirical data on how auspice influences human services in regard to availability, accessibility, quality, continuity of care, and cost-effectiveness? Are there data to support the boundary-blurring hypothesis? And if there are such findings, can the dysfunctional aspects of the findings be demonstrated (Demone and Gibelman, 1989)?

It would appear that some hybrid organizations are evolving. Have they been evaluated to determine their functions and dysfunction?

Martin Rein (1989) is not convinced that the theories which separate the nonprofits from the market or public sectors are adequately explanatory. He sees overlapping and blurring. Ralph Kramer (1989) is similarly inclined. He describes a mixed, pluralistic, and more competitive social service economy, making outdated the traditional view of the appropriate roles of government and the not-for-profit sectors and their individual and shared relation to the for-profit sectors. Both questions—what is private and what is public, and what should be so—are exceedingly complex. The dichotomy may be seen as increasingly invalid and instead be viewed as a two-way penetration, a continuum, and blurring (Shepsle, 1980).

Vigilance and constant monitoring are still essential. The critics of government are still essential, although at this time in the history of Western government, critics are hardly in short supply. More than general shotgun criticism, we need enlightened and competent criticism and advocacy.

A more pragmatic concern has to with agency viability. As fads and priorities shift, the contract of today may be the nonrenewal of tomorrow. Even in satisfactory continuing activities, the public agency may change vendors for the sake of change. The ability to appreciate the differences between soft and hard resources, to manage during cash flow problems, to be able to shift resources and staff as the situation demands, all require skillful management, flexible organizations, and an understanding board of directors (Demone & Gibelman, 1989).

There are other special subtypes of organizations, essentially quasi-public by purpose, not by accident. The Office of Economic Opportunity stimulated the development of hundreds of local agencies, often using the formal structure of a not-for-profit organization, whose fundamental purpose was to receive and spend governmental funds as those agencies so proscribed. In turn, as these agencies have matured, many of them have broadened their charter and functions and diversified their funding sources. Many of the classic not-for-profits have, de facto, become quasi-governmental. (See Levine, Chapter 6, for a unique examination of the impact of contracting on sectarian agencies.) Their income base is essentially limited to government. Thus, one concern has been the blurring of the distinction between the two sectors, public and private. Each could have had different constituencies, modes of operation, service philosophies, and methods of service delivery. Are these pluralistic differences to be valued, and if they tend to merge over time, how can we be sure that the best features are the ones preserved?

There is some reason to believe that the government's methods of budgeting and human resource management will dominate and since the existence of both is one reason for the growth of POS and privatization, the loss to the nation could be substantial. Kramer (1994) has collected several of the metaphors to describe this mutual interpenetration and dependence: Third-party government, indirect public administration, the contract state, nonprofit federalism, the new or mixed economy of welfare.

Another factor of great importance is the threat to both the welfare state and governmental financing of health services (Medicare and Medicaid) as well as the numerous programs supported by the several federal departments. As the government attempts to deal with devolution of programs with reduced resources and simultaneously also reduce taxes, the agencies serving the poor, elderly, and disabled are going to be the first to suffer, and this could likely be grievous. If the experiences in the District of Columbia are the benchmarks against which future developments are to be measured, both public and private human service sectors are in trouble (Gibelman, 1998, Vol. II).

In an era in which the marketplace economy is being freed from regulatory constraints on the assumption that benefits will trickle down to those less fortunate, some comments about this fiction are relevant. Are for-profit organizations always maximally efficient, designed to produce an outstanding product, clearly dedicated to the bottom line, effective planners, honest in their dealings with their consumers, and generally well-regarded by the general public? The experiences of American automakers in competition with the Japanese are revealing. The Japanese both produce a better product and do it more efficiently. The short-sightedness of many American corporations as they focus on immediate profits, even to the detriment of their enlightened long-term self inter-est, has been documented repeatedly. That in 1994 nearly 70% of the major Pentagon suppliers were under investigation for a variety of alleged major improprieties is not heartening (Pasztor, 1996). As noted earlier, the American corporate leader fares only slightly better than elected and appointed public officials in polls of public attitudes.

As for security and trust, references to Ivan Boesky and Michael Millken, the American banking scandals of the 1980s and those of Japan and the United Kingdom in the 1990s are constant reminders of the need for ever-vigilance.

Barber (1995) concludes that unfettered markets lead to poverty, and a reduction in the middle class, topped with a small layer of the very wealthy. The not-for-profit and governmental sectors have their flaws too, but all is not well exclusively in the for-profit quarter.

Cycles

Given the cyclical history of most social inventions, there is little reason to believe that government will be in permanent disfavor, or that POS and privatization will continue their limited current favored status. Examples abound. The American and the world's economy have methodically expanded and contracted over the years. Even the determination of what is private and what is public has gone through several manifestations (Evans & Boyte, 1990). More abbreviated cycles, sometimes resembling fads, are also common. Whether it is the choice of drugs or alcoholic bev-erages, choices shift back and forth. The press likes to report on the pop-ularity of elected officials. Single incidents may substantially influence the ratings. Pearl Harbor for Roosevelt, the Truman Doctrine for Truman, the Cuban Missile crisis for Kennedy, the Iran hostage-taking for Carter, and the Gulf War for Bush are examples of international events with sub-stantial positive influence for the incumbent (Kagay, 1991).

Arthur Schlesinger (1986) plotted 30-year cycles of rotating patterns of liberalism and conservatism in our society. Practices based on freedom, equality, and social responsibility alternate with private interests and retrenchment.

The histories of organized feminism or minority advocacy programs also demonstrate the limits of favor to which all events are subject. The competition is too great for any continuing long-term ascendancy. It is likely equally true for privatization and to a lesser degree for POS.

Institutional Futures

The distrust of government is commonly viewed in absolute terms. A more comprehensive view may contribute to a better understanding of what are largely relative issues.

Government does not operate in a vacuum, but rather is one of the essential institutions that powers all human societies. The family, religion, the economic system, education, and recreation are all essential fellow institutions which reflect and interact with each other. To function effectively, all of the institutions must contribute positively in an ever-exponentially ever-changing world. Dionne (1996) sees the revolt as targeted more to bad government than against big government.

The family is under great stress. Even its definition is under challenge. We see increasing rates of separation and divorce, a decline in the rate of heterosexual marriages, single-sex marriages, many more women in the work force out of the home, more single-headed households, and fewer children.

Organized religion in many of its guises is similarly strained. As with the political system, it has moved to the "right." Mainstream religions are declining in strength. They find it difficult to recruit clergy and parishioners. The growth is in the evangelicals and the fundamentalists. Christianity, Judaism, and Islam are all experiencing similar trends.

The distrust of economics as a discipline ("the dismal science"); the disintegration of Communism as an economic system; the continuing misgiving about capitalism in much of the world; the rapid growth of multinational corporations; the decline in the size of the middle class; and the increasing discrepancy between the wealthy and all other classes contain all of the elements for new class struggles.

The steady criticism of publicly operated elementary and secondary education (public higher education has escaped this broad brush criticism, to date) is consistent with the societal disenchantment of most of the major sectors of our life. The effort to privatize it is taking many forms around the country.

Only recreation has escaped this demonization. In its several forms—public and private, for-profit and not-for-profit, indoor and out-of-doors, individual and group, participant and observer, and organized and unorganized—recreation can certainly match the complexity of the other major institutions. Its partial immunity to the constant torrent of criticism faced by the other institutions may be a reflection of its perceived lesser importance to society and the failure to understand the important collective role it plays.

As important as all of these institutions are to the well-being of the pop-ulace, only one institution has the well-being of everyone assigned to it. All of the others have specific constituencies. Government is the only guaran-tor of equity and fairness to all the people all of the time, even though it may not perform this role well on all occasions. Galbraith (1994) sees gov-ernment, in its concern for economic and social amelioration, as uniquely essential in a society increasingly unequal. Dionne (1996) sees government as distinctively able to strengthen the institutions of civil society.

In this context, privatization is clearly symptomatic of the evolution of ideas permeating the worlds of all of our great institutions. The currently popular scapegoating of government with invective and vitriol, often led by newly elected officials, misses and displaces the essential target: a fun-damental disenchantment with life. The contemporary absence of a com-mon enemy to supplant the malaise makes it more difficult to face the essential problems of a world in great flux. The need to convert people with differences of opinions into enemies to be attacked with maltruths and mistruths, and to magnify modest differences, contributes to constant tension.

It is noteworthy that no major American jurisdiction has found both the executive and legislative branches formally endorsing privatization, or POS, by enacting specific legislation to that end. Thus it is likely that they will continue to be politicized and contentious and growth-constrained.

The essential task of the practical reformer given the extraordinary worldwide disquiet is to protect all of the basic institutions while sup-porting explorations on the margins. Pluralism is an important underly-ing conceptual base by which to experiment with matters such as POS/privatization. Since clear, unequivocal answers are not readily avail-able, alternative modes of service delivery are strongly advisable. At these times, interorganizational relations may take many forms. There may not be one clear superior method. The wise move may be to attempt several routes simultaneously. It may well be that the future of POS/privatization in the human services is best seen in a niche role. We suggest only that we be fully aware of the tenuous nature of our efforts and that we acknowl-edge, monitor, and measure the several experiments.

REFERENCES

How Americans judge basic institutions. (1976, September 13). *U. S. News and World Report,* p. 41.
Associated Press. (1991, April 2). German economic aide slain: Red army

faction suspected. *New York Times*, p. A26.

Ayres, B. D. (1996, January 2). A toll road in California offers a high-tech answer to traffic. *New York Times*, p. 1.

Banning, L. (1995). *The sacred fire of liberty*. Ithaca, N.Y.: Cornell University Press.

Barber, B. R. (1995). *Jihad vs. McWorld*. New York: Times Books/Random House.

Bass, A. (1996, July 11). Agency criticized over accreditation given hospitals. *The Boston Globe*, p. 19.

Blasi, J. (1994, June 30). Privatizing Russia—A success study. *New York Times*, p. A23.

Bendick, M., Jr. (1989). Privatizing the delivery of social welfare services: An idea to be taken seriously. In S. B. Kamerman & A. J. Kahn (Eds.), *Privatization and the welfare state*. Princeton, NJ: Princeton University Press.

Berke, R. (1996, January 7). Cease-fire: the mellowing of the American voter. *New York Times*, p. E1.

Broad, W. J. (1995, November 30). Panel of experts urges government to revamp science budget. *New York Times*, p. B15.

Brodkin, E. Z., & Young, D. (1989). Making sense of privatization: What can we learn from economic and political analysis? In S. B. Kamerman & A. J Kahn (Eds.), *Privatization and the welfare state.* (pp. 121–154). Princeton, NJ: Princeton University Press.

Brooke, J. (1995, November 21). Federal helium plant stays above the fray. *New York Times*, p. A18.

Browne, M. W. (1996, February 6). Helium won't fill future demands, physicists warn. *New York Times*, pp. C1, C7.

Coloradans propose repeal of church-property tax exemption. (1996, January 14). *New York Times*, p. B 12.

Cushman, J. H., Jr. (1995, December 26). Budget cuts leave E.P.A. facing layoffs. *New York Times*, p. 14.

Demone, H. W., Jr. (1998). Privatization, politics and the press. In M. Gibelman & H. W. Demone, Jr. (Eds.) *The privatization of human services, Volume II: Case studies in the purchase of services*. New York: Springer Publishing Co..

Demone, H. W., Jr., & Gibelman, M. (1989). The future of purchase of service. In H. W. Demone Jr. & M. Gibelman (Eds.), *Services for sale: Purchasing health & human services* (pp. 329–422). New Brunswick, NJ: Rutgers University Press.

Dionne, E. J., Jr. (1996). *They only look dead*. New York: Simon and Schuster.

Dillon, S. (1995, November 4). Mexico's lifeblood on the auction block. *New York Times,* p. 37.

DIY in Germany. (1996, March 2). *The Economist,* p. 60.

Dobbs, M. (1993, May 5). Russia's trickle down reform. *Washington Post,* p. A23.

Dowd, M. (1995, October 29). Identity crisis city. *New York Times,* p. E13.

Drucker, P. (1968). *The age of discontinuity.* New York: Harper & Row.

Dukakis, M. (1998). Personal reflections on purchase of services: A view from a state capitol. In M. Gibelman & H. W. Demone, Jr.(Eds.), *The privatization of human services, Volume II: Case studies in the purchase of services.* Springer Publishing Co.

Echikoson, W. (1993, May 27). French will privatize 21 state countries. *The Boston Globe,* pp. 45–46.

Editorial. Why not privatize city streets? (1983, December 20). *New York Times,* p. A30.

Elkins, S., & McKitrick, E. (1994). *The age of federalism.* New York: Oxford University Press.

Evans, S. M., & Boyte, H. C. (1990). *Free spaces.* New York: Harper & Row.

Flint, A. (1996, January 21). Liberalism lives! *The Boston Globe.* pp. 63–64.

Freudenheim, M. (1996, March 25) As Blue Cross plans seek profit, states ask a share of the riches. *New York Times,* p. 1.

Galbraith, J. K. (1994). *A journey through economic time.* Boston: Houghton Mifflin.

General Accounting Office. (1991). *Government contractors: Are service contractors performing inherently governmental functions?* (GAO/GGD–92–11). Washington, DC: Authou.

General Accounting Office. (1995a). *Budget issues: Privatization/divestiture practices in other nations.* (GAO/AIMD–96–23). Washington, DC: Author.

General Accounting Office. (1995b). *Government corporations: Profiles of existing government corporations.* (GAO/GGD–96–14) Washington, DC: Author.

General Accounting Office. (1995c). *Tax administration: IRS faces challenges in reorganizing for customer services.* (GAO/GGD–96–3). Washington, DC: Author.

General Accounting Office. (1996). *Budget issues: Privatization practices in Argentina.* (GAO/AIMD-96–55). Washington, DC: Author.

Gillers, S. (1996, July 5). "Filegate" was bad enough. Now this? *New York Times,* p. A23.

Glassman, J. K. (1994, December 21). How much would be offered for the 14th street bridge? *Washington Post,* p. D1.

Grunwald, M. (1996, February 3). DSS plan raises fear for children. *The Boston Globe*, p. 1.

Harris, L. (1973, December 6). Confidence grows in institutions. *The Boston Globe*, p. 18.

Harris, L. (1987). *Inside America*. (1987). New York: Vintage Books.

Heilbroner, R., & Milberg, W.(1996). *The crisis of vision in modern economic thought*. New York: Cambridge University Press.

Hernandez, R. (1995, November 21). Pataki urges state to sell some housing. *New York Times*, p. B6.

In trashmen we trust. (1973, December 3). *Washington Star-News*, p. 22.

Johnston, P.(1998). Personal reflections on the purchase of services in Massachusetts. In M. Gibelman & H. W. Demone, Jr. (Eds.), *The privatization of human services, Volume II: Case studies in the purchase of services*. New York: Springer Publishing Co.

Kagay, M. R. (1991, May 22). History suggests Bush's popularity will ebb. *New York Times*, p. E12.

Kaplan, A. E. (1996, January 28). Charities, under siege too, can't undergo market conversion. *New York Times*, p. E12.

Kramer, R. M. (1989). From voluntarism to vendorism: An organizational perspective on contracting. In H. W. Demone, Jr. & M. Gibelman (Eds.), *Services for sale: Purchasing health and human services*, (pp. 97–110). New Brunswick, NJ: Rutgers University Press.

Kramer, R. M. (1994). Voluntary agencies and the contract culture: "Dream or Nightmare?" *Social Service Review, 68*, 7–35.

Larson, E. (1995, October 23). Unrest I the west, *Time*, pp. 53–56, 63–65.

Lekachman, R. (1987). *America after Reagan*. New York: Macmillan.

Lewis, A.(1995, December 18). An atomized America. *New York Times*, p. A17.

Lynch, C. (1997, March 8). Soldiers for hire tempt war-weary. *New York Times*, pp. A1, A12.

Marriott, M. (1992, November 21). Study could be prelude to private owner for OTB. *New York Times*, p. B3.

Macer, S., & Jinks, C. (1995, November 9). War on poverty: No apologies, please. *New York Times*, p. A29.

Mexican bank privatization. (1991, March 9). *The Economist*, p. 81–82.

Morin, R., & Balz, D.(1989, May 26). Majority in poll criticize Congress. *Washington Post*, p. A8.

Morin, R., & Broder, D. S. (1994, July 3). Six out of 10 disapprove of way hill does its job. *Washington Post*, p. A1.

Nash, N. C. (1995, October 17). Privatizing in Hungary: Once more with feeling. *New York Times*, p. D1.

Neither snow, nor rain, nor fax... (1990, September 29). *The Economist*, p. 83.

Noble, K. B. (1995, December 22). U.S. studies wave of violence in Nevada. *New York Times*, p. A22.

Office of Management and Budget. (1973). *Federalism*. Washington, DC: Author.

Oreskes, M. (1990, September 19). Alienation from government grows, poll finds. *New York Times*, p. A26.

Overcoming the productivity paradox. (1995a, December). *PC Novice*, pp. 22–24.

Pasztor, A. (1996). *When the Pentagon was for sale*. New York: Scribner.

Perlez, J. (1995, November 2). Ukraine sells its companies, but buyers are few. *New York Times*. p. 1.

Perlez, J. (1996, January 6). Shaking up Czech industry. *New York Times*, p. 33.

Pertman, A. (1996b, February 11). Taylor: Plain speaking, simple solutions. *The Boston Globe*, p. 26.

Pertman, A. (1996a, July 15). Californians pay for edge at rush hour. *Boston Globe*, pp. A1, A29.

Peters, C. (1995, October 23). The politics of self-pity. *New York Times*, p. A15.

Phillips, K. (1994a). *Arrogant capital: Washington, Wall Street, and the frustration of American politics*. Boston: Little, Brown.

Phillips, K. (1994b, September 26). Fat city. *Time*, pp. 49–53, 55–56.

Political warfare in France. (1995b, December 13). *New York Times*, p. A27.

Privatization in eastern Europe. (1990, April 14). *The Economist*, pp. 19–21.

Protzman, F. (1994, August 12). East nearly privatized, Germans argue the cost. *New York Times*, p. D1.

Purdom, T. S. (1994, August 7). The newest Moynihan. *New York Times*,. pp. 25–29, 36–37, 48, 52.

Purdy, M. (1996, January 19). In jail business, Nashville company leads crowded field. *New York Times*, p. B4.

Putzel, M. (1993, September 8). Clinton embraces Gore blueprint to trim government. *The Boston Globe*, p. 1.

Reagan, R. (1982). *Public papers of the Presidents of the United States, 1981*. Washington, DC: U.S. Government Printing Office.

Rein, M. (1989). The social structure of institutions: Neither public nor private. In S. B. Kamerman & A. J. Kahn (Eds.), *Privatization and the welfare state*. (pp. 49–72). Princeton: Princeton University Press. .

Reuters. (1994a, November 4). Tories drop plan to sell postal service. *New*

York Times, p. A14.

Reuters. (1994b, November 7–8). Protesting privatization, French workers halt trading of futures, options in Paris. *Wall Street Journal,* p. 12.

Rezendes, M. (1995, November 12). Voters fear a gloomy future. *The Boston Sunday Globe,* pp. 1, 28.

Roberts, S. (1995, December 24). Alone in the vast wasteland. *New York Times,* p. E3.

Rocks, D. (1996, June 23). Privatization agency is closing its doors. *The Boston Globe,* p. 4.

Rohter, L. (1996, May 12). Split between Aristide and his successor. *New York Times,* p. 6.

Samuelson, R. J. (1996). *The good life and its discontents.* New York: Times Books/Random House..

Shlesinger, A. (1986). *The cycles of American history.* New York: Houghton-Mifflin.

Shapiro, M. (1992, October 2). Russia starts issuing privatization coupons. *The Washington Post,* p. A39.

Shepsle, K. W. (1980). The private use of public interest. *Society, 17,* 35–41.

Shriver, J. (1986). Quality of services. *Gallup report, 250,* pp. 2–15.

Staff. (1996, February 12). America's private army in Bosnia. *Time,* p. 20.

Stern, K. B. (1996). *A force upon the plain.* New York: Simon & Schuster

Stevenson, R. W. (1995, April 16). Britain is streamlining its bureaucracy, partly by privatizing some work. *New York Times,* p. 10.

Strom, S. (1995, November 12). Morgan Stanley gets a big role in privatizing uranium unit. *New York Times,* p. D6.

Study reveals southern California attitudes. (1989, Spring). *UCLA Institute for Social Science Research, 5,* 7.

Tierney, J. (1995, May 25). Bringing his gospel home. *New York Times.* p. B1.

Trust in government. (1985, January 7). *Time,* p. 26.

Turner, R. L. (1996, July 15). Lashing Clintons with fury, not facts. *The Boston Globe,* p. C10.

Will, G. F. (1992, April 12). Toward a renewed federalism. *Washington Post,* p. C7.

Will, G. F. (1994, May 12). The politics of minimalism. *The Boston Globe,* p. 15.

Williams, M. (1996, January 31). Public firefighting done privately. *New York Times,* pp. B1, B5.

Woodbury, R. (1993, July 19). Reno. *Time,* p. 54.

Index

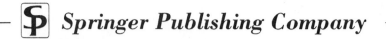

Springer Publishing Company

Total Quality Management in Human Service Organizations
Toward the 21st Century
John Gunther, DSW and **Frank Hawkins,** DSW

The total quality management (TQM) paradigm presents a unique opportunity for human service professionals to break away from traditional management approaches. In this useful supplemental text, the authors provide a clear overview of the tenets of TQM, as well as illustrative and extremely detailed case studies in an array of human service settings, including health care, public welfare, and education. The authors include two useful chapters on the emerging practices of benchmarking and reengineering. This text supplies the reader with a brief guide on how to implement TQM, as well as a useful glossary of terms for management students.

Partial Contents:

Overview of Total Quality Management. Total Quality Management and Human Service Organizations • Total Quality Management: A Model of Implementation • The Tools of Total Quality Management

Applied Total Quality Management in Human Service Organizations. Health Care • The St. Joseph's Health Center Story • Freeport Hospital Health Care Village • Public Welfare • "Quality Oklahoma" and the Oklahoma Department of Human Services

Emerging Practices. Benchmarking • Reengineering • Epilogue

Appendix A: Total Quality Management in Human Service Organizations: A Guide to Implementation • Appendix B: State of Oklahoma, Executive Order 92.3 • Appendix C: "Quality Oklahoma" Strategic Plan • Appendix D: A Brief History of "Quality Oklahoma"

1996   236pp   0-8261-9340-4   hardcover

536 Broadway, New York, NY 10012-3955 • (212) 431-4370 • Fax (212) 941-7842

§P *Springer Publishing Company*

Dilemmas in Human Service Management
Illustrative Case Studies

Raymond Sanchez Mayers, PhD, **Federico Souflee, Jr.,** PhD, and **Dick J. Schoech,** PhD

The authors have combined their experience as teachers and social workers to create actual case studies, with discussion questions to help prepare students for real world problems. A broad range of situations are discussed—from sexual harassment to ethical concerns and management theory.

Partial Contents:

- Human Services Management in Perspective
- An Accounting Clerk for DSS
- Developing an Information System
- Breaking Up Is Hard To Do
- Which Side Are You On?
- The Battered Women's Shelter of Aiken County
- Planning and the Politics of Inclusion
- Staffing a Planning Committee
- The Politically Correct Candidate
- Whose Values: The Politics of Planning
- A Sexual Harassment Complaint
- Inertia on the Board
- The Price of Serving
- "Creative" Grant Writing for Survival
- Too Many Chiefs
- Staff Meetings at Senior Citizen Centers of the Valley, Inc.

Springer Series on Social Work
1994   130pp   0-8261-7740-9   hard

536 Broadway, New York, NY 10012-3955 • (212) 431-4370 • Fax (212) 941-7842

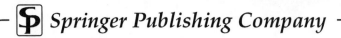
Springer Publishing Company

An Introduction to the U.S. Health Care System, 4th Ed.

Steven Jonas, MD, MPH, FACPM

"A brief overview encompassing all the diverse components of the U.S. health care system, focusing on principles, basic structure, and key unsolved problems.... This book can help everyone understand [the U.S. system of health care] — its characteristics, its problems, and possible improvements."

–by Founding Editor **Milton Roemer**, MD, MPH

"This is a brief, easy-to-read volume which is an ideal text for medical and nursing students who require a basic understanding of American health services, without a detailed exploration of their complexities. It's also a handy and informative resource for persons outside the medical fields."

–APHA Health Administration Newsletter

"May well be the ideal teaching tool for years to come."

–Inquiry

This classic entry-level bestselling text is a concise and balanced presentation of the domestic health care system. It explains the five major components of the U.S. health care system: health care institutions; health care personnel; financing mechanisms; research and educational institutions that produce biomedical knowledge and health personnel; and firms producing "health commodities" (such as pharmaceutical drugs and hospital equipment). The text has been completely updated, with new information on managed care and health care reforms - as they were planned, as they exist, and their future.

Contents:

1997   224pp   0-8261-3985-X   softcover

536 Broadway, New York, NY 10012-3955 • (212) 431-4370 • Fax (212) 941-7842